d𝒇

MARKETING AESTHETICS

The Strategic Management of
Brands, Identity, and Image

BERND SCHMITT • ALEX SIMONSON

Foreword by Tom Peters

THE FREE PRESS
New York   London   Toronto   Sydney   Singapore

THE FREE PRESS
A Division of Simon & Schuster Inc.
1230 Avenue of the Americas
New York, NY 10020

Manufactured in the United States of America

10   9   8   7   6   5   4

Library of Congress Cataloging-in-Publication

Schmitt, Bernd
    Marketing aesthetics : the strategic management of brands,
  identity, and image / Bernd Schmitt, Alex Simonson:
  foreword by Tom Peters.
       p.   cm.
    Includes bibliographical references and index.
    ISBN 0-684-82655-0
    1. Corporate image.   2. Brand name products.   I. Simonson,
  Alex.   II. Title.
  HD59.2.S357   1997
  658.8'27—DC21   97-9426
                                                            CIP

To the ultimate aesthetic experiences in life:

Schmitt: A Yoku Moku cookie, a cosmopolitan at sunset between the Grand Tetons, and a stay at any of the Amanresorts in Southeast Asia.

Simonson: A frozen Snickers bar, a hike down and up the Grand Canyon, and shopping in mega-supermarkets.

CONTENTS

PART II: IDENTITY MANAGEMENT
THROUGH AESTHETICS

FOREWORD

M y wife, Susan Sargent, is a textile artist. Trained in her craft for four years in Sweden, she has woven colorful, energetic tapestries that measure up to 9 feet by 17 feet. In 1993 she began to license her designs, and in 1996 she and I cofounded Susan Sargent Designs; she/we design, produce, market, and distribute rugs, pillows, bedding.

The market for our goods is huge. And amazingly fragmented and underbranded. I was determined from the start to take advantage of Susan's "look"/"vision" ("exuberant goods for exuberant lives," we called it) and create a distinct identity. We wanted to stand out . . . WAY OUT . . . from the crowd . . . at the start . . . even as a (very) wee company.

In short, in the last eighteen months I have become a branding/identity/voice fanatic. We have poured resources into the look and feel and sense of marketing materials, ads in trade journals, press kits, care cards for our goods, complaint cards, packaging for our bedding, trade-show booth design (and even invitations to trade-show parties). I did all this with a passionate belief in Susan's work and a big dose of . . . GUT FEEL.

And then I read galleys for *Marketing Aesthetics*. And went berserk. SO THIS IS WHAT I WAS TRYING TO DO I screamed aloud to my three dogs as I devoured page after page. NOW I GET IT.

For the last three years I have been on a crusade that I call . . . JUST SAY "NO" TO COMMODITIZATION. Quality is up, up, up in America . . . and around the world. Design consciousness is up too. Product development cycles have been slashed—dramatically. The (perverse) result: from Big Six accountancies to office-furniture makers and bankers we are awash in high-quality look-alike/me-too products and services, just as we face the toughest continuing global economic challenges in history.

There is no "the answer." At age 54, covered with bruises and scars, I am not that naive. But *Marketing Aesthetics* is no less than a breakthrough book. Okay, okay, the word breakthrough has been hopelessly overused . . . and thus cheapened beyond recognition. But . . . THIS IS A— NO BALONEY—BREAKTHROUGH BOOK.

Marketing aesthetics, the authors write, is the "marketing of *sensory experiences* [my italics] in corporate or brand output that contributes to the organization's or brand's identity." That is, marketing aesthetics is about experiencing a brand/company, e.g., Starbucks, ABSOLUT, Pepperidge Farm, Nike, UPS, LEGO, OXO, CAT. Experiencing=Look, feel, taste, smell, touch, color, texture, typeface, sound, etc.

The idea of marketing aesthetics per se is more than enough to warrant your reading this book . . . and carrying it around with you wherever you go as a physical reminder of the importance of the subject matter. But the book is much, much more. It provides (1) a clear conceptual framework, e.g., creating an "aesthetic strategy," "mapping the vision to sensory stimuli." It (2) walks you step-by-step through each development of sensory stimuli, e.g., texture, typeface, color, sound. And, best of all, it is (3) chock-a-block with examples, from mega-cases on the likes of Starbucks and Nike Town to a vignette about the creation of the dramatically successful/powerful logo for the International Wool Secretariat.

I am a pretty good student of both marketing and design literature. And as such, I can say unequivocally that this is the most important, original "marketing" book I've read (devoured/digested) in a long time.

Who should read it? Heads of seven-person training departments. And independent contractors. And nonprofit chiefs. And pastors. And Mom & Pop shop owners. And Inc. 500 entrepreneurs. And Forbes/Fortune/Business Week 1000 chairpersons. And me. It applies to all of us . . . urgently.

Tom Peters

PREFACE

The strategic management of corporate and brand identities is an integral part of general management, strategic marketing, and brand management. An attractive and lasting identity is created via the collaboration of strategic management and identity consultants; marketing and brand managers; product and graphic designers; advertising and public relations agencies; architectural and interior design firms; and many others in management and creative positions. The outcomes are corporate and brand aesthetics, i.e., attractive visual and other sensory markers and symbols that represent the organization and its brands appropriately and dazzle customers through sensory experiences.

Unfortunately, until now, these areas have been sorely neglected in the marketing and management literatures. This book is the first to offer a comprehensive strategic overview and implementation of corporate and brand identity management through aesthetics. It offers guidance for a variety of enterprises including packaged goods, industrial goods, technology goods and services, retail, not-for-profit, and more.

On the one hand, this book may be viewed as a natural extension of the literature on branding. On the other hand, it moves far beyond this by offering an entirely new management approach to the field of marketing, a new marketing paradigm. Marketing in the past has focused on isolated attributes and benefits. Then came the "branding phase," with a broad consideration of brand positionings but with—except for names—few guidelines for specific actions. This book focuses on the experiential benefits provided by a company or a brand as a whole and the aesthetic planning that is essential to developing and implementing a corporate or brand identity. We move beyond the "brand" to the overall aesthetic associated with marketing a product or service, i.e., the entire "trade dress" of the product or service.

The origins of the book date back at least eight years to 1989, when Alex Simonson, then an attorney focusing on marketing and trademark law, entered the Columbia Business School Ph.D. program and met then-Assistant Professor Bernd Schmitt. Simonson asked Schmitt whether marketers study customer reactions to packaging, to colors, to retailscapes, and other aesthetic-related reactions and how these elements create identities. Dr. Schmitt, trained as a psychologist, gave a distressing answer—a curt and quick "No." Yes, many studies about color and form surely existed in the psychology and arts literatures, but marketing had not been influenced by any of them.

That first conversation led to a systematic working relationship between Schmitt and Simonson focusing on the strategic nature of aesthetics in marketing. Some years and a number of published articles later, that endeavor has culminated in this book on marketing aesthetics.

The authors contributed equally to this book, and their names appear in alphabetical order. Schmitt and Simonson have different backgrounds concerning identity. Schmitt's training is in psychology and his prior consulting experience lies mainly in global image management. Simonson's training is in marketing and law and his prior consulting experience lies mainly in marketing research and strategy concerning protection of identity. The authors, however, worked together on the key concepts of each chapter, and each chapter is the result of multiple iterations between Schmitt and Simonson.

ACKNOWLEDGMENTS

We would like to thank the numerous managers from around the world, who took the time to discuss their companies' brands, identity, and image with us. We thank Beth Anderson and Robert Wallace of The Free Press for their editorial guidance and vision, and Julie Black, Robert Harrington, and Millicent Fairhurst, who helped us get the book to press. We also thank Joshua Marcus, who collaborated with us on prior research relating to identity, and Donna Eng and Puneet Manchanda, who provided valuable comments on a draft of the book. We acknowledge the work of many research assistants, especially Michael Meier, Richard Thomas, Maria Russo, Domenica Macri, Mitchell Behm in New York and Washington as well as Sally Lee, Ivy Fei, and Julie Zhang in Shanghai. Heike Matz has prepared all the graphics of this book except for the book jacket, which was designed by The Free Press.

We also wish to acknowledge the feedback received from Professor Schmitt's students who took his course on Corporate Identity at Columbia Business School and at the Hong Kong University of Science and Technology, and survey respondents at the Design Management Institute's 1996 Conference on Corporate Identity in Montreal. Finally, we gratefully acknowledge the support received from the Columbia Business School Faculty Research Grant, the B.A.T. Chair of Marketing at CEIBS in Shanghai, the Amedeo Research Grant, and Georgetown University Faculty Research Funding.

PART I

AESTHETICS AS A STRATEGIC TOOL

1

Aesthetics: The New Marketing Paradigm

A esthetics. From the moment we wake up to the end of each working day we are dazzled by what we see, hear, taste, smell, and feel. Our personal tastes guide our decisions in choosing our neighborhoods, decorating our homes, selecting our clothing, picking our appliances, and buying our cars.

But many managers and marketers have forgotten what provides value to customers; what truly satisfies customers; what turns them on. Business has been preoccupied with "quality function deployment" and "activity-based accounting," "business process reengineering" and "cost savings," "defining core competencies" and "strategic planning." Business processes do not provide value to customers. Core competencies do not. Even brands per se do not. Value is provided only by satisfying needs. In a world in which most consumers have their basic needs satisfied, value is easily provided by satisfying customers' experiential needs—their aesthetic needs.[1]

Aesthetics is not esoteric. The vitality of aesthetics in customers' lives provides opportunities for organizations to appeal to customers through a variety of sensory experiences and thereby benefit both the customers and the organizations through customer satisfaction and loyalty. These opportunities are not limited to industries such as fashion, cosmetics, and entertainment that are concerned with aesthetic products as such. They are not limited to exclusive, luxury products for high-end segments. Any organization whatsoever, in any industry, for any customer base, for profit or not for profit, governmental or private, consumer, industrial or service can benefit from using aesthetics.

ABSOLUT VODKA: AESTHETICS WITH A TWIST[2]

In the late 1970s, no one would have expected that the new Swedish vodka import would, a decade later, become one of the hottest-selling vodkas in the U.S. The odds were clearly against Absolut. It faced formidable competition by Stolichnaya from Russia, with a market share of over 80% in the imported vodka category. To make matters more difficult, Absolut had a brand name that lacked distinction; a product imported from a country not associated with a tradition of superb vodkas; and an old-fashioned bottle that looked as if it had come from an alchemist's laboratory. Not surprisingly, a marketing study warned against introduction.

In ten years, however, Absolut sales in the U.S. soared from 5,000 cases per year to 2.5 million. In the late 1980s, the Swedish upstart eclipsed Stolichnaya as the best-selling imported brand and commanded a market share of 60% among imported vodkas. It ranked third among all vodkas, surpassed only by U.S.-made Smirnoff and Popov.

How did Absolut do it? None of the common explanations for this kind of marketing achievement—product quality, efficient distribution, or price leadership, for instance—can explain Absolut's success. What happened is not miraculous nor mysterious, however. Absolut knew that the traditional ingredients of successful brands were no longer enough to lift a product above its competitors. The willingness to market its aesthetics moved Absolut into its enviable market position. Absolut's success followed a well-integrated identity campaign, termed "smart, showy, sassy, sophisticated, sometimes silly, though always stylish" that turned Absolut's weaknesses into strengths.

In the aesthetics strategy pursued by Absolut, the commonplace word that was the brand name and the product's distinctively shaped bottle became the center of an artistically imaginative campaign. The Absolut identity is cool, cutting-edge, yet playful and irreverent. The product is associated with a fashionable, arty scene, but without hype or pretension. In stores and on bar shelves the minimalist clear bottle, with its long, wide neck and the words ABSOLUT VODKA spelled out on the glass in evenly sized capital letters, stands out. The silver-and-blue Absolut package design reinforces the distinct product image—streamlined, straightforward, sophisticated. New product lines such as Absolut Kurant, Absolut Peppar, etc., are introduced naturally with minor appearance shifts such as a new lettering color, anchored by the stable simplicity of the ABSOLUT name on the bottle, the signature minimalist clear bottle and the trendy advertising campaigns that link the product to a hip, creative, high-end culture.

The typical Absolut ad displays the distinctively shaped bottle above a

EXHIBIT 1.1

Absolut Vodka Advertisement

Absolut, Absolut Bottle Design and Absolut Calligraphy are trademarks owned by V&S Vin&Sprit AB.©1995 V&S Vin & Sprit AB.

two-word headline that starts with the word "Absolut." The crucial element of this execution is the placement of the familiar bottle in unexpected and constantly changing settings. In each ad, the consistent minimalist style of the bottle and the lettering is given an unexpected touch—a twist that surrounds and emphasizes the stable visual elements. "Absolut Perfection" features the crystal-clear Absolut bottle depicted as jewelry topped by a halo (see Exhibit 1.1). "Absolut Original" features a stone bottle with cracks as if it had just been excavated from a prehistoric site. "Absolut L.A." shows an aerial view of an Absolut-bottle-shaped swimming pool.

In a nutshell, Absolut's sassy image is created through a sophisticated strategy that mixes consistent and simple refinement with planned and controlled unconventional executions. Not just the look of the ads but the way they use the advertising medium itself conveys this identity. Holiday campaigns always offer something special and unpredictable. One of the ads played tinny-sounding Christmas carols; another, multilingual holiday greetings from a microchip. The "Absolut Wonderland" ad was encased in a clear plastic package that contained tiny plastic "snowflakes" suspended in a mixture of oil and water. A more recent holiday campaign entitled "Absolut Warmth" included black wool gloves, cobranded by Absolut and DKNY, Donna Karan's hip line of casual clothing.

Absolut has restricted itself to print advertising. But in addition to a long roster of familiar publications, Absolut diverges from other national brands by advertising in unconventional trendsetting magazines that most media planners have probably never heard of, let alone considered: *Bomb, Details, Paper.* The Absolut campaign also abounds with unusual promotional tactics that reinforce the brand's aesthetic image as part of an upscale culture. Artists Andy Warhol and Keith Haring contributed to the campaign, creating artistic visions of the bottle marked by their own easily identifiable visual styles. Trendy fashion designers are called into service to design promotional clothing for Absolut, which is then worn by top models in the print advertisements. The image is also promoted through affiliating the name with a range of nonmainstream cultural events, which sport titles identical to the two-word advertising campaign—the "Absolut Concerto" series of new classical works; *Esquire*'s Absolut Story writing contest; and exhibitions at the Museum of American Folk Art in New York City.

Absolut also uses identity-reinforcement strategies that take its aesthetic image beyond print and out into real-life situations. This move brings to life the aesthetic elements of the print campaign—the familiar Absolut bottle, name, and headline phrase placed in unexpected settings. Cruising the streets of Manhattan and San Francisco, the mobile Absolut truck carries a giant reproduction of the Absolut bottle on a bed of acrylic ice. Billboards are placed near natural settings that are incorporated into the ad. The most dramatic one appeared in Dallas, where water may be more of a commodity than oil: The billboard was split down the middle by a cascading waterfall and read "Absolut on the rocks."

The Absolut campaign has revolutionized liquor marketing through its aesthetic strategy. Attesting to the campaign's success in creating a desirable visual image, and reinforcing its ties to the art world, individual items of the campaign (ads, promotional material and the bottle) have become collector's pieces; some are issued in "limited editions" that explicitly court this association with the art scene. A book published in 1996, the "Absolut Book," by Richard Lewis, memorializes the campaign from its inception until today. The Absolut campaign has been copied shamelessly by competitors, including Stolichnaya. It has been paraded and used for products unrelated to liquor. Yet more than fifteen years since its inception, the campaign seems as fresh as ever.

GAP, INC.: REVAMPING CASUAL RETAILING THROUGH AESTHETICS[3]

The Gap, retail clothiers founded in 1969, for many years had a solid strategy of selling Levi's jeans and identifying themselves with the lower-case swiveled "gap" logo. It was successful in the growth years of the enclosed mall in the 1970s and early 1980s, when identification, creating a brand, was the goal.

But as the look changed with the times, The Gap's did not. It became an icon of outdated (1970s-dated) retailing. Its turnaround is noteworthy for its heavy reliance on aesthetics. "Celebrating 25 years of style" was emblazoned on its 1995 25th-anniversary annual report. In 1983, it changed its logo dramatically with fine, straight, long black lines all in upper case—GAP—not only changing a logo, but creating an entirely new look and feel (see Exhibit 1.2). It created a new identity so strong that when one views the old Gap logo, it feels like another company entirely. By 1991, GAP had created an entire identity distinct from its prior

EXHIBIT 1.2

GAP Logo, GAP Kids Store Front, Old Navy Store Front

identity as a place to buy Levi's, and had dropped the Levi's line entirely. It succeeded in creating its own distinctive and self-sufficient identity.

The Gap brand is only one of GAP, Inc.'s success stories. GAP, Inc. also remade Banana Republic, which it acquired in 1983. After the idea of the novelty store (here, the jungle-theme store) became hackneyed and unprofitable in the late 1980s, GAP, Inc. in 1990 transformed Banana Republic's aesthetics. The company became a successful retailer of casual clothing; by 1995 it had moved into personal care products, shaping the identity further into an appearance center. The Old Navy Clothing stores were introduced in 1994, with their own unique identity using warehouse-like aesthetics and a rough and unfinished feel to convey the message and feel of low prices, good deals, sturdy clothing, and outdoor appeal. GAP, Inc. thus uses a stratified segmentation of creating three separate, distinct identities for three separate target markets. At the high end, there is Banana Republic; at the low end, there is Old Navy; and in the middle (or upper middle) segment is the Gap brand.

It is difficult to copy GAP, Inc. or match it, because it is a proactive company. GAP, Inc. maintains its aesthetic edge by rotating product lines numerous times each year for all its retail stores. If something looks good one season that does not mean it should be sustained. The Gap stores in particular have an identity that is related to timeliness; its aesthetic is flexible, communicating a solid message: The Gap helps you create a casual appearance appropriate for the times. The changes are quick and the rewards are solid.

GAP, Inc.'s performance is impressive. In 1995, it opened 225 new stores and expects to continue strong growth in the coming years. By March of 1996, GAP, Inc. operated 1,701 stores worldwide including 907 Gap stores, 444 Gap Kids stores, 211 Banana Republic stores and 139 Old Navy Clothing stores. Profit gains have averaged 28% per year for the last decade. The creative team has grown to 80 designers (for the GAP brand alone).

In 1995, foreseeing and perhaps helping to facilitate a change to the "stainless-steel" look, and shaping an identity as an image focus as was done with Banana Republic, the GAP stores launched a large line of personal-care products packaged with a distinctive stainless-steel and matte-glass look that dazzles people. Playing on aesthetic elements and styles, the December 1996 Christmas campaign claimed for Gap stores "every color—only GAP." Banana Republic urges: "Give color—Give

style—Give edge." Both fit with the times; both play on aesthetic qualities of forms and styles. Most recently it teamed up with Digital City to
produce scent samples on the internet. GAP, Inc.'s statement is clear; no
longer will it be caught outdated.

CATHAY PACIFIC AIRWAYS: THE HEART OF ASIA[4]

Cathay Pacific Airways was founded in 1946 in Hong Kong by two entrepreneurs, the American Roy Farrel and the Australian Sydney de Kant-
zow, who each invested HK$1 to register the airline. In 1948, Butterfield
and Swire, one of Hong Kong's major trading companies, bought into
Cathay Pacific and expanded operations. Today, Cathay Pacific is one of
the world's leading and most profitable airlines.

Cathay Pacific's corporate identity did not undergo a comprehensive
redesign for almost twenty years. In 1994, however, Cathay simultaneously revealed a new logo and livery and began a complete redesign of
the interior of its planes, ticket offices, and lounges. The new aesthetic,
designed by Landor Associates, came about after three years of market
research and design and cost Cathay about HK$23 million (US$2.95 million) over three years.

Although the previous logo and livery were well-known and associated strongly with Cathay, research indicated that they did not express
the airline's corporate positioning: an international airline based in Hong
Kong that represents the best of modern Asia. This complex aesthetic impression was created through the blending of a look and style with
themes and representations of core Asian values and cultural attributes.

The Cathay Pacific aesthetic is intended to be distinctly modern but

EXHIBIT 1.3

Cathay Pacific Aircraft (Boeing 747)

also distinctly Asian, to "reflect the changing tastes of our customers." By the start of the 1980s, most customers of Cathay were no longer the traditional set of Caucasian expatriates living overseas or those visiting Asia. Today, 75 percent of customers are Asian, with more and more passengers coming from Taiwan, Malaysia, Thailand, Korea, Singapore, and Japan. Mainland China represents Cathay's fastest growing market. Chinese customers are clearly one of Cathay's target markets for the future.

Cathay's new logo features a white brushstroke (the "Brushwing") that calls to mind Chinese calligraphy while simultaneously suggesting the wing of a bird about to take flight. The powerful-looking bird suggests aviation technology, while the Asian identity comes through in the graceful brushstroke, signaling Cathay's personal, Asian style of service. The new logo thus symbolizes Cathay's two core strengths: technical excellence and superior customer service. The color green— Cathay's signature color—was retained in the new identity but modified to a cooler, unique shade that appears more stylish and soothing (Pantone Green No. 323). The look reinforces Cathay's modern, caring image, its international scope, and its Asian identity.

Color schemes in the cabins and lounges are also designed to create a soft, relaxing, contemporary, and modern Asian atmosphere. The theme relates more to the natural elements of water, flowers, tree, stones, and slate.

The new identity is supported by a stylish new global advertising campaign: "Cathay Pacific. The Heart of Asia" (see Exhibit 1.4). Created by advertising agency McCann-Erickson Worldwide, the television advertising features a variety of Asian drummers celebrating the new look and colors of Cathay Pacific. Set to a pop soundtrack by renowned Japanese composer Ryuichi Sakamoto, the spot connects Cathay to its home in Hong Kong and closes with a special effect of the rendering of the new brushstroke logo. Print ads show a simple green background against which powerful metaphors such as a globe, a heart, a smile, and a bamboo reed (representing the Asian value of flexibility) are depicted with a calligraphic brushstroke similar to the brushwing in the company logo.

AESTHETICS AS A DIFFERENTIATOR

Absolut Vodka, GAP, Inc., and Cathay Pacific Airlines are all companies whose products deliver multiple benefits to their customers. Absolut is a vodka that performs well in blind tests with vodka drinkers. GAP, Inc.'s

EXHIBIT 1.4

Cathay Pacific Advertisements

multiple product lines across its different store names deliver quality casual clothing. Cathay Pacific is known for its superb operations, sound financial management, and attentive service.

Yet, product and service quality, superb craftsmanship and engineering, or excellent operations and financial management cannot explain the success of these products and companies in today's competitive markets. A focus on core competencies, quality, and customer value would not have been enough to create an irresistible appeal. Each company found a powerful point of differentiation through the use of aesthetics to create positive overall customer impressions that depict the multifaceted personality of the company or brand.

CUTTING-EDGE ORGANIZATIONS FOCUS ON AESTHETICS

Absolut, GAP, Inc., and Cathay Pacific are not alone. Several other smart organizations have gained a competitive advantage through aesthetics. Starbucks (discussed in Chapter 4) began as a local coffee store in Seattle in 1987. Ten years later, the company operates hundreds of coffee stores across the United States; has earnings above $450 million; is able to expand its product line into ice cream, books, and CDs (yes, compact disks!); can distribute its products on airlines and in supermarkets; and has entered the Japanese market. A major factor in the company's success is its systematic planning of a consistent aesthetic style that is carried through in everything the company does.

Consider Nike (discussed in Chapter 10). Nike has moved ahead of Reebok, Adidas, and other sports-shoe manufacturers. Its latest move is the retailing spaces called Nike Town. These high-tech flagship stores across the U.S. are experiential spaces, not just selling outlets. With the Nike logo—the swoosh—applied to everything from its athletic shoes and clothing to door handles and railings, Nike Town is propelling the company forward through aesthetics, enhancing emotional contact with the customers.

What is most impressive about companies such as Starbucks and Nike is their appearance in mature markets. Both have been successful by not doing what others have been doing, by leaving the traditional marketing to their competitors and by differentiating themselves through aesthetic experiences.

Even technology-laden firms like Lucent Technologies, AT&T's equipment spin-off, and IBM do not merely sell hardware and software any more. Lucent (discussed in Chapter 2) has positioned itself as an innovative, creative corporation through its unusual look and voice. IBM (discussed in Chapter 3) has staged an amazing comeback by changing its image from old-fashioned, bureaucratic "Big Blue" to one of the hottest tickets in the new media landscape. And even Bill Gates has discovered that appealing to customers' experiences can be a powerful tool. After his somewhat belated decision to embrace the Internet in December 1995, he has launched the Web-based Microsoft Network, which features a cutting-edge program viewer and original entertainment programming, and the MS-NBC cable program, both filled with unique aesthetics positioning.

FROM ARMIES TO OPERAS:
USING MARKETING AESTHETICS STRATEGICALLY

From armies to opera companies, organizations of every stripe are realizing the power of marketing aesthetics. The Israeli army has recently instituted an "aesthetic code" for its army bases. "Aesthetics is a profound concept that deals with culture and quality, not only decoration and service," says Yoram Rozov, who headed up the redesign effort for the bases. Traditional organizations in the arts that have always depended on aesthetics, including museums, theaters, and opera organizations, are becoming more strategic about using aesthetics for marketing the organization. The Metropolitan Opera in New York shifted gears in the late 1980s. Under its new CEO, Mr. Bruce Crawford, a former ad executive, star directors like Jean-Paul Ponelle, Franco Zeffirelli, and Otto Schenck transformed traditional Italian, French, and German opera into grandiose showpieces more on the Broadway than the traditional opera model: The Quartier Latin act of *La Bohème* with over a hundred people on a cramped stage, *Aida* with real horses in the "triumphal" scene, and an eye-dazzling *Turandot*. To the dismay of music critics (who claimed that the Met was "selling out art"), in most performances the decor received more applause than the singers. But the new approach paid off fully at the box office: Despite steady increases in ticket prices (each year proportionately higher than the previous year), the average occupancy rate at the 1995–96 season at the Met was higher than that of the best international airlines: 93%.

Source: Jerusalem Report, March 9, 1995; New York, 1996 (several issues).

Finally, aesthetics is relevant for producers of industrial goods as well. Like other firms, industrial firms create their image to customers through their products but also through packaging, brochures, delivery vans, trade advertising, etc. Differences between top-quality firms and less successful ones are immediately evident, not only in the machinery and organization of the work flow, but also in the overall appearance of the factory floor, the lighting, the uniforms of the workers, the "sound environment"—in short, in the aesthetics of the factory.

Traditional organizations provide products—the proverbial "selling the steak." But it has always been the case that good marketers, and particularly today's market-driven, customer-oriented organizations, focus on the perceived benefit of the product—"selling the sizzle." In the early 1980s, consumer researchers discussed an alternative to these approaches, the "hedonic" or "experiential" approach.[5] The cutting-edge organizations of today and the versatile organizations of tomorrow provide experiences—"selling the experience of consuming the steak." Any good steakhouse knows that beyond just providing a good steak, it must provide customers with a total sensory experience: well-crafted steak knives that feel right in the hand, dark wood decor, and low lighting, for example.

FROM BENEFITS AND BRANDING TO EXPERIENCES

The focus on experiences has evolved out of two earlier phases of marketing: the attributes/benefits phase and the branding phase. Many organizations still market their products using these earlier approaches. For some products the approach may be warranted; for most, it is outdated.

The Attributes/Benefits Phase

Open any marketing textbook, and its authors will tell you to focus on the benefits that product attributes provide to consumers. Customers express their needs, the story goes, as benefits that they seek from a product or service: decay prevention or plaque removal for toothpaste; safety and comfort for cars; on-time delivery and credit terms for industrial goods and services, for example. Kotler, in the ninth edition of his classic textbook *Marketing Management*,[6] views benefit segmentation, a

FIGURE 1.1

Focus of Marketing Approaches

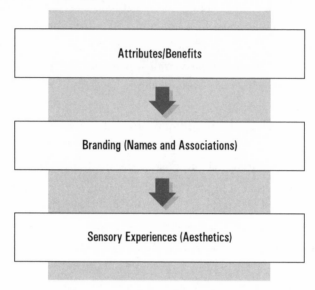

technique of classifying buyers according to the benefits that they seek from products, as "a powerful form of segmentation." Urban and Star, in *Advanced Marketing Strategy,*[7] stress the importance of formulating a "unique benefit proposition." They stated: "If we develop a unique competitive advantage on a dimension of importance to a significant portion of the market, we can enjoy a substantial share and high margin. We differentiate our product from competition in a way that generates utility for customers and profits for us." As a result, the marketing manager's task is to tweak product features using conjoint analyses and other models, until the product is well calibrated to customers' expectations and provides a solution to their problems.

Most customers today, however, are deeply unimpressed by isolated benefits offered by faceless products and hard-sell advertising of the problem/solution type. In the words of Larry Keeley, a strategist at the Doblin Group, "There is an overall trend away from product attributes towards lifestyle or value systems."[8] The consumer of today makes choices based on whether or not a product fits into his or her lifestyle or whether it represents an exciting new concept—a desirable experience. Similarly, business customers want to do business with innovative companies and require excellent quality and total solutions.

The Branding Phase

Brands provide an image. They assure us of quality. They offer total solutions. Branding moves beyond specific product elements (such as attributes and the utilitarian benefits they provide) to consider the product as a whole. According to David Aaker, author of *Managing Brand Equity* and *Building Strong Brands,* brands provide long-term values through their names and through associations that add to or subtract from the utilitarian features of a product.[9]

The concept of branding and brand management dates back to the 1930s when it was invented by consumer-packaged-goods firms like Procter & Gamble. It has waxed and waned throughout the century. In the late 1980s and early 1990s, an inordinate amount of energy has focused on "brand equity," "brand extensions," "brand image," "cobranding," "concept branding," "brand recognition," "brand awareness," and "brand associations" among others.[10]

At the time this literature was important. It reminded technically-minded managers that consumers' decision criteria fall short of the complex cost/benefit trade-off presumed in their analytical models. It told marketing managers to invest in brand building, i.e., advertising and communications, and to use price discount only as a last resort. It reminded brand managers accustomed to meeting short-term, fiscal-year financial targets to pay attention to the long-term value of their brands.

Proponents of branding also stressed the importance of symbols. As brand strategist David Aaker writes, "A strong symbol can provide cohesion and structure to an identity and make it much easier to gain recognition and recall. Its presence can be a key ingredient of brand development and its absence can be a substantial handicap. Elevating symbols to the status of being part of the identity reflects their potential power."[11]

Yet no attention has been paid in the branding phase of marketing to how a symbol is strategically created; and how the brand does what it does; how it conveys a positioning; how it provides tangible value; and how brands need to be managed on an everyday basis. The literature on brands focuses on naming and associations and broad strategic marketing issues—not on the variety of possible sensory elements that come together to create a brand identity.

More importantly, branding is but one small element of the larger picture of managing an identity and image. The work on brands often focuses on isolated brands and does not think in terms of the larger issues of forming corporate or multibrand identities.

Finally, while branding has become an integral part of marketing planning, it lacks the power to move consumers in a world marked by increasingly sophisticated communications. New media and technologies like multimedia, the Internet, and virtual reality provide immense opportunities for grabbing customers and providing them with satisfying combinations of text, pictures, and videos as well as sound, touch, and smell. In this world of heavy communications flow through a large number of media vehicles, through interactive and sensory-laden multimedia, product attributes and benefits, brand names and brand associations are no longer sufficient to catch attention, to draw consumers. Businesses that engage consumers are those that afford them a memorable sensory experience that ties in with the positioning of the company, product, or service. For all these reasons, the branding phase is losing its vitality and is being replaced by the marketing of sensory experiences, i.e., by marketing aesthetics.

MARKETING AESTHETICS

We coined the phrase "marketing aesthetics" to refer to the marketing of sensory experiences in corporate or brand output that contributes to the organization's or brand's identity. Today's environments are multimedia, multichannel, multisensory, and digital. Communications, transportation and products and services are becoming global. Worldwide, more people than ever are living in cities, and consumer lifestyles and preferences—especially among young people—are intense, short-lived, and ever-changing. These environments provide ideal conditions for marketing aesthetics.

Origins of Marketing Aesthetics

The term *aesthetics* was coined in the eighteenth century by the German philosopher Alexander Baumgarten from the Greek word *aisthetikos* (meaning "perceptive, especially by feeling"). According to Baumgarten, the term refers to a special branch of philosophy that aims to produce "a science of sensuous knowledge in contrast with logic, whose goal is truth." Baumgarten was interested, in particular, in the impact of physical features on individuals' experiences. Later on, the German philosopher G. W. F. Hegel (1770–1831) limited the usage of aesthetics to the study of the fine arts. In this book, we use the term in its original, broader sense.

The issue of how aesthetic gratification is provided is still a subject of debate in philosophical circles. According to the mainstream functional view of analytic aesthetics,[12] taking the aesthetic point of view means to take an interest in the aesthetic value of an object. Yet philosophers hold divergent views about how aesthetic value is provided. Some philosophers have argued that objects provide aesthetic value by virtue of possessing certain structural characteristics that appeal to people, such as formal unity, a good Gestalt, or other attractive qualities. Other philosophers have argued that objects provide aesthetic gratification by virtue of their referentiality—that is, by functioning as symbols that call to mind other pleasing things.

Psychologists wrestle with similar issues when they ask whether perception can be direct or must be mediated by a person's cognition. Early work in Gestalt psychology and the psychology of art, as well as recent research on visual priming, implicit memory, and automatic processing, suggests that colors and shapes may affect us directly without conscious processing.[13] Other work, studying consumer information processing, focuses on the inferences and conclusions that consumers draw when they are exposed to visual and other sensory stimuli.[14]

The term *marketing aesthetics* refers to the structural *and* the referential qualities of an organization's or a brand's aesthetics, working together. Some of a consumer's perceptions are direct, while others are cognitively mediated. In the realm of corporate and brand aesthetics, both the philosophers' and psychologists' two schools of thought are at play. Gratification can be provided by the inherent qualities and structural features of an organization's or brand's aesthetics or by the meanings communicated via an organization's or brand's aesthetics.

Marketing Aesthetics: Form, Peripheral Messages, and Symbolism

Marketing aesthetics draws from three disparate areas: (a) product design, (b) communications research, and (c) spatial design. Each of these areas is characterized by dichotomies.

In product and graphic design, a distinction is made between function and form. This dichotomy, stemming from the Bauhaus design movement, has become a well-known distinction. *Function* refers to the utilitarian benefits or attributes of a product or service, and *form* refers to the packaging of the product or service.

In communications research on persuasion, a distinction is made between two kinds of messages, the central message and the peripheral message. *The central message* refers to the main persuasive issues or arguments, and *the peripheral messages* refer to all other tangential elements that are not attended to as the main message cues—typically those that package the message, such as the attractiveness of the presenter, the color of the room in which the message is given, or the music surrounding the presentation.

In spatial design, *structure* and *symbolism* are differentiated. *Structure* relates to such issues as the way people interact with their environment on a practical level: how many floors, elevators, traffic patterns, etc.—much of an architect's inquiry. *Symbolism,* on the other hand, refers to the nonfunctional experiential aspects of the space.

Marketing aesthetics cuts across each of these disparate areas; it is designed by numerous professionals engaged in these general areas. Marketing aesthetics focuses on one pole of each of the above dichotomies. As shown in Figure 1.2, it deals with form, with peripheral messages, and with symbolism. It does not deal with function, central message, or structure.

FIGURE 1.2

The Domain of Aesthetics

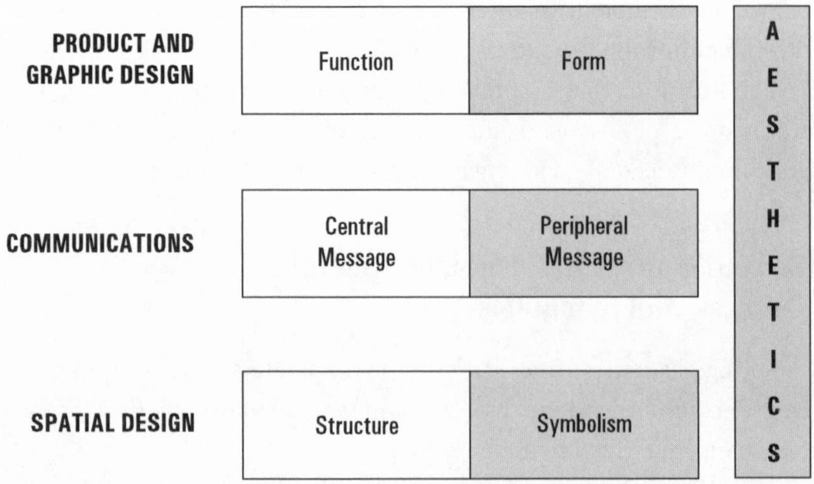

AESTHETICS PROVIDES TANGIBLE VALUE
FOR THE ORGANIZATION

Why are we arguing that aesthetics is so important? Because aesthetics offers multiple, powerful, specific, and tangible benefits to organizations.

Aesthetics Creates Loyalty

Aesthetics is one of the major "satisfiers" in consumers' experiential worlds. When products or services are perceived as undifferentiated in terms of their typical attributes, intangibles like experiences become the key selling points. As we have seen, Absolut has managed to offer consumers a striking contrast in a product that is virtually undifferentiated in terms of its features. Ralph Lauren offers paint products with names like "Candlelight Silver," "Buffalo Creek," "Nantucket Yellow" and "Workshirt Blue" to differentiate this commodity.

Aesthetics Allows for Premium Pricing

How can Nike charge over $150 for running shoes or Starbucks $3 for a cup of iced coffee? The answer that managers, business school professors, and others in marketing uniformly provide is that these organizations have strong, well-recognized, respected brands—"They have brand equity." But what is it about their brands that allows them to price at a premium above the competition? The answer can be found in the unique aesthetics that surround these brands: Nike's aesthetics of performance and Starbucks coffee-house experience. When your company or product provides specific experiences that customers can see, hear, touch, and feel, you are adding value and you can price that value. As a result, an aesthetically attractive identity enables premium pricing.

Aesthetics Cuts Through Information Clutter

Our environment is becoming increasingly cluttered with messages. Consumers have numerous TV programs to choose from, are bombarded with logos and messages in their daily lives, and can access millions of stimuli via electronic media. But an attractive aesthetics cuts through this clutter. It uses every medium to its fullest potential. It has distinct

FIGURE 1.3

Tangible Benefits of Aesthetics

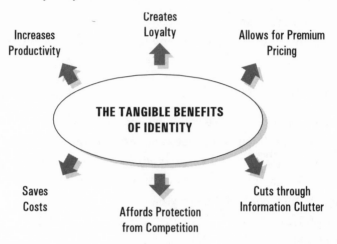

symbolism that identifies and relates to the company. Forms of repetition increase the memorability of these visual marks in consumer minds. As a result, products are more easily recognized and selected at the point of purchase. A strong identity achieves a higher communication impact with the same exposure, or it achieves the same impact with fewer exposures and thus saves costs. It achieves more with less.

Aesthetics Affords Protection from Competitive Attacks

Brand names and logos may not be copied. Legal and technical remedies can be used to fight any such counterfeiting. The stronger the aesthetic and the more it is manifested in more and more identity elements, the easier it is to protect from a practical point of view. It is unimaginable that a competitor could imitate the whole of the sensory elements and aesthetics of a successful company. Moreover, as we discuss in Chapter 8, not only names and logos, but trade dress (the legal term for a brand's distinctive stimuli) is legally protected under federal and state laws.

Aesthetics Can Save Costs and Increase Productivity

Once a firm's aesthetic guidelines are intact, employees and outside firms need to spend less time creating new layouts and messages. The visual system provides structure and guidance. Moreover, ads, labels, and promotional materials often have constant elements; they do not need to be redesigned for any new campaign. Finally, an attractive aesthetic is also a powerful internal marketing tool. It attracts topnotch creative personnel, which is a key concern when entering new foreign markets. Aesthetics motivates your staff—and it beautifies the work place.

AESTHETICS MUST BE EVERYONE'S CONCERN

Virtually all marketing activities involve aesthetics, including new product development and planning, brand management, category management, service management, advertising and promotion, packaging, interactive media communications, and public relations. Yet in most organizations aesthetics does not even appear in a job description, and in most top business schools it does not appear in the curriculum.

Managers have stories to tell about their organizations, their products, or their services. These stories can be managed by placing them into multisensory communications that provide aesthetic experiences.

TOM PETERS ON DESIGN AND AESTHETICS

Of all the management gurus, Tom Peters is the most sensitive to design and aesthetics issues. Peters' *Liberation Management* devotes a whole chapter to issues of design. Those who have seen his video, "The Peters Experience," know the enthusiasm Peters brings to the subject. In an article in the *Design Management Journal,* the veteran identity consultant compiled a list entitled "Design is . . ." Here are some of the 142 items on Peters' list.

1. an easy-to-use FedEx airbill
2. the formal position of the chief designer on the corporate organization chart
3. the number of times the CEO calls the chief designer in the course of the average week or the number of times the CEO stops by the chief designer's office (not vice versa) in the course of the average week (and the proximity of their offices)
4. the binder you use in your introductory training course
5. found equally on farms and in high-fashion dress shops

(continued)

(continued)

6. part of the everyday vocabulary throughout the organization, in the training department as well as in engineering and research
7. the care with which winery logos are reproduced on wine-bottle corks
8. total consistency (a design sense that pervades every single thing an organization does)
9. business calling cards
10. whether (or not) design is directly or indirectly mentioned in the corporate philosophy statement
11. consistency (looks familiar—and good)
12. inconsistency (startles—and breaks with the past)
13. what you most remember about what you've produced
14. the nifty engineering that went into effective fresh-fruit labeling
15. great brochures
16. great tractor seats
17. about relationships (i.e., with a product or service)
18. the ability to discard received wisdom about the way things work (and are used)
19. about LOVE and HATE, not like and dislike (research shows that long-term consumer attachment is tied to an emotional reaction to a product or service—"like" does not a long-term relationship cement)
20. EVERYTHING

Source: Tom Peters, "Design Is . . ." *Design Management Journal,* Winter 1995, pp. 29–33.

These communications are managed through an aesthetics strategy across various identity elements like logos, typefaces, packages, lighting, buildings, grounds, fixtures, uniforms, stationery, business cards, promotions, advertising, point-of-purchase displays, event posters, product configurations, scents, musical backgrounds, ornaments, textures, and many other viable media for creating and sending communications.

These identity elements have the potential to provide gratification. But they frequently do not. Whether corporate or brand elements do or do not provide aesthetic gratification depends to a large degree on proper management. As we will see, this type of management involves a clear understanding of the elements of an aesthetics strategy and how these elements create overall customer impressions.

AESTHETICS STRATEGY

This book is about using aesthetics strategy to create and market corporate and brand identities. Aesthetics strategy includes the strategic planning and implementation of identity elements that provide sensory experiences and aesthetic gratification to the organization's multiple constituents. An organization's constituents include its external customers (suppliers, wholesalers, distributors, and end consumers), its employees, its investors, and the general public.

An aesthetics strategy is different from a corporate or marketing strategy. As part of its corporate strategy, the organization decides on its core business strength, its corporate structure, and where it wants to go in the future (e.g., whether it wants to grow through acquisitions or by exploring new markets). As part of its marketing strategies, the organization makes decisions regarding market segments, customer targets, and key competitors. An aesthetics strategy takes corporate and marketing strategies as input to express the company's mission, strategies objectives, and culture through visual (and other sensory) means. An aesthetics strategy, successfully implemented, creates an identity for the organization and its brands.

2

Creating Identity and Image Through Aesthetics

In 1995, when AT&T split into three separate companies, one of the key challenges was to create an identity and image for the new AT&T equipment spin-off. The new company was an unusual start-up: it had $20 billion in revenues and a long history of technological innovations. Bell Laboratories, the research arm of AT&T, which would be the core of the new company, had produced seven Nobel-Prize winners and invented such everyday necessities as the dial tone and voice mail. The challenge for this new entity was to capitalize on the positive characteristics associated with AT&T while at the same time developing a new identity as an innovative player in the highly competitive telecommunications and equipments market.

Selecting a Name and a Visual Identity. Landor Associates had only three months to research and design a new name and visual identity for the company. It started the identity and image-creation process with in-depth interviews with senior managers, heads of businesses, and marketing staff. Soon it became clear that management would not be satisfied with a simple, mainstream solution but was committed to establishing a distinct, clutter-breaking identity for the new company.

26

FIGURE 2.1

Numbers of Companies with Name Elements Shown

	ALL CLASSES	TELECOM	HIGH TECH
"Net"	11,665	1,625	1,890
"Sys"	12,742	172	2,436
"Tech"	10,237	143	1738
"Tel"	7,909	870	1227

It was decided to avoid technically sounding names that are common in technology-driven businesses and to create a more unusual, user-friendly name instead. As Figure 2.1 shows, in 1995 there were thousands of companies (and several hundreds in telecommunications and high-technology alone) using the "net," "sys," "tech," and "tel" letter combinations as part of their corporate names, products, or services. Another name with these types of letter associations might have given the company a stodgy image and would surely not have differentiated it from its competition.

A similar decision was reached by analyzing the logos of current and future competitors. Key competitors in various businesses and services (such as Nortel, Siemens, IBM, Microsoft, NEC, Sony, Texas Instruments, Motorola, and GE) all employed blue, gray and black logos. To stand out from its competition, the decision was made to use a more unusual corporate color than is commonly used in the telecommunications, equipment and high-tech industries.

Finally, desirable and undesirable associations and images for the company were identified. Figure 2.2 shows the associations from AT&T that managers wanted to keep, those associations that they wanted to lose and, most important, the new image that they wanted to add.

Based on this input, Landor developed and evaluated a total of 700 names. It then formulated a short list of 12 names and arrived at three serious name as well as logo finalists. Some of the names worked better with some of the logos. Landor then tested the names in the U.S., Argentina,

FIGURE 2.2

Elements of Lucent's Desired Image

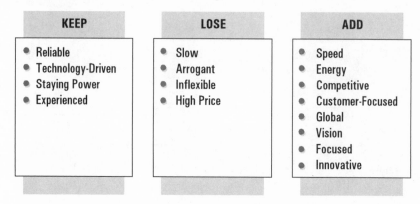

KEEP	LOSE	ADD
• Reliable	• Slow	• Speed
• Technology-Driven	• Arrogant	• Energy
• Staying Power	• Inflexible	• Competitive
• Experienced	• High Price	• Customer-Focused
		• Global
		• Vision
		• Focused
		• Innovative

Brazil, Mexico, the U.K., Germany, France, Japan, and Singapore. The names were screened for cultural and linguistic problems in 13 languages (English, French, German, Danish, Arabic, Cantonese, Thai, Italian, Spanish, Swedish, Japanese, Mandarin, and Hindi).

The Name and Visual-Identity Launch. The new name was to be Lucent Technologies and the new visual identity a hand-drawn red circle (see Exhibit 2.1). The announcement came in February 1996. Employees received a short brochure that explained the new name and logo as well as guidelines of their usage. "The word lucent means 'glowing with light' and 'marked by clarity.' It suggests clear thought, brightness and energy. Our bold, new symbol, the Innovation Ring, suggests movement and completeness. A symbol of knowledge, its hand-drawn quality reflects the creativity of our people." Superimposed on this write-up were the words: "innovation," "simplicity," "intuitive," "light," "clarity," "creativity," and "movement."

The identity builds in flexibility for the future. The core of the company name is "Lucent" which is already used by customers without "technologies." So, "technologies" may be phased out over time. The same may be decided for "Bell Labs Innovations" which at this point is provided underneath the name to show the link to AT&T's former research lab. Bell Lab Innovations, however, like Technologies, is subordinate to the Lucent name. The new visual identity also affords flexibility: the Innovation Ring can change in scope and size, and can become a white ring against red background in color reverse. In black and white it becomes a distinct gray.

EXHIBIT 2.1

Lucent Logo on Truck

The Advertising Campaign. The $50 million advertising campaign that accompanied the launch of the new identity was designed by McCann-Erickson. Based on focus groups and in-depth interviews with large and small business customers, industry analysts, employees, investors, and consumers, a target group called "The Doubters" was identified. "It became clear that the one common bond that they all shared was some degree of skepticism about the new company," explains Sal Randazzo, senior vice president at McCann-Erickson. "Who are you? What can you do? Are you 'hot'? What's your market potential? What have you done? Will I want to work for you?" The objective of the advertising was to convert the doubters into believers.

McCann-Erickson made the new identity the focus of the print campaign and used the underlying concepts of the visual identity as selling points in its television advertising. The first step of the campaign was to create awareness, letting customers know that the Bell Labs people who sold phones and chips are now part of Lucent Technologies. To do so, print advertisements showed a business card of Lucent Technologies and explained its components, e.g., the Bell Lab association (see Exhibit 2.2). The TV ads used an ironic voice-over, saying a former division of AT&T was "going freelance" after 125 years. The new slogan, "We make

EXHIBIT 2.2

Lucent Advertisement

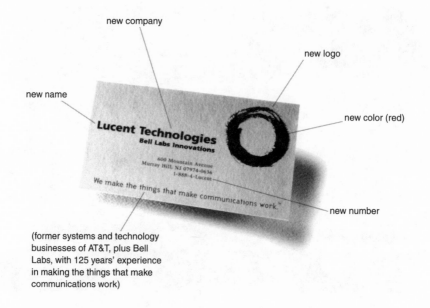

the things that make communications work," appeared in both the TV and print ads. The campaign for this star company was highly innovative and distinctive without even a hint of arrogance. It stood out well among the frequently used futuristic high-tech imagery that is commonplace among competitors.

The Web Site. The Web site makes prominent use of the name, logo, and advertising as well. As in the ad campaign, viewers who access the Web site first see the Lucent business card with user-friendly markers referring to the components of the Web site. They are formulated in straightforward English: "search us," "contact us," "what we do," "work @ lucent," "ideas, ideas, ideas," and "news & info." The markers have round circles attached to them which glow and beam. When the user clicks the business card, it turns and reveals its back side of handwritten messages such as "take a look at our new on-line stock ticker."

Outcomes of the Campaign. Within a year after the spin-off from AT&T, Lucent has achieved its objective. Through its innovative identity and image campaign, it has established itself as a powerful, yet innovative and flexible, friendly and approachable company. In the first six months, Lucent reached 91% awareness among the financial community, one of the key constituents of the company. Its stock price increased by 85%, and it received $7 billion in new contracts.

CREATING A NEW IDENTITY

Lucent is a good example of the creation of a new identity through aesthetics. The well-integrated new-identity program for Lucent Technologies was motivated by a dramatic change in AT&T's corporate structure: the splitting of AT&T into three separate companies. This situation presented the unique challenge of creating an identity for AT&T's equipment spin-off, a new company that would immediately rank among the Fortune 100.

The boom in mergers and acquisitions of the mid-1980s is returning with a frenzy in the mid-1990s. Any corporate or brand restructuring, whether by merger, acquisition, or spin-off brings great opportunity for creating, modifying, and tailoring identities that requires a major undertaking. Corporate restructurings raise core identity questions relating to the birth, death, and union of identities that arise through such restructurings. Consider, for example, New York's Manufacturers Hanover Bank, which merged with Chemical Bank in the early 1990s. Numerous decisions had to be made concerning what name to continue with what colors, what styles, themes, etc., to push. Differing target markets can make the process all the more difficult. Should separate identities continue as stand-alone brands? In this case, a hybrid identity (a "merger of equals"), nonetheless favoring the Chemical Bank identity was created, by the De Sola Group, an identity firm, and named Chemical. A few years later, the new company itself merged with Chase Manhattan Bank. The choices were all the more complicated considering that Chemical's customers might have already been subjected to an identity change. The choice was the opposite this time: Chemical was extinguished and the new identity was again an aesthetic hybrid, called Chase. These sorts of decisions need to be managed carefully.

The motivations for creating new corporate or brand identities or updating existing ones are not always structural ones. There are a variety of other reasons that act as major drivers of identity management.

DRIVERS OF IDENTITY MANAGEMENT

Driver 1: Low Loyalty or Losing Market Share. Organizations or brands experiencing low loyalty or increasing defection need to consider what their identity means to their customers and how identity might enhance customer loyalty. Valuable corporate and brand identities are created through corporate aesthetics that are attractive and strategically well managed. Without an identity, there is no attraction, no premium pricing, no hook for loyalty. There's only the self-destructive option of competing on price. In the words of Michael Porter, "A strong sense of corporate identity is as important as slavish adherence to parochial business-unit financial results."[2]

Driver 2: Outdated Image. Proactive management of identity can prevent "identity crises." Identities can become dated and tired; they can appear out of sync with the times. Since certain aesthetics are associated strongly with various time periods, it is easy for corporate or brand identities to be conflated with an era's identity (like the Sixties, the Seventies, etc.). To appear innovative, many organizations and brands shy

FIGURE 2.3

Drivers of Identity Management

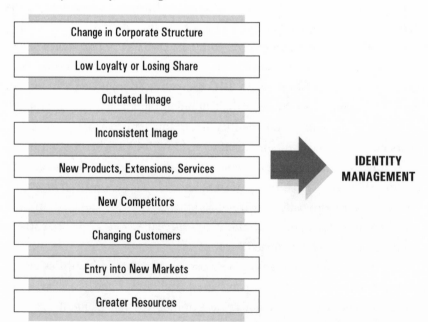

away from a classic design that could afford greater timelessness. The downside of this choice is that neglecting to update identity can result in unintended associations with the organizational or brand image.

Driver 3: Inconsistent Image. Organizations often are lax in maintaining image or identity consistency for similar target markets. Consider Sloan's supermarkets in New York City. Virtually any store has a distinctive facade, yet appeals to the same target markets. The result may be an overall impression of shabbiness or sloppiness. Exhibit 2.3 depicts two storefronts for Sloans within a ten-block area. The looks, logos, and names (Sloan's vs. Sloans) are different across the stores. Moreover, take a good look at the store on the top. Three separate typefaces are used on one storefront.

Driver 4: New Products, New Extensions, and New Services. New product development, new variations or product lines, and new services require identity creation decisions. Also, cobranding requires careful attention to relationships between the identities of the cobranded products or service. Sometimes the decision is simple, such as when a brand extension plays on the existing identity; most situations are more difficult, particularly in areas beyond consumer packaged goods.

Driver 5: Change in Competitive Landscape. The introduction of competitors to a market means the introduction of new identities to the playing field. Organizations need to assess how their identities compare and interact with those of competitors. They need to assess whether the new identities will alter customer impressions of their own identities. More broadly, organizations need to monitor "aesthetic competition," even in product and service categories different from their own. Since customers experience aesthetics throughout their day in various environments, they do not necessarily compartmentalize them into product categories, and their impressions of a company's identity can be based on their impressions of identities in different categories. Changes in hotel interiors may affect perceptions of airline interiors. Thus, changes in any arena can impact customers' impressions of your organizational or brand identity.

Driver 6: Change in Customer Characteristics. Attitudes and behavioral patterns can change over time and require changes in identity. This

EXHIBIT 2.3

Sloan's (or Sloans) Storefronts

is particularly the case for organizations and brands catering to certain demographic segments, like the young, the elderly, the poor, the wealthy, etc. The categories may remain your interest, but the customer characteristics of those in the categories are always changing. Identities for teens, for example, need constant updating as successive cohorts of teens have different attitudes and behavioral tendencies.

Driver 7: Entry into New Markets. Companies moving into new markets (foreign or domestic) or into different kinds of businesses require identity management to determine whether to create new identities, related identities, or identical identities. They need to manage their expansion to enhance the potential for success and to be able to ensure that the expansion will add, not detract, from their image.

Driver 8: Greater Resources. In recessions in the past, corporate identity management has suffered the results of the "ax." As more resources are available for organizations, attention should be paid to identity, as it might have been neglected for too long a period of time. Moreover, small-scale identity management is less expensive than ever before due to computer programs that can manage (at least) visual identity for a small organization.

IDENTITY MANAGEMENT
IS NOT BRAND MANAGEMENT

As the above drivers suggest, identity management is much broader than brand management. Brand management focuses exclusively on the marketing of a brand as a stand-alone item—a lone soldier as it were. Brand and marketing managers expend a great deal of energy on tactical decisions concerning pricing brands, promoting brands, and advertising them. They spend much less energy on the long-term, strategic aspects that determine a brand's survival—the brand's identity and image. They spend virtually no time creating interbrand identities or corporate identities.

In the past few years, many organizations have become disenchanted with the parochial focus on the brand as an isolated element and have moved managers toward thinking in terms of category management, focusing attention on the broader idea of working with retailers to increase entire-category sales, working on an entire line of goods or services. The result has been an increase in organizational awareness relative to brand awareness. In a 1997 telephone survey conducted by the research firm Louis Harris & Associates, consumers were asked to give the names of the best U.S. brands. As *Business Week* noted, the public recalled a surprisingly large number of names that were not strictly brand names (such as General Motors, Procter & Gamble, Johnson & Johnson). They

concluded that "the poll confirms the tenet that a strong corporate identity helps a brand."[3]

Identity Creates Image

Identities create a corporate and brand image. But there are, of course,
many marketing activities besides an organization's or brand's identity
that contribute to image. These include, among others, sponsorships,
public relations, crisis management, and advocacy advertising.[4] All
these activities affect the public image of a brand and its reputation, and
of a company and its value to investors. In contrast to these other activities, identity management concerns visual and other sensory components. Aesthetics is an extremely powerful and robust source of the
impressions that customers have of an organization or a brand. A strong
identity based on aesthetics must therefore be the starting point—not
the residue—of any effort to win and keep customers.

Who Plans Identity?

To manage an identity requires a careful mapping of a strategic vision to
create sensory stimuli and communications that evoke that vision—that
instantiate the identity. Identity management requires all the skills of
the manager in addition to know-how in working with creative teams
that include graphic designers, industrial designers, architects, interior
designers, copy writers, art directors, and artists.

Typically, identity projects of any scale are implemented with the aid of
four groups: (1) in-house design staff, (2) graphic design shops, (3) strategic
identity and communications consultancies, and (4) advertising agencies.

In-house design is frequently used for small budgets and for routine
procedures like retailer's print inserts in newspapers. Graphic design
shops, part of an extremely fragmented industry (estimated at over 6,500
in 1990), take on much of the package design for start-ups, menu design,
logo design for small industrial organizations, basic signage for small retailers, and much of business-card and stationery design. The strategic
identity and communications consultancies take on a hybrid role: that of
management consultant regarding design and that of designer. They often
afford to the company with resources a solid approach including hand-
holding, experienced design staff, and at least some research to support

the design process. Ad agencies manage an identity through communications. Finally, other firms often play a role in addition to the typically visually-oriented role of the identity management and advertising firms, such as architectural firms, interior designers, and industrial designers.

Small-Scale and Large-Scale Identity Projects

Anyone in business will sooner or later face aesthetic issues. A brand manager needs a new package; an account executive needs to work with creatives to come up with a new campaign; a manager needs to work with strategists to determine how design specs for a logo will relate to a proposed ad campaign; an entrepreneur needs to hire a designer for a new restaurant; an editor needs to work with artists to create meaningful visuals to accompany stories; a CEO needs to plan global identity; a hotel chain needs to reassess the aesthetics of its properties; an airline wants to revitalize its image; a school wants to create striking, high-impact promotional materials. The list goes on.

Organizations usually employ marketing managers who work with designers when needed. Even when working with strategic design firms, it is common for a marketing manager to hire them for an isolated task: to create a new package for the launch of our new line, or to create a new package to bolster market share for an ailing brand. Much of this kind of work is generated by middle-level managers, but it still requires painstaking attention to identity issues because even small-scale decisions, in aggregate, can impact the company's overall identity in major ways. That is, even though many identity projects are on a small scale, the big picture must always be kept in mind. Without the big picture, the company's identity can quickly become convoluted and diffuse and no longer reflect the company's true intentions.

A large corporate-identity renovation project entails a full-scale attack on every communications element and a large series of processes to create new standards for the identity.

CONTINENTAL AIRLINES:
A COMPREHENSIVE IDENTITY OVERHAUL[5]

A recent large-scale identity renovation program was the comprehensive management of Continental Airlines' new identity by Lippincott &

Margulies, one of the leading firms in identity management. The first phase of the program, begun in February 1990, involved intensive interviews with management, employees, customers, and travel agents about current perceptions and strategic goals. This research phase resulted in the formulation of a strategy to project the image of a "world-class, top-quality airline, consistent and professional in both its operations and its service, yet personable, dynamic and responsive." Research also revealed that the company's red, orange, and gold colors, red-and-black logo, and other identity elements failed to express the desired image.

Lippincott & Margulies redesigned all of Continental's identity elements including corporate communications materials, signage, advertising, plane interiors, uniforms, serviceware, the aircraft exterior, ticket counters, airline tickets, and promotional pieces. The program was phased in over a four-year period.

To express the new positioning, the aircraft interior featured blue and gray hues used in a variety of textures and materials to give a relaxed, comfortable, yet professional impression. The logo colors were changed to blue, white, and gold, and a distinctive globe on the logo conveyed the idea of an international airline. The serviceware design was based on the geometry of the globe. For uniforms, Lippincott & Margulies worked with designers from Fashion World Corp. to create a comfortable, professional look in navy blue and gold. The final paint color scheme for the aircraft consisted of blue and gold on a white aircraft body with a three-dimensional globe on the wing and a new typography for the company name. To reaffirm Continental's commitment to its own employees, 5,000 of them were invited to witness the unveiling of the new identity at a special event inside an airport hangar against a backdrop of a blue sky with hanging clouds.

———————

IDENTITY PLANNING: PAST, PRESENT, AND FUTURE

Identity Planning in the United States

Corporate identity has its origin in industrial design.[6] The half century between 1925 and 1975 was a period of growing material comfort for much of the American people. In 1927, right before the Great Depression, in an increasingly competitive market advertisers and manufacturers began to argue that styling or changing the appearance and presentation of products could encourage consumer demand. This trend created a new breed: industrial designers. The objective of this new idea was to encourage consumers to replace products with new models of different colors, forms, and materials—to displace them with others that are not more efficient but more attractive, as Ernest Elmo Calkins, a renowned advertising executive, put it in 1930.

American industry began to hire industrial designers to style manufactured goods. These designers were often European emigrants and familiar with the design and art movements of the time: Art Nouveau and Art Deco, Bauhaus, Cubism, Russian constructivism, German expressionism, and Italian futurism. Ten years later, at the 1939–40 New York World's Fair, these designers created educational exhibits and corporate displays showcasing the latest consumer goods. It was a sensational theatrical presentation in which the products of America's industry czars—refrigerators, dishwashers, televisions, and cameras with color film—took center stage, entertaining fairgoers and making them believe in the American dream.

The year 1941 saw the founding of Landor Associates by German-born, London-educated Walter Landor. Landor focused on commercial graphic design, not traditional product design. The son of a Bauhaus architect, Landor began as an industrial designer, then turned to graphic design and established a reputation for long-lasting logos. In the fifty years since, Landor Associates' clients have included Levi Strauss, Miller Beer, General Electric, McDonald's, Bank of America, Fuji film, and Lucent Technologies, as well as Cathay Pacific and many other airlines. For almost twenty years, the firm operated aboard a retired ferryboat in San Francisco that Landor had bought in 1964 on a whim and that he used as the firm's logo. Landor's design philosophy: "If the effort does not show, then it's good design. It must never look designed. And a good design should last."[7]

Along with Landor, Gordon Lippincott and Walker Margulies pioneered the field of package design and brand identity in the 1940s, 1950s, and 1960s, completing assignments primarily for East Coast firms like Tucker, Waterman, Mead Johnson, Coca-Cola, and Xerox. The firm trained many identity consultants and designers who went on to form their own firms (e.g., Anspach Grossman Portugal [AGP] in 1969). In the 1970s a nonprofit organization, the Design Management Institute, was founded in Boston. Its mission is to demonstrate the importance of design through various teaching activities. The Design Management Institute has a strong bias toward product design, just like the Corporate Design Foundation, a second nonprofit organization formed in the mid-1980s.

In the 1980s, other firms, like Siegel & Gale, established a strong foothold in the industry. Siegel & Gale first focused on simplifying communications and then on "corporate voice." In establishing the concept of a "corporate voice," Alan Siegel, chairman and CEO of Siegel & Gale, broadened the concept of identity management and strengthened its link to corporate planning and strategy:

> A Voice is a lot more than corporate identity. It is more than the logo, a slogan, the annual report, or even an advertising campaign. Although it drives them all. Voice is your character and personality. Voice is what integrates and insures the consistency of the company's behavior. Voice is a sustainable point of difference. That is how Voice helps position the company for the long term and helps deposition your competition.[8]

Events in the mid-1980s foreshadowed a change in the industry. Siegel & Gale was acquired by advertising giant Saatchi & Saatchi, symbolizing the joining of two key communications vehicles. This first major acquisition set the stage for others at a time when design was facing what we call "the great fallout of the early 1990s." In a recessionary environment, managers were quick to lose identity planning, not considering it a "key" element of the business function. Identity was viewed as "merely aesthetics."[9] So when designers were hurt the most, advertisers lunged at what they saw as cheap but vital resources. Acquisitions followed: Marsh & McLennan acquired Lippincott & Margulies; in 1988, AGP become part of the WPP group (a marketing services company); and in 1990 Young & Rubicam bought Landor Associates. While some firms were planting themselves abroad and expanding, others closed shop. But what has evolved is interesting: a world where design, identity, and aesthetics is viewed as part of integrated marketing communications; a world where designers and identity consultants must not only be concerned with graphic art and design but also with consumer behavior and marketing strategies; a world in which an organization and its brand's identity has become the concern of everybody involved in the strategic planning of corporate direction and brand value.

Identity Planning in Other Countries

In the last 25 years, there has also been a surge of interest in identity management through aesthetics in Great Britain and Central Europe, in Japan and to some degree in Southeast Asia.

In Europe, interest in this field has been particularly strong in Great Britain. Most of the leading European corporate identity firms are based in Great Britain. But a significant literature on corporate identity has also appeared in Dutch, French, and German, most of which has not been translated into English. In contrast to the English literature and consultancy work, Dutch, French, and German authors and identity firms often take a broader view of identity. For example, Zintzmeyer & Lux, a Swiss identity firm whose clients include Asea Brown Boveri

---

NATIONAL DESIGN AND AESTHETICS

In Britain, the British Design Council has taken a central role in integrating design issues in all phases of industry. The organization stresses that, in the 1990s, a focus on design is essential for competitiveness. What this coordinated effort acknowledges is that innovative and creative activity is not only the province of designers and creative people.

The entire organization must be made aware of—taught to speak the language of—aesthetics. In this effort, the government can take an interest in these issues as a crucial part of its competitiveness strategy. The British Design Council's mission statement reads: "To inspire the best use of design by the UK, in the world context, to improve prosperity and well-being."

Other European countries such as Germany and Switzerland have similar agencies that coordinate national efforts to promote design, but the United States has yet to pick up on this key aspect of promoting industry. The debate in the U.S. is over whether such a council is practical or not for such a big, diverse, complex country. Statewide initiatives may be the best solution, but there is still little consensus on how to link these into a national effort. The future of U.S. competitiveness may be at stake in this debate.

Source: "Trends around the World," *Design Management Journal,* Spring 1996.

(ABB), Nestle, BMW, and German Telecom, views organizations and brands as more than economic units: it views them as influencing the values, perceptions, policies, and culture of our time. Like Siegel & Gale in the United States, Zintzmeyer & Lux place prime importance on the development of an identity as an expression of a company's mission and culture, including its social responsibilities.[10]

A key mover in Japan has been the firm PAOS and its founder, Motoo Nakanishi; their interest is mainly in large-scale corporate identity projects. After graduating from Tokyo's prestigious Waseda University with a degree in fine arts in 1968, Nakanishi established PAOS and gained a name as the pioneer of Japanese-style corporate-identity (CI) consulting. Nakanishi undertook projects for numerous Japanese corporations, including Mazda, Matsuya Department Stores, Bridgestone, INAX, NTT, Ricoh, Sumitomo Bank, Kirin, and Kenwood. Nakanishi is the author of many books on Japanese and global corporate identity and communications programs.[11]

Nakanishi was the first to point out the seminal role of aesthetics for identity management. He defines "corporate aesthetics" as "a quality control program which seeks to upgrade the aesthetics of all objects associated with the company, serving to stimulate the business environment." In the PAOS consulting practice, design is not limited to graphics, company logos, product design, or packaging. Any form of corporate output is seen as having the potential to provide aesthetic value and gratification, and thus as having the potential to differentiate the company and its products from competitors. Moreover, the organization is not only seen as a product and profit creator but as a "culture-creator" for customers, employees, investors, and society at large. As Nakanishi states,

> Today's excellent company must find a balance between quantitative management, humanistic management and aesthetic management. In other words, the corporation must be an economic machine that provides aesthetic and social values, as well as profits. Organizations that can synthesize these spheres will have the edge in the century to come.

Finally, in Southeast Asia it was Henry Steiner who created graphic design and identity management step by step. Mr. Steiner founded Steiner & Co. in 1964 in Hong Kong and now has clients from Singapore to Shanghai and from Seoul to Jakarta. Like Alan Siegel and Motoo Nakanishi, Henry Steiner has a broad and strategic view of identity.

"What you want is a personality, history, a special approach. I call what I do corporate definition."[12]

Building the Future with Identity Management

At the turn of the century identity management worldwide has moved away from its narrow origin in product and graphic design to face broader societal issues of corporate mission and culture. Identity is increasingly used strategically. The core of identity management is the creation of a corporate (or brand) aesthetic that expresses the organization's (or brand's) "character" through attractive identity elements. In turn, these expressions result in predictable, satisfying customer experiences that build stable relationships. Identity management, with aesthetics at its core, should be the concern of many internal and external functions, departments, and people from graphic design to communications and spatial design. Thus, the systematic, comprehensive, and strategic integration of various identity elements through aesthetics is at the core of future identity management.

HOW THIS BOOK WILL HELP MANAGERS

Committed to this broad and strategic view of identity management, the purpose of this book is to provide a new look at the goal of marketing. This is not a design book. What we do here is set forth a strategic framework through which managers and consultants are able to plan and implement an aesthetics strategy for their organization and brands. The systematic, comprehensive, and strategic approach to corporate aesthetics that we provide in this book offers executives clear guidelines for enhancing an organization's or its brands' appeal, thereby providing value for the organization and its multiple constituents.

The need for a framework through which to approach identity through aesthetics has been expressed for some time now, but no such framework has been forthcoming. The problem is that so far marketers, strategic consultants, and academic researchers have simply failed to develop concepts that are relevant for the strategic management of corporate aesthetics. Most concepts developed in the field of strategic management (such as portfolio models, models of competition, and models of the firm) are ill suited to managing corporate aesthetics. Artistic and design concepts and

AN ACADEMIC CONCEPTUAL FRAMEWORK FOR DESIGN

One attempt to conceptualize consumer reactions to a product's design from an academic consumer research perspective was made by Peter Bloch in 1995, in an article, "Seeking the Ideal Form," published in the *Journal of Marketing,* cited below. Bloch distinguishes the three basic consumer responses (cognitive, affective, and behavioral). Product form is seen to influence cognitive and affective responses, which in turn influence behavioral responses. This approach relies on the standard cognitive-response approach to consumer behavior, where behavior is seen to be influenced by cognition and affect as opposed to the other way around. The model incorporates variables that moderate such causal links as individual preferences and tastes, consumer "design acumen," personality, "cultural and social context," etc.

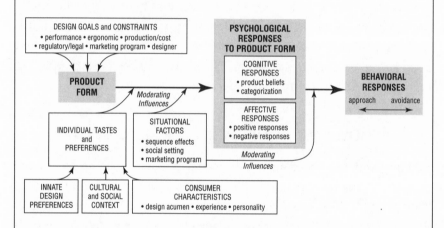

The model helps consider the question of design in the context of potential academic streams of research relating to consumer behavior of design. Bloch creates propositions, some of which are too intuitive for designers or managers to consider, like "The stronger the positive (negative) psychological responses to a product's form, the greater the propensity to approach (avoid) the product." Some of the propositions, however, are potentially useful and can be tested, like "The relationship between form and psychological responses to that form is moderated by the perceived aesthetic fit between the product's form and that of other objects in relevant ensembles." The article could be a forerunner to a potentially useful line of research in the area of product aesthetics and identity.

Source: Reprinted with permission from *Journal of Marketing,* published by the American Marketing Association, Peter Block, Vol. 59, July 1995, p. 17.

techniques on their own are often too esoteric and hard to integrate into a strategic approach. To make matters more difficult, the aesthetic aspects of corporate and brand identity have not been factored into marketers' measurement and evaluation systems. Design firms, for their part, are averse to testing their creative product—in their eyes, creativity can't be measured. As a result, organizations looking for guidance in designing and implementing aesthetic strategies have been at a loss.[13]

Four Objectives

Following are the four objectives of this book.

Objective 1: Provide Basic Analyses for Aesthetics and Identity Planning. Each year, numerous organizations change logos, and each year organizations undergo aesthetic changes, from their promotions and publications to their properties and presentations. Despite the overwhelming volume of this sort of work, there is a scarcity of literature for managers that introduces them to, and guides them through, the issues and processes in changing and updating identities through aesthetics and design. *Marketing Aesthetics* is intended as a systematic, comprehensive, and strategic guide for identity management through aesthetics.

Aesthetics management should begin with a thorough status quo analysis of every aspect of a company's or a brand's visual and sensory identity. The objective of this analysis is to get a clear understanding of the identity that the organization wants to project for itself and its brands in its aesthetic output (its corporate expressions) and how customers perceive the organization's current aesthetic output (customer impressions). Researchers, along with designers and managers, can discover gaps and mismatches by comparing corporate expressions to customer impressions and can also benchmark their own aesthetics against aesthetics leaders.

Objective 2: Provide a Conceptual Framework for Managing Aesthetics. In Part II, we present a framework for managing corporate and brand aesthetics. The identity project represents a process from "corporate expressions" to "customer impressions." Customer impressions are dependent on how expressions are created in various identity elements. These expressions are manifested through two major aesthetics concepts: styles and themes.

Chapter 3 focuses on the management of expressions of organizations or its brands. In Chapters 4 and 5, we present the key elements of the aesthetics strategy for manifesting the desired expressions: styles and themes. In Chapter 4, we introduce the basic concepts of aesthetic elements and styles, and we will show how individual aesthetic elements can be integrated into an overall aesthetic style that best reflects the company's desired identity. Themes, the subject of Chapter 5, infuse meaning into styles. Themes represent the company or its brands' central positioning. Themes are thus a key building block in forming an identity. They communicate the values of the organization, the personality of its brands, and other messages it desires to put forth. Themes can be communicated in a variety of ways, including stylistic elements such as color (Apple's upbeat rainbow color scheme, for example) or corporate icons such as Merrill Lynch's bull, a powerful symbol that expresses the firm's stance in the financial markets.

In Chapter 6, we show how themes and styles together create overall impressions in the minds of the organization's customers. Customer impressions can convey broader concepts that a company wants to invoke—a time dimension, such as traditional or contemporary, or a place dimension, such as rural or urban. We will introduce these broader dimensions and explain the implications of overall customer impressions for corporate and brand identity.

We devote Part III (Chapters 7 and 8) to helping managers understand the research and legal tools that may be useful for identity planning. In our view, research must be used at every stage of the design process to inform managers, to guide designers, and most importantly, to understand customers' reactions. An understanding of legal issues is key to afford adequate protection of corporate output and "trade dress."

Objective 3: Familiarize Managers with Aesthetics Strategic Thinking.
The book is filled with applications and with examples of the best practices in aesthetics, identity management, and design, including traditional consumer packaged goods, financial services, industrial products, global products and services, and retailing, among many others. We discuss examples in numerous settings such as products, packaging, advertising, Web sites, promotional materials, logos, brand names, store front signage, and retail spaces, among many others. We provide numerous examples from companies in the United States, Canada, Europe, and

East Asia. These examples highlight the breadth of the world of aesthetics and identity but, more importantly, they allow the manager to see common threads that run through all the situations.

We dedicate the remaining three chapters of the book (Part IV) to the three major areas that are critical for comprehensive identity management: global identity management (Chapter 9); the management of retailing and retail spaces (Chapter 10); and the management of identity on the Internet (Chapter 11).

Objective 4: Improve Communication Between Managers and Designers. An important purpose of this book is to facilitate interaction and communication between managers, consultants, and designers. A complaint we often hear from managers is that they are unable to communicate well with designers, they are unable to work in teams to accomplish marketing objectives, they are unable to get their designers to see the "big" strategic picture, and most of all, they are afraid to encroach on the creative freedom they think designers need. Designers, on the other hand, tell us a different story. They often feel unguided in the process of creating a design for business. They would welcome helpful guidance, but often do not receive anything but broad guidelines that could mean anything or nothing to them. Designers also complain that managers feel that design is "art"—in the best case meaning that intuition and skill are paramount, in the worst case meaning that only intuition and innate ability count. What managers often lack, we are told, is an appreciation for the designer as part of the strategic team, as a strategic player.

This situation is no surprise. Marketing managers and strategists are often trained at business schools, engineering schools, or law schools. They have a marked "analytical" bent, often with little or no knowledge of the world of design or art. They often feel uncomfortable dealing with questions of design; this discomfort is only heightened by the typically large differences in personality and style between the managerial types and the creative types. Top managers often ignore or avoid the aesthetic aspects of their strategies in favor of more familiar territory like traditional marketing segmentation, positioning, and planning.[14]

Of the many managers we contacted, the vast majority often defer to the creative judgment of the designers, not because they think that this is smart policy, but because they have no training or knowledge in the area. This forces them to do one of two things: speak up and fear sounding foolish or keep quiet and defer to the designers' expertise. But today this won't do; the trained marketers find themselves in an environment marked by increased need for full sensory planning and a high degree of interaction with design professionals.

THE CORPORATE EXPRESSIONS/CUSTOMER IMPRESSIONS FRAMEWORK

Our framework for analyzing corporate expressions and customer impressions is modeled after a long tradition in psychological research on person perception. The CE/CI Framework is based on the management of two major parts: corporate expressions and customer impressions through aesthetic styles and themes. Each chapter of Part II, entitled "Identity Management through Aesthetics" (Chapters 3–6), will present one of the four relevant concepts: corporate and brand expressions; styles; themes; and overall customer impressions.

Expressions and Impressions

The terms "expressions" and "impressions" were first related to each other by the Austrian sociologist and social psychologist Gustav Ichheiser in the context of person perception.[15] Ichheiser was interested in the question: how do we create judgments about individuals in our daily lives? All we observe directly is others' facial expressions, their appearance, their behavior, their choices of friends, etc. We assume, however,

FIGURE 2.4

The CE/CI Framework

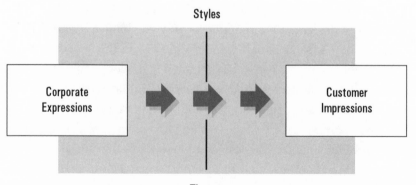

that these expressions are related to something behind the facade: a "private self" composed of a person's character and personality, of his or her beliefs, feelings, and intentions.

Ichheiser's ideas were subsequently expanded by other psychologists. Egon Brunswik extended Ichheiser's idea to the well-known lens model of person perception, and Fritz Heider elaborated on it in his *The Psychology of Interpersonal Relations.*[16] Both of these psychologists were most interested in the integration process, i.e., how isolated impressions are put together into an overall perception of a person's personality.

Corporate Expressions and Customers Impressions

This model of person perceptions is a useful analogy for the perceptions of organizations by their multiple constituents (see Figure 2.4). Customers do not have direct access to an organization's or a brand's culture, missions, strategies, values, to the "private self" of the organization or the brand. However, customers do see the public face of the organization or brand—its expressions. This public face is projected through multiple identity elements with various aesthetic styles and themes. It is usually never seen in its totality, but the various perceptions are integrated into overall customer impressions of the organization or its brands. In Part II, we elaborate on this framework for managing corporate and brand expressions to create customer impressions.

PART II

IDENTITY MANAGEMENT THROUGH AESTHETICS

3

Corporate and Brand Expressions

IBM'S CORPORATE AND BRAND EXPRESSIONS[1]

In the early to mid-1990s, IBM went through a remarkable transformation. The company shed its impression as a static and outdated corporate dinosaur through the use of refreshingly new and consistently integrated identity elements. Through these new expressions, IBM regained the design and aesthetics leadership that it had acquired in the 1950s, 1960s, and 1970s but had gradually lost in the 1980s.

Until the late 1970s IBM was primarily a supplier of mainframe computers and related products and services. In that business IBM had established a formidable market position as an undisputed product leader. During this early period IBM was also known for managing its identity extremely well. From 1956, the year of the inception of the IBM design program, through the mid-1970s, a few individuals were responsible for design and aesthetics management. They included IBM Chairman and CEO Tom Watson; his vice president for communications, Dean McKay; Elliot Noyes as architectural and product design consultant; Paul Rand, who designed IBM's famous logo, as graphic design consultant; and Charles Eames as the consultant for exhibits and films. This highly personalized management system established IBM positively as Big Blue, an impressive model of a contemporary technology company.

But in the mid-1980s, the situation changed dramatically for IBM: the mass-marketed IBM personal computer was introduced, and IBM's target market suddenly spread from information systems professionals to end users. IBM's personality as the king of mainframes worked against the company's new marketing goals. IBM now gave the impression that it was a dated, old-fashioned, slow company. IBM's attempt to change these impressions through playful advertising executions—such as a campaign that used Charlie Chaplin—was only partially successful. One problem was that CEO John Akers, in the portfolio-models' spirit of the times, ran the company as a series of strategic business units, with each unit responsible for its own advertising and identity activities. Altogether, IBM used approximately 40 different advertising agencies. Moreover product design, responding to the pressures of shorter and shorter product life cycles and cost pressures, was producing new products that were unimpressive in their design—in contrast to competitor Apple, for example. Virtually no new facilities were created; instead, existing buildings and offices were refitted in the most cost-efficient way.

In graphic design, internal resources were gradually reduced. Ninety percent of IBM's graphic design work was outsourced to vendors, which were hired by thousands of individuals worldwide with little experience in graphic design. Also, IBM had become increasingly nonchalant about the use of its logo, theme lines, and advertising and promotional materials; there were several hundred different logos and slogans in circulation. As *I.D.* magazine noted in 1993, "In 1989, four years before the company would post record losses, IBM's management was well aware that it was no longer perceived as an innovator in the highly competitive computer industry, even though it remained one of the nation's strongest research and development laboratories." Following PC Expo 1994, a major personal-computer trade show held annually in New York City, a reporter for *Brandweek* joked: "Want some fun? Count the slogans in the IBM booth."

IBM Today

In early 1993, Lou Gerstner took the helm at IBM. He took steps to capitalize on the value of IBM as a brand and to streamline its communications and identity activities. In May 1994, Ogilvy & Mather was hired as IBM's sole advertising agency. In October 1994, after PC Expo 1994, 8,000 copies of a publication entitled "The Spirit and Letter of IBM

EXHIBIT 3.1

IBM logo and ThinkPad 560

Brand Identity," developed by IBM Corporate Design in collaboration with Lippincott & Margulies, were printed for internal distribution within each division of IBM. The first section, "The Spirit," laid out the principles on which the IBM identity was supposed to be based. The second section, "The Letter," provided specific instructions for applying the IBM brand worldwide. It prohibited varying logos, displaying 22 such variations, many of which had been used or were in use, and which clearly diverged from the traditional logo. One example was a logo with a picture of an eye, a bee, and the letter "M." Adoption of the standards discussed in the memorandum became mandatory for each division. The following passage appeared at the beginning of the memorandum:

> To create a clear, consistent and understandable brand identity in customers' minds, brand attributes and the way they are expressed must be closely linked. Companies that present a cohesive, distinctive, and relevant brand identity can create a preference in the marketplace, add value to their products and services, and may command a price premium.

New television advertising was used to express simple themes, with "Solutions for a small planet" as the anchor theme in most TV and print ads. The ads stressed that IBM provides solutions to all customers world-

EXHIBIT 3.2

IBM Aptiva S

wide. The best-known commercial, using English subtitles to show two French retirees in the streets of Paris conversing in computer jargon about hard-drive failures, was first shown during the Superbowl of 1995. It was recognized by *Adweek* as one of the best commercial spots of the month. Other spots of the same campaign include subtitled shots of two nuns in Prague discussing their Internet experience; surfers in Australia discussing the AS/400; and monks sitting on a hill in Italy discussing interoffice mail. The ads were clutter-breaking and attention getting; they established IBM as a player at the cutting edge of the computer industry.

The print ads all shared a common look and played on the "solutions" theme of the television advertisements. An important word (a concept) that IBM wanted the reader to focus on was magnified in large font and colored in IBM's corporate blue. At the start of the paragraph was a tab icon similar to an action button in a Windows application. The ad looked similar to a Web page; through this identity element, IBM again established the company as a cutting-edge, media-versatile company. The IBM home page was introduced in October 1994 and was highly praised in a *Business Week* article of November 14, 1994 as "nonstandard." The Web page also plays on certain themes of the ad campaigns and follows guidelines established in the "Spirit and Letter."

In terms of products, 1994 saw the introduction of a series of ThinkPad notebook computers with an unusually compact design based on a keyboard that is expandable once opened. The product introduction was accompanied by an original ad campaign that called the product "The Butterfly" and placed pictures of small butterflies on different pages of major newspapers. This playful approach illustrated the features of the computer in a persuasive way. The product was perceived and remembered very well by consumers and created a separate brand identity endorsed by IBM. Although the product was not very successful in terms of its performance relative to its development costs, it played a significant role in establishing IBM as an innovator after years of disappointing new-product introductions in the PC market. The ThinkPad line of computers has also dramatically improved IBM's image.

In 1996, IBM introduced a new consumer desktop computer, the Aptiva S. This computer features an innovative approach to reorganizing traditional desktop components. Media access (disk drives, CD-ROM) are contained in a compact pop-up unit on the desktop, while the PC processor sits below the desk. This enhanced functionality packaged in a dynamic black design form is another recent example of IBM reclaiming design leadership.

In 1996, IBM introduced a lightweight, slim series of beautifully designed ThinkPad 560 notebooks, targeted to customers who are increasingly looking for products that they can take from the office to their homes and on the road. In October 1995, *Brandweek* reversed its earlier dismissal and praised the "unified look and tone of IBM displays at major trade shows which feed off the same messages contained in IBM ads." New IBM corporate buildings are under construction.

Had this book been written ten years ago, we would have featured Apple Corporation as a leader in the consistent expression of an attractive identity and Big Blue as a stodgy, old-fashioned corporation paying little attention to the management of its identity. Ten years later, the roles have almost flipped. Since the introduction of its PowerBook series, Apple has tried to look more corporate, but has thus far not succeeded. IBM is perceived increasingly as reliable, original, fun, and innovative. The overall image of IBM is that of a growth company on the cutting edge of the computer industry.

IBM tracks customer impressions through telephone surveys on a regular basis and uses focus groups and other research techniques as part of the design process, especially for consumer products. Through the systematic use of some highly successful corporate expressions, the company has successfully changed customer impressions of itself and its products. In 1995 and 1996 several articles appeared in the business media, praising IBM as a growth company. In July 1995, Interbrand Schechter, a London-based identity firm, valued the IBM brand at $17 billion, just behind Coca-Cola and Marlboro. The brand had been ranked at position 282 just one year before. And brand value is a direct function of the management of brand identity.

MANAGING EXPRESSIONS

Large corporations like IBM have a tremendous variety of identity elements from which to communicate an identity about the company and its brands (the IBM brand as such, ThinkPad, and Aptiva, for example). All these identity elements, whether they are explicitly managed or not, have the potential of producing multiple aesthetic experiences for various groups of customers (business customers or end users). Therefore, an organization's visual (and other sensory) output must be managed in such a way that its planned expressions produce the desired customer impressions.

Regarding corporate expressions, managers may ask themselves the following questions: If we are a hotel, should we analyze and manage the aesthetics of the hotel as a whole, analyze and manage parts of the hotel (e.g., the lobby), or focus on the colors of the flower arrangements in the lobby? If we are a car manufacturer, should we assess the interior of the car as a whole or the feel of the fabric? If we are considering an ad for a pain reliever should we plan the ad as a whole or the tone of voice of the spokesperson or voice-over?

Moreover, how can we express through our identity system that we are a diversified, decentralized company with stand-alone brands, rather than one big, centralized corporation? What are our corporate missions and values and how can we express them visually? How broadly should we manage identity? Is it enough to create a new logo and signage system or should we also manage and perhaps streamline our advertising, packaging, the uniform of our service personnel? Should we be entirely consistent in our aesthetic expressions, repeat elements, styles, and themes throughout our identity elements, or should we introduce some variety?

As these questions illustrate, key expression-management issues include

1. determining the appropriate level of analysis for identity management;
2. selecting and structuring identity elements in such a way that they convey the structure of the organization, its divisions and the role of its brands;
3. expressing internal characteristics of the firm (what it does and stands for) through various identity elements;
4. determining the breadth with which identity and image should be managed;
5. choosing the appropriate degree of consistency and variety among identity elements.

This chapter focuses on these key expression-management issues. Before discussing them, we describe the public face of a firm and its brands—i.e., the identity elements at the disposal of most organizations for managing the identity of their firms and brands. At the end of the

FIGURE 3.1

Key Expressions—Management Issues

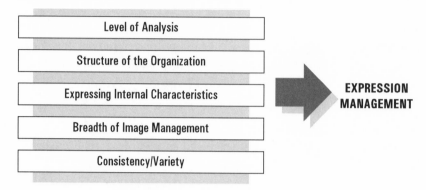

chapter, we provide a list of structural, procedural, and task requirements for managing expressions successfully.

THE PUBLIC FACE OF THE ORGANIZATION
AND ITS BRANDS

The public face of the organization and its brands manifests itself
through a variety of identity elements. These include corporate seals
and stock certificates, business cards, invoices, the greetings on voice
mails, letterheads, news releases, uniforms, vehicles, plants, showrooms, sales bulletins, sites on the Internet, print and TV ads, background sounds and smells in offices, signs on streets and office
buildings, merchandising aids, sales kits, instruction manuals, products
as such, packaging, point-of-purchase displays, coupons, videos, and on
and on. The list is long and unwieldy. How can we give some structure
to this list? Can we sort these identity elements into categories that entail common management tasks?

As Figure 3.2 shows, these identity elements may be viewed and analyzed at various levels of generality. We suggest that managers differentiate at least three levels: the level of the Four P's of identity and image
management (Level 1); and two levels of basic elements.

The Four P's

By analogy to the four P's of the marketing mix, we can distinguish four
major P-types of identity elements: Properties, Products, Presentations,

FIGURE 3.2

Hierarchy of Identity Elements

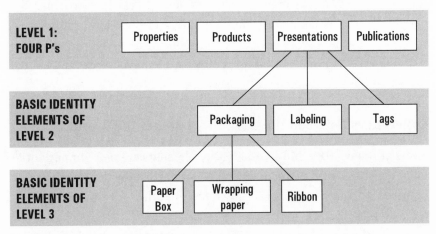

and Publications. The Four P's are the highest level of analysis. They constitute the four major expression components of identity and image management. They correspond to levels of expertise among those who manage our aesthetics: aesthetic specialists with expertise in spatial design (e.g., architectural firms and interior designers) for Properties; brand and product managers and engineers for Products; graphic design and packaging firms for Presentations; ad agencies, PR agencies, and corporate identity firms for Publications.

Basic Identity Elements

Basic elements of Properties are buildings, offices, retail spaces, and company vehicles. Basic elements of Products include specific aspects or attributes of the good or service. Presentations are the surroundings of the good, such as packaging, labeling, and tags, or surroundings of the service, such as shopping bags, place settings, napkins, and the appearance of employees. Publications include promotional materials, advertising, business cards, and stationery.

It is sometimes useful to view these basic elements as being themselves composed of several different levels. That is, basic elements may be further subdivided. For example, a corporate building (a basic element among properties) may be subdivided into the entrance area, elevators, conference rooms, etc. Conference rooms may be analyzed in terms of the desks and chairs inside the room, the screen, the artwork on the wall, etc. The same applies to other basic elements. As shown in Figure 3.2, Packaging (an identity element among Presentations) may be subdivided into paper box, wrapping paper, and ribbon, for example.

Identity elements vary dramatically according to the type of organization. Figure 3.3 provides examples of basic elements for three types of firms that have applied our categorization.

Differences Between the Organization and the Brand

Some of the Four P's and basic identity elements are more important to manage for the parent organization's identity than for the identity of its brands. For example, Properties are more important for parent organizations than for brands.

Also, the types of elements differ. For organizations, key identity ele-

FIGURE 3.3

Identity Elements in Three Organizations

	APPAREL RETAILER	FOUR-STAR HOTEL	INDUSTRIAL WHOLESALER
PROPERTIES	• Headquarters • Offices • Retail • Stores	• Building • Gardens • Limousines	• Showrooms • Offices • Delivery Trucks
PRODUCTS	• Line of Casual Wear • Line of Cosmetics	• Guest Rooms • Lobby • Shops • Restaurants	• Industrial Products • Industrial Services
PRESENTATIONS	• Packaging • Tags • Wrapping Paper • Background Music	• Staff Clothing • Lighting • Scents	• Signage • Logos • Product Displays
PUBLICATIONS	• Consumer Advertising • Catalogues • Brochures	• Consumer Advertising • Stationery • Forms	• Trade Advertising • Brochures • Stationery • Forms

Adapted from Bernd H. Schmitt, Alex Simonson, and Joshua Marcus, "Managing Corporate Image and Identity," *Long Range Planning*, Vol. 28(5), pp. 82–92. © 1995 Elsevier Science. Reprinted by permission.

ments of Publications are brochures, business cards, annual reports, and corporate advertising. For brand Publications, image advertising is perhaps the most important P-element. For brands there are no important Properties; however the Product aesthetic and its presentation in the form of packaging and wrapping is key.

The brand may be linked to the parent organization and its other brands. If this is the case, then identity elements of the organization and the identities of its brands are interlinked. In this case, the organization should establish management structures that facilitate this type of management (e.g., by establishing the position of a corporate identity manager that manages across product lines or by establishing cross-functional identity teams).

Allocating Resources: Expansion vs. Concentration

There are often so many possible outlets for corporate expressions that it would be impractical and inefficient to devote resources to all of these identity elements. American Express uses aesthetics in a wide variety of elements, an approach that one may term an "expansion approach." An expansion approach maximizes reach—that is, it has the highest probability of reaching a diverse range of customers. At the other end of the spectrum, the concentration approach, certain identity

---

AMERICAN EXPRESS AND THE CENTURION

American Express reveals its corporate identity in numerous basic elements, including the look and feel of its Travelers Cheques, the lilt and attitude of its telephone operators, advertising through mail solicitations, and customer contacts in its travel offices. These corporate expressions create millions of customer impressions every day, each influencing the way American Express' current—and prospective—customers perceive the company's products, service, and overall image. Taken together, these expressions represent American Express's public face in the minds of its customers.

For most customers today, however, American Express is known through its charge card. It is the company's most important identity element, the public face of the company imprinted in a single piece of

---

(continued)

(continued)

plastic. The cards come in various varieties such as personal, government, and corporate cards. In 1994, 36.3 million cards were in use worldwide. Charges on all cards totaled $141 billion. AMEX card-holders charged an average of $4,000 per year versus $1,500 for Visa and MasterCard. Anspach Grossman Portugal Inc., the design firm that has created several card identities for American Express, has found in research that the design of a card can serve as a primary differentiator and also influence the frequency of use.

All card expressions have a few common elements: the centurion, the AMEX logotype, the black embossed user identification and a "Member Since" area. There is also some variety, e.g., in background patterns: the personal card features an etched AmEx pattern; the corporate card has a horizontal stripe pattern. The card comes in progressively more expensive-looking shades of green, gold, and platinum.

The familiar etched image of the helmeted and caped centurion depicts the leader of a 100-man unit in the army of ancient Rome. The symbol was first introduced on American Express Travelers Cheques in 1950. Eight years later, the centurion became a signal part of the design of the company's first charge card, intended to be an expression of power, leadership, and resoluteness in action.

The cards' colors and the centurion symbol clearly express some of the core features of American Express's private self very well. But are they also perceived that way? Do customers notice the centurion? Do they pay attention to him? And do they perceive and interpret the colors of the cards as signaling increased levels of exclusivity?

Source: Student paper by Barbara Breza, Jessica Brown, and Gil Fuchsberg submitted to Bernd Schmitt as part the class "Corporate Identity" at Columbia University Business School, December 5, 1995.

elements are selected to stand out, to create the identity, leaving numerous others untouched. Local retailers, for example, often pay aesthetic attention only to certain elements of their retail spaces, like shelves or lighting, shopping bags, and local newspaper ads. Even large corporations often fail to use all their possible aesthetic manifestations meaningfully.

Aesthetic Elements

Aesthetic elements are embodied in identity elements. An example is the paper box, which we may isolate as a basic element to be analyzed in terms of its color, size and shape, material, the typeface on the lid, etc.

Corporate and brand aesthetics are created through primary attributes (such as color, shape, material, and others) and symbols, which taken together constitute styles and themes (see Chapters 4 and 5). Therefore, we advise every manager to pay attention to aesthetic attributes, their qualities (Which color? Which shape? Which typeface?) and whether they should be repeated in other identity elements. In other words, an analysis of an organization's identity should start at the highest level of the Four P's, then move through the different layers of the basic identity elements and ultimately identify the key aesthetic elements that are inherent in them.

Aesthetic Consistency vs. Aesthetic Variety

The consistency vs. variety decision concerns the degree to which the aesthetic elements in different basic elements should be the same or different. That is, should the aesthetic elements of one identity element (colors, shapes, or whole styles and themes) be repeated in other identity elements, or should they differ from one another? The choice between consistency and variety influences the impressions customers receive of the company, its products, or its services. Variety leads towards perceptions of flexibility but can also convey sloppiness and lack of identity, while consistency creates impressions of one well-managed image but can also be interpreted as rigidity.

Consistency increases the probability of reaching target customers effectively. Consumers are bombarded with hundreds of visual and verbal identity elements every day—with promotional material, advertisements, packaging, etc. Since they cannot possibly notice and pay attention to all the manifestations of a corporate or brand identity, they selectively choose to focus on some of them and ignore others. Memory errors commonly result: customers cannot remember a color, a shape, the interior of a space, or an advertising slogan. In the worst-case scenario they may confuse it with a competitor's. Consistent expressions increase the likelihood of remembering the expressed identities.

Suppose the American Express centurion were displayed as prominently in the print ads and in the TV ads as he currently is on the credit cards. Further, imagine him accompanied by a slogan referring to strength, security, and protection and made dynamic in TV ads. In this case, customer memory of the centurion as a symbol of strength linked to American Express would increase.

Aesthetic variety may be used to appeal to different customer segments. In those cases, the company needs to identify the key identity elements for each target segment and to express its identity with that segment by means of those identity elements consistently. However, in other identity elements a different expression may be conveyed because a second target group is exposed to these elements. For example, an organization may decide to give different impressions to end consumers than to business customers and may manage basic elements of presentations/publications and properties accordingly. Multiple expressions, however, would tend to cause harm if target customers are exposed to several of the varied visual manifestations at the same time.

MANAGING DIFFERENT TYPES OF IDENTITIES

Identity consultants distinguish three types of identities, which are illustrated in Figure 3.4. Some companies use the same name and logo, signage and aesthetics for all their divisions and on all their brands. This constitutes a monolithic identity in which the organization *is* the brand. On the other hand, if the company is known by its name and aesthetics only to business customers but by its brands to end consumers, then the company expresses itself in the form of a branded identity. Other types of relations fall between these two extremes. For example, a company may select degrees of endorsements for its various divisions and their brands. It then uses an endorsed identity structure.[2]

Monolithic Identities

Organizations with a monolithic identity often have divisions in closely related businesses. Monolithic identities are most common for industrial conglomerates or business service companies. The acquisitions benefit from adopting the organization's identity and have therefore

FIGURE 3.4

Types of Identities

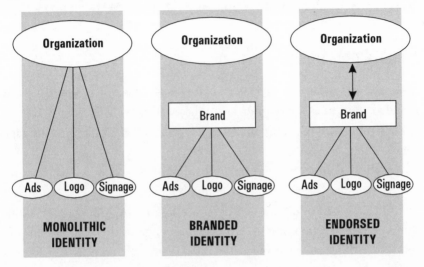

Source: Wally Olins and Elinor Selame, "The Corporate Identity Audit," pamphlet (Uster-Zurich: Strategic Directions Publishers Ltd).

adopted it. A disadvantage over time is that the identity becomes amorphous: the company stands for anything—and nothing. Or the identity is tilted toward certain businesses. In these cases, the company may decide to switch to another identity form.

Branded Identities

Companies with a branded identity, often found in the packaged consumer goods industry, have established noticeable brand identities in the marketplace. However, the parent company is hardly known to consumers because its identity is not present in the marketplace. Identity elements are used extensively for brands (in the form of attractive packaging, labels, promotional materials, ads) but sparsely for the parent company. Its logo, color scheme, and other aesthetic elements are different from those of the company. Branded identity may have been created intentionally (e.g., in the case of Procter & Gamble's brand-management system) or by acquisitions of major brands that had immense brand equity. A company may also decide to create a stand-alone brand because the brand image may not benefit from a link to the company or to appeal to different market segments (as is the case with Miller Breweries' Red Dog or Estee Lauder's Origin, Clinique, Aramis and MAC brands).

Endorsed Identities

Endorsed identities are hybrids of the ideal types of monolithic and branded identities. They often offer the best of both worlds: under an endorsed identity the company benefits from the brand identity and vice versa.

After its identity revision in the mid-1980s, General Electric presented itself to the public as a company with multiple GE-endorsed identities. General Electric had been a modern corporation with thousands of innovative products, from aircraft engines to TV programming services. But as a survey suggested, by Americans and other customers worldwide, GE was perceived as old fashioned and out-of-date; it was associated only with light bulbs and appliances. To broaden its identity in the customers' minds, GE decided to link its subsidiary businesses and brands to itself as parent. An identity system was created that displayed both verbally and visually their degree of closeness to GE.[3]

An endorsed identity is also quite common in the fashion industry. The Armani label has four verbally and visually linked lines: Giorgio Armani, Emporio Armani, Mani (a brand sold through department stores), and AX by Armani (also called Armani Exchange). There is a verbal and visual consistency throughout the four brands (the minimalist, casual Armani style) but there is also variation: Giorgio Armani is formal, Emporio Armani is upscale casual, Mani is everyday business, and Armani Exchange is very casual (and positioned against The Gap). Other designers have followed suit: there are Donna Karan and DKNY; Gianni Versace, Versus, and Versace Jeans Couture; Ralph Lauren, Polo and Polo Sport; and many others.

MANAGING IDENTITY CHANGES

In Chapter 2 we discussed drivers of identity change. In terms of structural management issues defining the relation between organizations and brands, two situations are of particular relevance: corporate changes such as mergers, acquisitions, or spin-offs; and international expansions.

Mergers/Acquisitions and Spin-offs

Structural issues are raised in the case of mergers and acquisitions and spin-offs. When Boeing and McDonnell-Douglas merged in December 1996, the new entity could have been chosen from a variety of models: create a new identity, with a new name and signage; use either the Boeing name or the McDonnell-Douglas name; or create brands under a new corporate umbrella. The decision was made to continue doing business only under the Boeing name. In contrast, when pharmaceutical companies Ciba-Geigy and Sandoz merged in early 1996, they took on a new name, Novartis, and a new identity as "the world's leading Life Sciences company."

In the case of a spin-off, the question is whether (or to what degree) to distance the new company from the parent. Lucent Technologies, discussed in Chapter 2, is an interesting case of a spin-off that created an identity from scratch while still benefiting from its association with the more established parent AT&T company. Imation, a new, independent company, spun off in 1996 from 3M, also uses an association to its parent by using as a tag line "Born of 3M Innovation." The imagery, used in its advertising campaign, however, is, just as in Lucent's case, innovative and cutting-edge, and quite different from 3M.

Global Expansions

Key identity issues are also raised when an organization decides to expand internationally. For example, in East Asia, monolithic and endorsed identities are more common than branded identities.[4] Large corporations are more trusted when they introduce new products and brand extensions than new start-up companies are. Therefore, it may be necessary for a company that uses a branded identity structure to change to an endorsed identity when it enters East Asian markets. The key management issue is which identity elements should be adjusted in order to achieve a localized endorsed identity without sacrificing the global image of a branded identity. P&G, which uses a branded identity in the United States, has switched to an endorsed identity in Asia by changing two identity elements: its advertising, which ends with the P&G logo for each brand ad, and the packaging, which displays the P&G name in bigger characters than in the small print used in the United States.

SCHIZOPHRENIC IDENTITIES

When two major milk producers in the New York region, Tuscan and Dellwood, merged in the early 1990s, the question of how to create the new identity could have led to problems with the new entity's corporate expressions. The options were to (a) keep separate identities, (b) create a new identity, or (c) merge one identity into the other. Tuscan and Dellwood, however, took a novel approach, a cost-effective way to identify the relation between the organizations without losing customers loyal to a particular brand. It was, to our knowledge, the first "schizophrenic brand identity"—as managers in the

company referred to it. The milk container (shown above, folded open), the core identity element for both organizations, was identical to the old Tuscan container on one side and identical to the old Dellwood container on the other. Milk could be delivered centrally without regard to package considerations so retailers could rotate the containers to face the consumer showing the Tuscan face, the Dellwood face, or some combination of the two.

The schizophrenic packaging was a clever way to unite two identities while maintaining their familiar separate appearances so as to

(continued)

(continued)

create no recognition challenges. The dual-brand packaging, however, was an interim step toward unification. The final packaging used Tuscan, the more recognized, and felt to be the "stronger" brand, as the main brand name, with the Dellwood name directly below, using smaller letters to connote its relationship but deferring to Tuscan as the core identity. The package design was revolutionary, moving from standard graphics and minimalist style to an illustration of a cow jumping over the moon, trying to evoke an organic image.

Source: Telephone interview of Tuscan marketing managers; Spring 1996 (Simonson).

EXPRESSING THE PRIVATE SELF OF THE ORGANIZATION OR ITS BRANDS

Aesthetics is not used only to express the structure of an organization. Another core task in expressions-management is to express what the organization does, what its values are, its mission—i.e., to express its private self. For a single brand, the task is similar—namely, to express the brand's character.

According to corporate identity expert Wally Olins, a corporation can project four (inner) things: (1) who we are, (2) what we do, (3) how we do it, and (4) where we want to go.[5] Olin's categories roughly correspond to what management theorists have called (1) "corporate personality" and "core competencies," (2) "products and markets served," (3) "corporate procedures," and (4) "mission" and "vision," respectively. In the context of a market and society, these four elements make up the core positioning of a corporation. The key task of an aesthetics strategy, then, is to express this corporate positioning in the form of an aesthetic positioning (as we discuss at the end of this chapter).

Olins' definition is limited to the organization (the corporation) as a whole. It describes the different facets of the private self of an organization. However, identity management is concerned not only with organizations but also with brands.

A brand also stands for something. It is composed of attributes and features. It is manufactured, or in the case of a service, planned. There are marketing strategies associated with a brand, a target market, a positioning. A brand has a certain quality. It leaves a certain mark. It has a certain character (In Greek, *character* means "mark" and "sign"). The private self of the brand is its character.[6]

RELATING THE PUBLIC FACE AND THE PRIVATE SELF

The objective of expressions-management is to express the private selves of organizations and brands appropriately through their selected identity elements. But often they do not match perfectly: the private self of the organization or the character of a brand are not adequately projected in the various identity elements that constitute the organization's or brand's public face. These mismatches we call *projection gaps*.

These projection gaps occur for different reasons. The company's managers may select inappropriate identity elements to express the organization or brand. Or they may neglect (and not use) a key identity element. Or the projection gap may result from the wrong type of expression.

The process that transforms the private self of the organization into its public face is aesthetics planning of identity elements. Digital Equipment Corporation provides a case application of how an examination of the private self of the organization can be the starting point of an identity transformation.

APPLICATION: DIGITAL CORPORATION[7]

Massachusetts-based Digital Equipment Corporation offers a complete range of information-processing solutions from personal computers to integrated worldwide networks. The company does business in over 100 countries and develops, manufactures, and markets its products in North and South America, Europe, and the Asia/Pacific region.

Since the foundation of the company in 1957, the engineering-oriented and entrepreneurial spirit of Digital put products first and the Digital brand a distant second. Marketing dollars were allocated accordingly, and communications were not directed to as wide an audience as they should have been. With every new product, promotional material was designed with little concern for what information it contained and whether or not the message was in line with other Digital promotional material. Like IBM in the early and mid-1980s, Digital went through a series of significant internal and environmental changes. The company significantly downsized and reorganized itself into several business units, each with its own profits/loss responsibility. As these businesses were decentralized, emphasis was at the same time placed on increasing connectivity and total solutions to customers and on transforming a traditionally engineering-driven company into a market-driven, customer-oriented company.

In the mid-1990s, Digital was working on a worldwide identity program to establish the corporation as a major global brand. It commissioned several firms, including Sampson Tyrrell of London for logo design, Total Research of New Jersey to conduct research on perceptions of the company and promotional material, New York-based strategic-design firm Siegel & Gale to define the private self of the organization in terms of its character or, to use Siegel & Gale's terminology, its "voice," and Boston-based Sametz Blackstone Associates for developing general guidelines for its verbal and visual communications across disciplines (promotional literature, public relations, investor relations, environmental graphics, etc.).

Research indicated that the Digital corporate brand was not as well known and as clearly defined as its major competitors. Some respondents thought that DEC, Digital, and Digital Equipment Corporation were three separate companies.

In defining Digital's private self (or "voice"), Siegel & Gale identified traits that stood for the corporate culture, reflected core competencies, and excluded other more undesirable values. The emerging brand personality to be expressed in Digital's identity elements included the following traits: "customer focused," "honest," "collaborative," "accountable," "practical," "straightforward," "innovative," "smart," "aggressive," and "professional."

Sametz Blackstone used these traits as a starting point for developing internal guidelines for communications (which can be accessed by all Digital employees in an Intranet part of the Internet Web site as "Brand Communication InfoCenter"). The link between the corporate personality traits and the guidelines can be seen clearly in the guidelines for communications. "Does your communication look and sound like Digital?" employees are asked in the brochure entitled "Digital brand Identity Guidelines," followed by a bullet-point checklist: "honest and straightforward," "aggressive, robust, innovative, externally competitive," "professional, polished," "collaborative, open, teamed."

These guidelines were flexible principles and not rules; approaches and not recipes. As Roger Sametz put it, "We developed building blocks, not prescriptions. These building blocks could be applied in different media and different opportunities as appropriate, but the result would be distinctly Digital." Employees were provided with examples of promotional industry material that met the principles. For example, Digital's traits can be expressed well in promotional material that uses active verbs, demonstrates benefits, uses type dynamically to point readers to content, favors photography over illustration, includes people whenever possible, and uses stand-alone silhouetted images of products (untouched by the typeface) to make the product "the hero."

PLANNING DEVICES FOR MANAGING EXPRESSIONS

Managing corporate expressions requires planning devices. The planning process starts with the selection of team members. The team managing an aesthetics project must then follow certain procedures to be effective and pursue certain tasks.

Structure: The Aesthetics-Strategy Team

Identity management means coordinating decisions regarding aesthetics across identity elements. That is, identity management focuses on strategic issues not addressed by any of the individual aesthetics specialists. Top-management involvement is critical for the success of larger-scale corporate-identity projects.

Many aesthetics specialists, architects, interior designers, advertising agencies, public relations firms, Web designers, graphic designers, and identity consultants are involved in decisions that concern an organization's identity elements. The selection of the right team is key. To project the company's private self in its public expressions, managers and design professionals have to speak the same language. The language of managers

FIGURE 3.5

Planning Devices for Expressions—Management

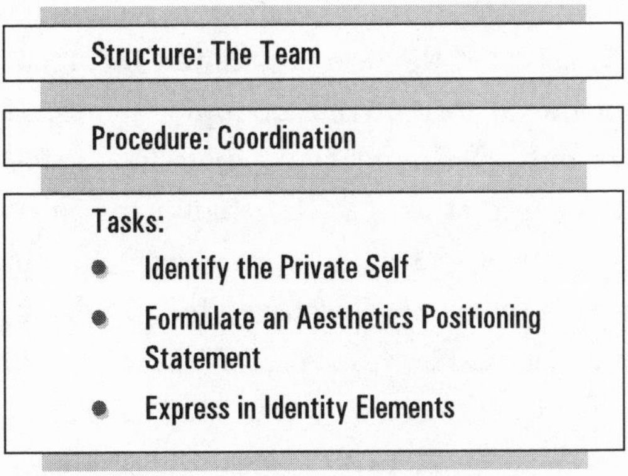

Structure: The Team

Procedure: Coordination

Tasks:
- Identify the Private Self
- Formulate an Aesthetics Positioning Statement
- Express in Identity Elements

needs to be translated for designers, so that the creative team can fully understand the strategy. This means that adjectives describing the positioning need to accompany a discussion of design; designers need not only to understand what information needs to be conveyed, but what feeling or thoughts managers intend to convey along with the information.

The team must set itself clear objectives. In the identity-planning project for Bell Canada considerable time was spent on defining the objective of the identity project and the role of research.

> Our strategy from the outset was to leave nothing to chance, to develop a systematic approach to corporate identity development based on extensive research and analysis. After months spent probing the issues, we concluded that, beyond a new logo, what we needed was a coherent and consistent brand identity. This would entail the development of a complete communications strategy ranging from a comprehensive nomenclature and branding system to standards for the interior and exterior design of our retail outlets.[8]

Procedure: Cross-functional Coordination

Corporate or brand identity management projects are often compared to an orchestra. Gianfranco Zaccai, president of Design Continuum, wrote:

> We are like an orchestra playing together when we work well with a client. We know if they have a strong violin section or if they need to add our violinist. To work well together requires that we and our clients understand our own and each other's core competencies. This shared knowledge comes with a long-term relationship.

The 1994 Winter Olympic games in Lillehammer, Norway represent a successful example of cross-functional cooperation. The International Olympic Committee rated the design program the most developed and coherent one in the history of the Olympic Games.[9] The games displayed a creative and consistent visual expression to over a billion viewers worldwide. The aesthetics of the Lillehammer games were embodied in the logo of the games, tickets, interior objects, buildings, sports arenas. The games gave the whole country an image renovation.

The organizing committee was staffed with 480 employees and hired 200 other people in various capacities. During the games, 30,000 people were involved in the organization. The central producer of the aesthetics created was the design section of the Lillehammer Olympic Organization Committee and the design teams commissioned as creators and makers of the design work. Marketing and information teams collaborated as close partners to promote acceptance and use of the visual system. An outer group of designers (e.g., colleagues of hired designers and designers for licensed companies) also provided key input. A group of external design consultants, who formed a limited company, Design Group '94, created a flexible set of limited visual elements and a handbook of principles for the design program. Design managers also took on the role of design promoters. The design section kept regular contact with 40 of the 45 units of the project organization to improve cross-functional integration. The idea was to "infuse" design into any activity of the project. These visions, structures, and activities created the distinctiveness of the Lillehammer Olympic Games through aesthetics.

Tasks

Identify the Facets of the Private Self or Brand Character. As we have seen in this chapter, the aesthetics strategy-formulation process must start with a consideration of the private self of the corporation or, in the case of a branding project, with the brand's character. Without a clear understanding of an organization's mission and vision, personality, and core competencies, any aesthetics strategy for a company must fail. Without a clear understanding of the qualities of a brand, and how far these qualities may be stretched in consumers' minds, any aesthetics strategy for a brand will fail. This part of the process requires an internal as well as external analysis of the organization's strengths and weaknesses using portfolio models, growth-path analyses, value analyses, or other general management tools. It requires an external and internal corporate identity audit.

When Caterpillar, the manufacturer of earth-moving equipment and diesel engines, decentralized its operations, it faced a crisis of corporate identity. The company realized that it had to define its essential attributes and character—before it was lost. As Bonnie Briggs, the manager of Caterpillar's corporate identity program, explains, "First, the team considered the company's personality—a composite of qualities, some evolving, some unchanged since the beginning. Discussing, refining, and agreeing on Caterpillar's evolving personality helped to eliminate confusion about the company's character." A statement was drafted to define the company's identity: "Caterpillar enables the world's planners and builders to turn their ideas into realities. We are proud of our ability to create and support the best equipment and engines on earth. It's not only what we make that makes us proud—it's what we make possible."[10]

Formulate an Aesthetics Positioning Statement. After the prior analysis, the next objective is to formulate a positioning statement that can be used for aesthetics management. Most positioning statements (for companies or brands) are vague and largely verbal. The aesthetics positioning statement should be simple, but provide guidance and coordination to the aesthetics management.

One of us (Schmitt) consulted on a project for a luxury hotel in Hong Kong that underwent a change and required a new positioning statement. Most luxury hotel chains, especially in Asia, use experiential and aesthetics elements increasingly as part of their positioning. The right aesthetic positioning allows these hotels to create an attractive image with customers, enhance occupancy rates, and command premium room prices. The hotel was an established landmark property in Hong Kong, and management desired a gradual change rather than a radical one. The business traveler had been identified as the target customer. Interviews with management indicated that a standard positioning as a hotel for the business traveler with many business-related amenities such as business centers, fitness clubs, etc., did not seem to provide a competitive advantage. Thus, a new aesthetic strategy emerged, namely to position the hotel in a simple light, as providing a pleasant experience and a contemporary atmosphere where the business traveler feels at home.

The positioning was implemented for the public face of the hotel by redesigning the lobby to make it look warmer and more homey, the uniforms to look relaxed yet professional, and the guestrooms to include books and a home-video collection, and instructing the staff to treat guests in a casual yet efficient way.

Express the Aesthetics Positioning Appropriately in Identity Elements. One public manifestation (e.g., in a logo) is usually not enough to project an aesthetic positioning or to signal change. Corporate expressions benefit from multiple—yet consistent—expressions. The organization must decide, however, on what elements are most appropriate for expressing its positioning and how to best allocate resources.

In the case of the change of an identity, the question of how to time the transformation is also important. Consider an airline. What should be changed first: The aircraft exteriors? The aircraft interiors? The lobbies? The waiting rooms? The staff uniforms? One good strategy is to first change the identity element with the most noticeable impact in terms of effective contact frequency. A new corporate aesthetics should be introduced with a big splash: It should be announced through special events, PR, and advertising media. At least two or three key elements should be changed at the same time, in order to demonstrate some critical mass of consistency. Once the new aesthetics is launched, the speed of transfer should be rapid. United Airlines in the mid-1990s looks inconsistent—both old and new logos are in evidence. Some planes are renovated, some are not; some airport facilities have been redone, while others have not.

SUMMARY

Corporate expressions, as we have seen, are put forth as the public face of an organization or brand. These expressions are part of identity elements. To produce the appropriate impressions in customers, all of the organization's expressions need to be managed strategically. This process occurs through the management of the styles and themes that form the core of the identity.

4

Styles

In just a few years, the name Starbucks has emerged as a leader in a new consumer pastime, relaxation in a coffee house. Starbucks was founded in 1971 as a start-up venture in Seattle, selling whole beans and ground coffee but no coffee beverages. When Starbucks president Howard Schultz visited Milan in 1983, he decided to export the concept of the European coffee shop to the United States. "He saw Italians congregate at hundreds of streetcorner espresso bars and thought he could export the idea to the States."[2] In 1987, Starbucks began its move from a small local coffee store in Seattle to what has become a nationally recognized icon of expensive gourmet coffee. The Starbucks success story is dramatic: earnings of less than $1 million in 1990 rose to $4.1 million in 1992 and then to $26.1 million in 1995; sales vaulted from $93 million in 1992 to $465 million in 1995. For the fourth quarter of 1996, Starbucks reported earnings of $12.7 million, more than double the profits of the previous year. As of November 1996, Starbucks had 1,034 outlets. The financial pundits' average estimate of Starbucks' future five-year growth rate sits at 36.8% per year, higher than most companies across all industries—including the fast-paced semiconductor industry.

How did Starbucks single-handedly usher in one of the largest shifts in consumer socialization and leisure of the 1990s? Marketers try to explain such phenomena in terms of consumer behavior, time of entry, and the strategic choices of marketing-mix elements. Their analysis goes as follows: Starbucks has discovered and capitalizes on a hitherto unmet need. Starbucks has a pioneering advantage; Starbucks combines marketing-mix elements in a unique way; it uses branding to create unique identifications such as the "frappuccino." All that may indeed be true. But what explains the attraction to Starbucks? What explains the "feeling" of being in Starbucks? What explains the appeal? Starbucks' emergence as the premier choice of coffee drinkers centers around its successful aesthetics—one that is largely based on style, the focus of this chapter.

Starbucks and Styles

Coffeehouses and teahouses have been with us for hundreds of years, but they had associations that did not seem conducive to a mass market. They brought to mind mysterious seedy dealings late at night, or pretentious French writers discussing existentialism over endless cups of coffee on the Left Bank. The other side of the coin was the all-American coffee shop, synonymous with diners, family restaurants, breakfast and lunch spots, all places that emphasized function over style.

EXHIBIT 4.1

Starbucks Logo

Part of the difference in Starbucks' approach lies in the creation of a look that is relatively consistent throughout the United States. The 1950s ushered in chain restaurants such as McDonald's, with its clearly unique and standardized style, but Starbucks is different. It is part of a genre of chain stores like the Body Shop, H$_2$O, and Bath and Body Works that use style to create an aesthetic. As they see, feel, and experience soothing collections of things that seem to fit together, the customers are seduced by the aesthetic. Whether the customer appreciates art or not, the lure is in an aesthetic that delivers harmony on the one hand and planned contrasts on the other. First and foremost, these consistent systems of visual forms tantalize the eyes.

Organic and Inorganic Blends of Aesthetic Elements

While the designs vary in any particular store to match the local market, the typical Starbucks works around a planned mix of organic and manufactured components: light wood tones at the counters and signage areas, brown bags, and a green icon that features a female human figure with long flowing hair all create a natural, environmentally conscious feeling. These organic-inspired elements are blended with more sleek, modern touches: the wood has a very smooth surface that makes its "natural" tone seem finished and comfortable; polished dark-marble counter tops seem imposing and high-tech; glass shelves, thin modern white track lighting, and pure white cups all create a contemporary feeling. The logo's human figure also delivers the double organic/modern message: she is earthy looking, yet she is rendered in a modern-looking abstract-representational form, in black and white with a band of color around the center only. The colors of the lamps, walls, and tables mimic coffee tones, from green (raw beans) to light and darker browns. Special package and cup designs coordinate to create livelier, more colorful tones for holidays.

Borrowing and Improvising Aesthetic Elements and Styles

Is Starbucks innovative and new? Starbucks has won numerous design awards; it has sued competitors for trade dress infringement when its look has appeared to be copied. Yet, on second glance, the Starbucks style has been with us for many years—in fact, it has its roots in the hallways of corporate America. Starbucks transformed the world of coffee-

EXHIBIT 4.2

Authors Taking a Break at Starbucks

house leisure by echoing the precision and artistic level of modern, well-designed office spaces, law firms, corporate boardrooms, and libraries. The similarities are remarkable. The use of smooth, varnished light woods, dark marble, and a blend of organic and high-tech textures and tones has been a staple of office design for over ten years.

The Starbucks aesthetic does not stop there. Touch is also brought into play: the packages that hold Starbucks coffee beans are smooth and straight, soft to the touch but with strong support. The consumer can feel the product's substance through a velvety, firm, but pliable "skin," making the hard product feel smooth, almost buttery. This is the matte-feel packaging texture favored by hard-cookie brands such as U.S. market leader Chips Ahoy. Oddly enough, dry-dog-food packaging has also used this approach for years. But the Starbucks coffee purchaser does not make strong associations to dog food; only the feel, not the look, is similar.

The Starbucks packaging is accessorized through assigning a different visual design to each type of coffee in the collection. Each type has its own colorful stamp, icon, color scheme, and graphic that identifies it. These stamps offer planned variation, planned divergence from a basic uniformity of style. It is a poster-art look that uses a minimalist base accessorized by a touch of ornamentalism. In grand style, the 1996 Annual Report is made of textured coffee-colored paper created from espresso grounds. The report, sporting a colorful array of photos and illustrations, urges "Look closely, you can actually see coffee bits in those pages."

Starbucks also keeps its look lively with rotating variations based on timely themes. In 1996, for example, Starbucks introduced its "25th Anniversary" theme. The paper cups had a 1970s "psychedelic" pattern, rendered in appropriately "seventies" neon colors. Signs hung in the coffee bars used these same attention-grabbing colors and pattern and recast 1970s slogans to be about coffee: "Give Beans a Chance," for example.

The Starbucks style draws customers in because it offers a planned, familiar vision, neat, organized, and systematic, but uses a changing variety of elements to create alluring visual stimuli. Starbucks' style tends to be abstract and stylized but highly recognizable. The style is not new; it borrows from several artistic looks. The effect, however, is dramatic. Aesthetic changes, identity shifts, and full-blown corporate identity projects need not be novel to be successful. What is needed is an overall vision, and vision can be honed through understanding. In this chapter, we introduce the idea of a style, focus on the elements of styles, discuss broad style dimensions and, finally, explain how to create successful styles.

WHAT IS "STYLE"?

When we refer to a *style,* we mean a distinctive quality or form, a manner of expression. According to art historian Meyer Shapiro, style is "the constant form—and sometimes the constant elements and expression—in the art of an individual or a group."[3]

The concept of style has been used in a variety of disciplines, from art history and literature to fashion and design. CNN's "Style" show by Elsa Klensch covers trends in a myriad of "style" domains including fashion design, jewelry design, interior design and home furnishings, architectural design, food presentations, and many more.

Functions of Styles

Styles serve a number of important functions for organizations. They create brand awareness; they cause intellectual and emotional associations. They differentiate products and services; they help consumers categorize products and services as being related. They help subcategorize variations of products within product lines; they fine-tune the marketing mix across target markets. For society, styles beautify our surroundings, mark off areas for pleasure and relaxation, reduce stress, and facilitate socialization. One of the foremost tasks of identity management through aesthetics is to associate the organization and its brands with a certain style.

Elements of Style

Styles are composed of primary elements, and can be analyzed in terms of them. Color, shape, line, and pattern are key elements of a visual style. Volume, pitch, and meter are some elements of auditory style. Buying and consuming are multisensory experiences. In retail spaces, for example, basic elements need to be managed, such as sound or scent. Background music and sounds, fragrances and tastes, materials and textures, all surround and influence consumers whether they enter department stores, grocery stores, or boutiques. Much of marketing aesthetics, however, still revolves around visual elements and style.

In what follows we present the primary elements corresponding to their basic sensory domains: sight, sound, touch, taste, and smell (see Figure 4.1). Later, though, we discuss how elements come together to create styles across their sensory domains. For example, the aesthetic element of texture contributes to a visual style even though it relates most directly to the domain of touch.

SIGHT: ALL PERCEPTIONS START WITH THE EYE

The most prevalent primary elements of styles in the marketing-aesthetics arena are visual. Aristotle's maxim that "all perception starts with the eye" is especially true for corporate and brand iden-

Figure 4.1

Primary Elements

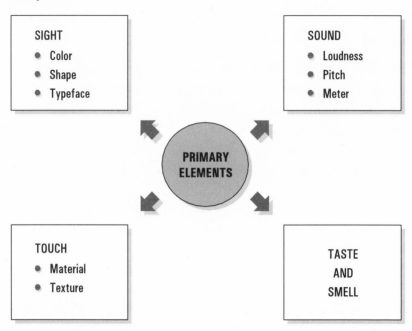

tity. Psychological research has shown that people have excellent memories for pictures. Compared with words, pictures are highly distinct, and thus may be recalled for a long time.

Consider the results of an experiment by Erdelyi and Kleinbard[4] on visual memory over time. They presented people with 60 pictures of common objects or with 60 names of the objects. Subjects in the experiment were asked to recall the words and pictures again and again up to seven days after they first saw the items. Interestingly enough, average recall of the words stayed constant after one hour. Subjects did not always recall the same words; they recalled some at certain times, and previously recalled words might drop out again over time. But when the items were shown as pictures, average recall increased up to four days.

That effect has been attributed to the higher degree of discrimination of pictures compared with words. Pictures are complex stimuli that always offer new cues. They are highly distinct and thus can be recalled relatively easily.

In this chapter we shall see that, from the perspective of marketing aesthetics, major visual elements consist of shapes and colors. We will also briefly discuss typefaces, since they are an aesthetic element that appears in numerous identity elements such as brand names, packaging, point-of-purchase displays, advertising, promotions, brochures, catalogs, business cards, and stationery.

SHAPE

Product and packaging shapes can be very powerful. As in the Absolut example in Chapter 1, the mere shape of a bottle can have dramatic marketing effects. The Calvin Klein fragrance CK ONE® has a "downmarket chic" identity conveyed in the product's simple screw-top bottle with a shape more suited to cheap liquor than to fragrance (see Exhibit 4.3). When a

EXHIBIT 4.3

CK ONE® Fragrance Bottle

© 1994 Calvin Klein Cosmetic Corporation.

handle was added to the Murphy's Oil Soap plastic bottle, sales began to soar, without any special advertising or promotion. With the old package shape, the brand was associated with old-fashioned housework drudgery; the handle made the product seem easy to use and convenient. The old-fashioned, natural identity suddenly became an asset. A bottle can become a trademark or an icon; it can create an identity almost single-handedly.

Three other bottle shapes that are easily identified with particular products are Coca-Cola, Chanel No. 5, and Heinz Ketchup. This identification is derived from only one aesthetic element—a shape—of one identity element—a bottle. Yet most consumers will have immediate associations, immediate feelings, about each bottle shape. Indeed, the importance of shape as an aesthetic element can even override functionality as a factor in corporate decisions. The H. J. Heinz ketchup bottle, advertised in the 1950s as "the best-known bottle in the world," capitalizes on the value of its bottle shape despite its obvious impracticality.

The original success of the Marlboro cigarette brand was due not only to its cowboy theme but also to the clever combination of primary attributes perceptions in the redesign of its cigarette package. Until 1955, Marlboro was an obscure niche brand for women. Then it was repositioned as the epitome of machismo, in major part by developing a rugged box with a flip-up top that changed the shape of the packaging.

Shapes can also be crucial elements of distinctive logos, as is illustrated by the logos of Apple, Nike, and many others. Distinctive shapes in properties or product design, such as the Transamerica Pyramid in San Francisco (Exhibit 4.4), can achieve instant recognition or "awareness," a marketer's dream come true. Transamerica's corporate identity has been closely linked with its headquarters building, which serves as its logo, as a prominent visual on its Web site and has been featured in advertising campaigns, including a "pop-up" ad in *Time* magazine and a series of magazine spreads.

As visual symbols, shapes are also an important source of a global identity. Unlike names, shapes cross cultural boundaries with relative ease. But marketers need to identify why particular shapes create certain impressions. Beyond specific objects that shapes can emulate, shapes are composed of a few key dimensions that give rise to specific associations.

Dimensions of Shape

While shapes appear to come in an infinite variety, there are four key dimensions of shape that should be considered by managers in planning

EXHIBIT 4.4

Transamerica Ad Depicting the Transamerica Pyramid

an aesthetics strategy (Figure 4.2). Tinkering with these dimensions can have a dramatic impact on customers' perceptions.

Angularity. Angular forms are those that contain angles (triangles, squares, rectangles, etc.), while rounded forms have no sharp corners. Both of these categories carry a set of rich associations. Angularity is

FIGURE 4.2

Dimensions of Shape

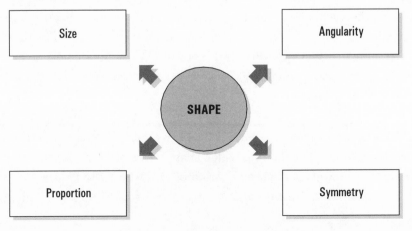

associated with conflict, dynamism, and masculinity; roundness evokes harmony, softness, and femininity. Similar to this distinction is that of the straight form versus the curved form. Straight shapes are often perceived as masculine, sharp, abrupt, and choppy, while curved shapes are perceived as feminine, soft, and continuous.

Symmetry. Symmetry refers to mirror identity of form or arrangement on the two sides of a dividing line (axis) or plane. Symmetry creates balance, an important factor in how we evaluate the visual appeal of an object; for example, it has been found in various past and recent psychological studies to be a key factor in how we judge the attractiveness of a person's face. But the appeal of symmetry has its limits. A touch of asymmetry can make a face even more appealing by adding an element of uniqueness and individuality. Cindy Crawford (whose face is an important identity element for Revlon) does not remove the mole on the side of her mouth because it adds to the attractiveness of her face; her otherwise symmetrical features are thrown into relief by the asymmetry of a mole on one side. Symmetry somehow provides order and relieves our tension; asymmetry does the opposite, creating agitation and tension—but often a little tension saves a visual image from monotony. Symmetry is often itself juxtaposed with a hint of asymmetry to provide the sense of balance with a touch of excitement or movement. We see this in the display of clocks or watch faces. In advertisements, brochures, catalogs, and all other displays, watches and companies' clock hands are set to the 10–2 position (symmetry on the vertical axis) with a hint of movement provided by the second hand at 35 seconds, a bit past the axis of symmetry (the 30-second mark). Most other combinations could create partial symmetry, like 9–3 with the second hand at the 60-second mark. But, with all three hands, the 10–2, 30-second position creates complete (vertical) symmetry with the same distance between each hand (corresponding to exactly 20 minutes). In the opposite (equivalent to 8–4 and 60 seconds) another perfectly vertical symmetrical position exists, a symmetry used by Mercedes-Benz as its logo.

Proportion. Proportion is another major variable influencing the way we perceive shapes. Long angular shapes and oblong shapes (which were prevalent in the baroque period of art) extend the field of vision, thus appearing to capture more of a particular scene, creating a dominating aesthetic. Short angular shapes can seem more timid and meek. With round shapes, proportion and symmetry are often blended, since perfectly circular shapes are also naturally symmetrical. Thus, circular shapes appear less powerful than oblong shapes, but they create perceptions of harmony, resonating with softness and perfection.

Size. Personalities are often read into particular shapes. This is readily apparent when we focus on size. Large shapes, tall or wide, are often perceived as powerful and strong while small shapes, short or thin, appear delicate and weak. Nobody understood this principle better than the Dutch painter Piet Mondrian, whose thick black lines marking off large blue, red, and yellow squares and rectangles have inspired the designs of a wide variety of consumer products, including shower curtains, beach towels, and the L'Oreal Studio line of hairstyling products. With their large and angular shapes, these product designs project strength, energy, and effectiveness.

More than other dimensions of shape, the way size is evaluated varies strikingly depending on cultural and regional norms. In the West, small size is often viewed as having little stature—our outsized national folk heroes like the huge Paul Bunyan are testaments to this cultural preference for largeness. But in the East, large size is often viewed as awkward and unwieldy. In any region, the effect of size can vary; sometimes stout is considered unsophisticated and unintelligent, while thin is considered orderly and sharp.

Distinctiveness of Shapes

The power of shapes in an aesthetics strategy is overwhelming. This power is directly related to the distinctiveness of the shape. The distinctiveness is related to (a) the extent of exclusive pairing of the shape with the company or brand and (b) the inherent quality of the shape.

Pairing, Repeating, and Protecting Shapes. A shape can take on various meanings depending on the context in which it appears. The shape alone of a trademark or other emblem does not identify a particular product or company in an unambiguous fashion. Thus, the goal is not to form a trademark or logo to fit a product, but to pair a potentially appropriate shape with a product. In other words, avoiding poor shape-product matches is the key goal in analyzing shapes in corporate and brand identity. For example, consider the wool trademark designed by Francesco Saroglia for the International Wool Secretariat.

The wool logo's supple, flexible, smooth but intricate shape portrays a generic quality that is appropriate for, but not specific to, wool. The interlocking strands suggest yarn, and the roundness is vaguely feminine, which goes well with wool's associations with feminine themes such as fashion and knitting; but the logo does not rule out a masculine identification, which could perhaps be made with the "optical illusion" look of the logo that calls to mind the scientific, optics-oriented work of the artist M. C. Escher.

Shapes become associated with a product or company through repeated pairing. Through repetition over time, the pairing of a product and a shape can become a familiar part of an identity. As a result, as with other primary aesthetic elements, shapes should be considered as proprietary identity elements that are consistently used and reinforced via corporate communications. Indeed, nonfunctional, aesthetically valued shapes are afforded legal protection as valid trademarks. Coca-Cola's contoured bottle, Chanel No. 5's square bottle, and Perrier's curved bottle are examples. The movement away from focusing on names to focus on looks—on trade dress—accords with the notion that the law protects not merely the name but the identity. Managers should pair product and shape, repeat the pairing over time, and protect the pairing from appropriation by competitors.

COLOR

Color pervades corporate and brand identity. Logos usually appear in color, products have colors, the fabrics of company uniforms are color coordinated; the walls of the exteriors and interiors of buildings have color; ads have color schemes; and packages lure us with various colors. Gone are the days of Henry Ford, whose Model T was offered in "any color, as long as it's black." An enormous range of colors is available for virtually all identity elements. When tights were first marketed in the 1960s, only six shades were available. By the end of the 1980s, Christian Dior sold tights in 101 colors. The trendy cosmetics company MAC (Make-up Art Cosmetics) broke into the crowded cosmetics industry with a novel strategy that included no advertising and simple packaging—but a huge range of colors in its product lines, with 140 shades of lipstick, including the more sophisticated earth tones that customers preferred to the traditional pinks and purples. Even this seemingly large number of colors is drastically multiplied for many materials. In January 1996, the Japanese fabric company Kanebo held an exhibition in the prestigious Spiral Design Building in Tokyo, exhibiting its 3,600 dyes. Black may be the primary (or only) color in the collection of some avant-garde fashion designers, but this is a result of careful choice rather than of necessity.

USING COLOR FOR IDENTITY

Company and Brand Identification

Companies can make color the major focus of their identity by utilizing a single distinctive color or a color palette as part of their visual identity. If a color is consistently used across a variety of identity elements, it becomes part of a company's signature; Kodak's yellow, Tiffany's light blue, IBM's darker blue, and Mary Kay's pink are good examples. Coca-Cola uses the color red in an effective way; the company makes sure that the color is reproduced appropriately on an infinite number of materials and surfaces worldwide and is very protective about the use of its color.[5] Indeed, as we will see in Chapter 8, colors can be legally protected.

Colors signal categories, so colors are strategically chosen for uniforms and other physical surroundings. A full-blown identity can be generated for a conglomerate by using color as well. For example, Best Foods, a division of CPC International, one of the 100 largest industrial companies in the United States and one of the largest corn refiners worldwide, uses the color yellow prominently on the packaging of all its major products, including Mazola corn oil, Hellmann's mayonnaise, Best Foods' mustard, Mueller's egg noodles, Argo cornstarch, Niagara spray starch, and Knorr soup mixes.

Product Line Identification

Color can also be used to separate product lines into subcategories. Bayer brand aspirin uses the strategy, familiar in over-the-counter health care products like shampoo, of putting related product lines in the same bottle and package design but distinguishing variations, with different colors. The identity of the Bayer brand with its relation to various product lines is created primarily through color.

Associations

A color can be chosen for the specific associations it carries with it. The brown of United Parcel Service's trucks, uniforms, and other identity materials signals the company's no-nonsense, behind-the-scenes, reliable identity. Frequently, color marks a brand so that it stands out from similar products. Red is popular for brands. Dewar's uses red; Mobil uses red; Coca-Cola uses red; and, among others, Campbell's uses red. When we walk down the soup aisle in the supermarket, we do not need to look for the Campbell's or Progresso names; we merely need to look for red (Campbell's) or blue (Progresso): one way these two companies differentiate is through their color identities. Color can call attention to a product that traditionally does not employ color. Cooper Industries' Plumb brand hammers achieved success by giving the hammer handles a bright orange color, making them easy to spot in the toolbox—and on the retail shelf.

Companies may also invent new colors, or rather, new color terminologies, to market their products. To illustrate "the subtle tones that make all the difference" in their line of color laser printers, Canon invented colors such as "fog" and "moss." The all-green ad copy of "moss" reads: "Between yellow and green there's olive. Between olive and gray there's fern green. Between fern green and gray there's slate green. And if you keep finding the colors between the colors, you get to a color called MOSS."

WHAT DOES COLOR MEAN TO CUSTOMERS?

The Composition of Color

Beyond mere identification and association, color can be used to create experiences. The human eye can distinguish among 10,000 hues. Three basic dimensions—saturation, brightness, and hue—can be used to relate perceptual experiences to physical properties. Saturation refers to chromatic purity, or freedom from dilution with white. Brightness has to do with intensity, or energy level (akin to loudness or amplitude in music). Hue refers to the wavelength, the particular shades of color that we see (royal blue versus teal blue, for example).

We can see the possibilities for using these various aspects of colors when we look at how the color pink is used. Pink, a less saturated tone of red, is often associated with children's products. The pastel shades of pink often used for infants' clothes and toys are less bright than the neon pink of older children's toys. To get an idea of the differences in hue of the color pink, consider the full line of varying pink hues evident at a lipstick display.

THE STRUCTURE OF COLOR CATEGORIES

Affective, Cognitive and Behavioral Reactions to Color

"Colorful" Colors. Each dimension of color seems to be related to different behavioral reactions. For example, the more saturated a color, the greater the impression that the object is moving. The brighter the color, the greater the impression that the object is closer than it really is. Hues at one extreme end of visible light (reds, oranges, and yellows) tend to be perceived as more energetic and extroverted, while those at the other end (greens, blues, and purples) appear calmer and more introverted. For example, reds tend to be perceived as adventurous, sociable, exciting, powerful, and protective. Yellows are often seen as cheerful, jovial, exciting, affectionate, and impulsive. Greens and blues are viewed as calm, restful, and soothing. At the same time, reds, oranges, and yellows are perceived as warm colors, while blues, greens, and violets come across as cold colors. Different hues also produce varying impressions of distance: blue and green seem farther away than red, orange, and brown.

The Prestige Colors: Black and White, Gold and Silver. Black and white represent extremes of saturation and often of brightness. Thus, the color white, particularly if it is bright, is perceived as sunny, happy, active, and sometimes as pure and innocent. The color black is often perceived as dark and mysterious and sometimes as impure or evil. Metallic colors such as gold and silver have lustrous images; they take on the qualities of the metals gold and silver. Thus, they convey the qualities of inorganic materials, but they also create feelings of brightness, luxury, and elegance due to their associations with opulence and precious metals. This is why imitating gold or some other standard such as marble is difficult. An imitation must evoke the underlying image of value, or it will backfire and seem to be an imitation, or "cheap."

Reactions to Color Combinations

We have been focusing on the use of particular colors in isolation. Ironically, using an array of colors can create an identity that is often less complex than one created through one color. Apple Computer's user-friendly, playful image is expressed not only in its apple-shaped logo but also in the rainbow-style array of colors within it. The rainbow or any other particular combination of colors creates a unified Gestalt that can overshadow the associations of the particular colors within it.

CREATING LUXURY THROUGH STYLE

The German-based Montblanc Inc.'s line of writing implements is an example of an identity that uses style to appeal to customers' aesthetic sense. The company produces a full line of writing implements and accessories such as leather desk calendars and date books. The main color of the Montblanc products and other identity materials such as brochures is a rich black, with the white star symbol adorning all the products. The black-and-white color scheme is accented by touches of gold on the pens and leather products, adding to the "luxury" image. Only the most lustrous materials are used in the company's identity materials, from the thick, smooth paper with embossed letters that is used for the "Your Personal Montblanc Guide" that comes with every product, to the velvet that lines the boxes in which products are sold. Montblanc emphasizes the idea of an overall style that they offer their customers in order to enrich their lives: "All the writing instruments and accessories of the Montblanc collection fit together harmoniously and perfectly complement each other. This sophisticated combination forms the most cultivated writing environment: the world of Montblanc."

Source: Company materials.

Often a combination of colors can conjure a very specific image. For example, the Phoenix airport's use of various umbers and other earth tones combine to create an association with the desert. Color combinations can also evoke specific meanings by their associations with national flags. Red, white, and blue are used together to build an all-American identity, whereas red, white, and green conveys an Italian identity and is thus often used for packaging Italian foods.

TYPEFACE

Typefaces are everywhere we look: on publicity materials, cards and stationery, advertising (both print and broadcast), point-of-purchase displays, bags, and packaging. A typeface is an aesthetic element that is composed primarily of other aesthetic elements. A typeface has shape, color (and material) that need to be considered separately and together. As with shapes, typefaces come in an infinite variety and can convey an infinite number of images. (Numerous design books display the multitude of typefaces.)

The Look of Typefaces

Typefaces are a unique aspect of style, since they add representational qualities directly to words or letters, which of course themselves already convey meaning. A typeface can be given a particular shape in order to create certain perceptions. Tall, narrow letters with precise serifs seem elegant; rounded, full letters without serifs seem friendly, even cuddly. The "metropolitan" Art Deco-style typeface of the *New Yorker* magazine is indelibly paired with the qualities associated with literary New York: sophistication, wit, style, the avant-garde. A typeface that seems almost handwritten will convey a company's people-oriented, unthreatening, low-key identity. Cursive rather than print letters, as in the logo of the Crane's paper company, seem fancy and celebratory, appropriate for Crane's identity as the paper of choice for special occasions and formal letters. Choices such as whether to use capital or lowercase letters matter as well. Capital letters convey authority and aggressiveness; but use of all-lowercase letters can make a daring, understated impression.

Often the feeling and perceptions accompanying the look of the letters in a particular word or group of words relates to other uses of a similar typeface. Consider the Benetton store in the Georgetown neighborhood of Washington, D.C. It uses gold uppercase letters in a bold style such as we would find on a federal building or in other official national contexts. For Washingtonians, the imagery is stark and familiar: the Benetton sign evokes qualities associated with the federal government, such as power, strength, harmony, trustworthy, strong moral values, and international leadership.

Perception and Memory for Typefaces

Consider the following name: Hyatt. Without looking ahead in the book, write it down exactly as the letters appear in the logo. The Hyatt logo was designed by Landor Associates, as displayed in Exhibit 4.5 a few pages later. As the exhibit shows, the letter "A" uses an untraditional horizontal bar stroke. The lack of the true horizontal bar stroke is one small element that contributes to the modern impression of the corporation. Though as your own attempts to recall the logos may have demonstrated, it is clear that these sets of variation may not be consciously perceived and remembered. The same is the case for many other logos designed by Landor (e.g., the logos for Saturn and JAL).

Sometimes identity elements are literally misperceived by customers. Some stimuli (e.g., an advertisement) may not impact the intended customer target correctly or may have an insufficient impact. The perception of the company in the customer's eyes can be reduced, sometimes even impoverished. Mazda's original logo was a stylized representation of the letter "m," but it was perceived by most consumers outside Japan as an "l."

SOUND

Sounds and music matter in two ways for corporate and brand identity: as background, they enhance identity in retail and other spaces; and in advertising and other communications, they can be identity-creating elements.

As Leonard Bernstein explained in his Norton Lectures at Harvard, sounds are based on harmonic series. If sounds are highly structured, we call them music. To the question posed by MIT's computer scientist Marvin Minsky, "Why do we like certain tunes?" Bernstein answered crisply: "Because they have certain structural features." One such structural feature is melody. Melodies (or their more rudimentary form, melodic contours), are sequences of single pitches organized as a musical whole. The basis of jingles that are frequently used in communication messages, melodies are the most salient, easily recognized, and easily remembered musical feature.

Establishing a Sound Identity

According to philosopher David Burrows, "Background sound . . . gives the world a texture of microactivity."[6] It can relax people, hurry people, make them happy or make them sad. Designers of retail spaces and restaurants are expert creators of this texture of microactivity.

Many services are sound-intensive. Hotels, restaurants, supermarkets, department stores, hairdressers, airlines, and professional service providers such as doctors, lawyers, and accountants make heavy use of auditory stimuli to connect with customers. Sound pervades the service encounter over the telephone, on the selling floor, in the waiting room, and any place the customer visits. Voices for advertising need to be chosen carefully to create various tonalities and accents leading to recognizability and favorable associations, feelings, and evaluations.[7]

Sounds also create identities in advertising. In its TV ads, "Campbell's Garden Vegetables and Pasta" brand illustrates the freshness of its ingredients with the snapping sound of fresh vegetables.

Background sounds and music can enhance a corporate or brand identity because sound is a powerful emotional and behavioral cue. While visual aesthetics can be vivid and arousing, visual elements are difficult to change without associated production costs; and with the exception of video, visual aesthetics are stable unless changed. Sound, on the other hand, is easy to change and is also inherently variable and changing. Music has highs and lows, fasts and slows, and louds and softs.

The inherent variability and ease of change makes sound a flexible, low-cost identity enhancement and creation device. The effects of sounds are, like visuals, highly dependent on the impressions that customers have. A "noisy" doctor's office might hurt sales, whereas a noisy restaurant might be desirable and appropriate to achieving a youth appeal and identity.

ENHANCING IDENTITY THROUGH MUSIC

For years, United Airlines has been using George Gershwin's "Rhapsody in Blue" in an identity-creating fashion. "Rhapsody in Blue" has been featured in United's advertising, when customers are on hold for the Reservations toll-free phone number, and on the safety tape played before each flight. Gershwin's music is contemporary, dynamic—an American classic; its connection with the metropolis of New York City was augmented when the music was featured prominently in Woody Allen's *Manhattan.* The tune is an ideal aesthetic tool to express United's positioning as a contemporary U.S.-based international airline that takes business travelers to major destinations around the world.

TOUCH

Materials can create a certain "feel" for a product. Ericsson, a company that sells cellular phones, claims, "Hold it [the phone] and you're hooked ... It feels like part of you." Materials used are important sources of identity in print communications, office exteriors and interiors, and company uniforms. Glossy versus matte paper for stationery and business cards, marble versus plastic at a check-in counter, wool versus polyester on a uniform all provide stark dichotomies.

APPLICATION: S. D. WARREN'S MATERIAL AESTHETIC

A company that understands the power of materials is the S. D. Warren Company, a subsidiary of Scott Paper Company. Warren is particularly strong in manufacturing a variety of paper for offset printing. Paper for offset printing can be judged in terms of strength, smoothness, printability, brightness, and opacity. Strength, smoothness, and printability are utilitarian criteria. Brightness and opacity are both utilitarian and aesthetic. Brightness creates contrast and intensifies color, while opacity prevents images printed on one side of the paper from showing through on the other side.

To illustrate the aesthetic value of its papers and convey its identity,

EXHIBIT 4.5

Hyatt Logo

Warren uses its own brochures as both a promotional material and a product showpiece. Utilizing Warren's impressive variety of paper materials, the different brochures feature a number of breathtaking photographs and illustrations. For example, one product, "Lustro Gloss," is illustrated with striking black-and-white and color photography taken at Carnegie Hall. Each page displays different versions of the paper such as "Lustro Dull," and "Lustro Dull Cream" showing subtle shades in the bright red seats of the concert hall and brilliant details on some of the instruments. Another brochure for "Pointe Clear Matte" ("nothing fancy in knock-out style") uses shots from the sport of boxing to make the point. Still another brochure illustrates the smooth, uniform surface with crisp, brilliant reproduction of "Cameo Dull" by explaining various garden concepts (such as the formal garden, the Japanese garden, the English garden, the roof garden). The description of the Formal Garden reads:

> What is a garden? Whether a simple window box or the manicured forests of Versailles, a garden is where man controls nature for aesthetic reasons. Pleasing to the eye, soothing to the senses, a garden rewards one's efforts much like the paper this is printed on, Warren Cameo Dull.

The brochures are not only visually appealing but also pleasing to the touch. One brochure for a rough surface, entitled "The Spirit of Discovery," has an elevated surface made of leather that engages the senses of sight, touch, and even smell.

Associations from Materials

Materials carry strong associations relating to warmth, strength, and naturalness. A range of associations are evoked by choices such as what

OXO: BRINGING AESTHETICS TO KITCHEN TOOLS

The Oxo brand of kitchenware items is a perfect example of design leadership that capitalizes on creating an aesthetic experience for consumers. In Oxo's Good Grips line of kitchen tools, the sense of touch was brought into play, complimenting a striking visual look. These kitchen gadgets were designed by Sam Farber, retired founder of the CopCo cookware company, when he realized that existing cooking tools were not comfortable to use or aesthetically pleasing. Farber worked with designers on the Good Grips line, keeping the experience of the consumer in mind at every step. The handles of the implements were designed to be oversized and easy to grip—Farber's wife, who suffers from arthritis, was the inspiration there—and Oxo used a material called santoprene® that is composed of plastic and rubber and has a pleasingly warm, smooth, nonslip feel. Flexible sections on the sides called "fins" offered "fingerprint softspots" that help the handles to bend to an individual's finger grip and that give extra cushion and control.

These sensory considerations of "feel" were the starting point for a visually striking design that sets the product apart from the competition. The bulky shape added a "masculine" touch to a traditionally "feminine" product, extending the appeal of the product beyond the usual market for kitchen tools, 30-to-40-year-old women. Black was chosen as the color for the signature handles of all Good Grips products, giving them a high-tech, sophisticated look. The Good Grips products have won countless design awards.

Source: Company materials, interviews with managers, and speech delivered by Sam Farber, "The Oxo Story."

type of wood to use for a product. A 1996 Lexus advertisement boasts, "Pine was too stark. Birch, too thin. Oak, far too bland. So we decided on California walnut. . . . At Lexus, we scrutinized 24 different types of wood for the interior before we found one that made the cut." These types of associations apply equally to the materials themselves and to pictures and drawings of the materials or their patterns, which can be used in all sorts of marketing communications (advertising, packaging, or product design).

Inorganic materials such as marble, glass, or metals are perceived as cold, and hard, while organic materials such as wood or leather are perceived as warm, and soft. Rough materials have been traditionally perceived as outdoors-oriented, whereas polished materials have been appropriate for indoors. Changes in these design orientations, however, can be seen with the change, for example, in floors and laminated tops, which used to mimic polished marble and wood grains but now are likely to resemble rough marble or other rough or matte surfaces. Rough materials have moved indoors, suggesting strength combined with an outdoorsy, free feeling, unfettered by order and symmetry. Inside or out, organic materials such as flowers, woods, and the like can be used to make people feel relaxed and in harmony with nature. But color and shape can also work with the texture of the material to create feelings. Bricks (or brick-like prints or photos), which are an inorganic material perceived as hard and strong, nonetheless also convey warmth because of their red color—suitable for fireplaces, interior walls, cozy terraces, and the like.

Materials and Textures

Textures of certain materials can be powerful sources of sensations. In a 1997 mailing campaign, Brooks Brothers, a men's retailer, included fabric samples so that customers could experience the materials firsthand.

SCENT: TASTE AND SMELL

Taste is highly derived from smell. Smell is the most powerful of the senses. Scents are omnipresent in our environments. Stores that specialize in scented products, like Crabtree & Evelyn or The Body Shop, rely on scents to create identities in their products as well as in their retail spaces. Except for these cases in which they act as identity creators, scents have the advantage of subtlety; they often do not draw attention to themselves. Like background sounds and music, scent can enhance an identity rather than create it.

Smell is based on a small number of components that can produce thousands of sensations. Smells are often divided into seven distinct categories: (1) minty, (2) floral, (3) ethereal, (4) musky, (5) resinous, (6) foul, and (7) acrid.[8]

Scent Reactions

Research shows that females react to certain smells differently from males. It is also clear that certain smells appear to be uniformly offensive, while others are uniformly appealing. Aromatherapy promises physiological and psychological benefits based on specific aromas. Neurologists test various scents for use in keeping gamblers at slot machines. Andron by Jovan (an allusion to "androgen," a male sex hormone) was a cologne for men touted as pheromone-enhanced, designed to lure women.

The Power of Scents

Human beings have an excellent ability to distinguish smells. The memory of smell is perhaps the strongest memory we have. We all recall excruciating details about an experience when we smell a scent that we smelled at the time of the experience.

Scent experiences and evaluations and our perceptual learning of smells may depend largely on verbal labels. There may be nothing inherently "eternal" smelling about Eternity, or "obsessional" smelling about Obsession, or "unisex" smelling about CK ONE®. The differentiability of smell, the strong memory for smell, and the ability to create unique associations all make smells and tastes an ideal tool for enhancing a corporate or brand identity. Again, "pair and repeat" becomes the rule to create the association.

We typically describe smells not necessarily in terms of their own properties but by comparing them to other things that the smell evokes in memory. We often perceive scents as smoky, fruity, spicy, or floral and evaluate them as intoxicating, delightful, pleasing, or their opposites. We also associate them with seasons—spring scents might be fruity or floral, while winter scents can be piney or cinnamon-based. Given the strong memories scents evoke, it is easy for marketers to build on scents to create their desired perception or feeling when creating or enhancing an identity.

CREATING A STYLE: SYNESTHESIA

What Is Synesthesia?

The stimulation of one sense by another sense is called synesthesia, from the Greek *syn* (together) and *aisthanesthai* (perceive). Composers Scriabin and Rimsky-Korsakov associated colors with music: E major with blue, A flat with purple, D major with yellow. The writer Vladimir Nabokov reported smell and touch associations when he uttered a vowel sound: for him the long "a" of the English alphabet had a tint of weathered wood; the French "a" evoked polished ebony. The notion of synesthesia is used consciously in many art forms from the Japanese tea ceremony to Wagner's *Gesamtkunstwerk,* and contemporary performance art.

The Japanese tea ceremony consists of serving special tea in a ritual manner with carefully selected utensils in a room of certain proportions containing a painting and a garden view. Certain stylized movements are used by both the server of tea (the host) and the participant in the ritual (the guest). The ceremony thus appeals to multiple senses and incorporates concepts of product design, ceramic design, interior design, art, and movement.

Similarly, Wagner's *Gesamtkunstwerk,* as embodied in his famous *Ring* opera cycle, is supposed to integrate acting, symphony, and operatic music, and Wagner had a special theater built for the performance of this unique art form in Bayreuth, Germany. Modern performance art also appeals to multiple senses by using features of several art forms such as acting, dance and movement, music and sounds, and in some cases taste and smell.

The Holistic Nature of Style

Synesthesia creates an integration of primary elements such as colors, shapes, scents, and materials into "systems of attributes" that express a corporate or brand aesthetic style. Though identities are composed of the primary elements that we have discussed, a holistic perception is the result. The holistic nature of perception has been the central tenet of a movement in psychology called the Gestalt movement. Gestalt psychologists believed that the whole, or Gestalt, is more than the sum of the parts. Planning corporate and brand identities require the manager to pay meticulous attention to the parts that create the whole. What ultimately counts is the entire Gestalt, but slight changes in underlying dimensions or their interactions can cause massive changes in the Gestalt.

APPLICATION: GILLETTE

Successful corporate or brand aesthetics, even in the design of a single product, uses synesthesia as a design principle. Multiple primary attributes (loud and aggressive colors; dynamic, rhythmical music; bold shapes and typefaces) are combined to create a holistic perception—a style.

The Gillette series of razors and toiletries (deodorants, shaving creams, and aftershaves) represents an example of synesthesia. The Sensor razor, launched worldwide in 1989, is a visual and tactile experience. The experience is further enhanced by the mega-brand identity system created by Anspach Grossman Portugal, an identity firm. To capitalize on the success of its Sensor razor, its best-selling shaver system, Gillette then selected the design firm Desgrippes Gobe & Associates to develop a line of fourteen toiletry products for men, scheduled for a simultaneous launch in the United States and in Europe. Gillette had traditionally been outsold by rivals. In the U.S., Gillette trailed S. C. Johnson's Edge brand gel in the aerosol shaving cream and gel category by fourteen share points and Procter & Gamble in the deodorants category by nine share points. It had largely ignored aftershaves. Its toiletries business accounted for 20% of sales but only 12.6% of operating profit.[9]

Desgrippes Gobe applied its proprietary research process, termed "SENSE" (an acronym for Sensory Exploration and Need States Evaluation), to identify the key design elements (shapes, colors, and materials) that relate to and express the Gillette products' identity: masculine, traditional, but technologically progressive. In the new products, the company's inherent values were related to the act of shaving. The firm viewed shaving as a rite of passage linked to a man's daily transformation from private to public space; the meaning of colors, shapes, materials, typefaces, and fragrances were related to this context. The design, developed by Desgrippes Gobe in collaboration with Gillette's in-house design team, incorporated existing Sensor equities in the colors silver and black together with grips, but they also added some key innovations. As they explain the rationale behind the product, packaging and graphic design:

> The color blue communicates the cleanliness of shaving. . . . Black communicates universality and a gutsy, masculine lifestyle. Silver, with its metallic sheen and industrial presence, reflects the performance aspects of razor blades and Sensor. A revolutionary thin-walled, crystal clear container showcases the clarity of a new transparent product. Structural designs are proportional to fit a man's hand and [are] slick and cylindrical or ribbed and reminiscent of a man's broad shoulders. . . . Gillette's bold Futura logo reinforces the Company's masculine heritage and leadership position. . . . Domi-

EXHIBIT 4.6

Gillette Sensor Razor

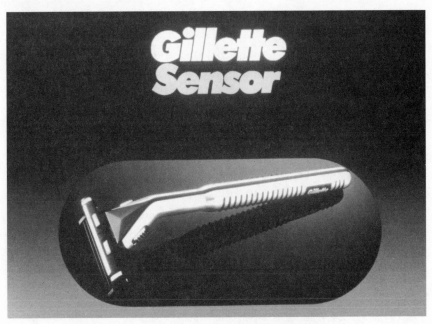

nated by citrus with a mossy, woodsy base, Cool Wave (the name of the product) unifies the functionally based Gillette Series.[10]

Two Managerial Approaches to Creating Style

At Gillette, as at most organizations, a style is usually born through the vision, creativity, and intuition of designers. They work in two ways: a bottom-up approach entails selecting key primary attributes and then combining them to create a unifying style; a top-down approach, on the other hand, involves selection of a style and then implementing the style through the selection of primary attributes.

The bottom-up process is often easier when a brand is being repositioned. Here, customers may be quite familiar with certain key attributes (for example, a corporate color) that provide familiarity to customers

---

LICENSING STYLE

The leap from designing clothing to designing a signature scent is now *de rigueur* for fashion designers. But after these extensions into body products have come extensions into virtually every aspect of customers' aesthetic environment. Expanding their lines of products to include their customers' entire physical environment, these fashion designers are creating and marketing an aesthetics that their customers can experience through products as diverse as jeans and candlesticks. Familiar fashion names such as Guess?, Ralph Lauren, Calvin Klein, and Donna Karan have all produced housewares lines that stay true to each designer's aesthetics. Italian designer Missoni produces rugs with its distinctive geometric patterns (for $4,500); Ralph Lauren produces pillowcases and sheets that repeat the subdued colors, stripes, and plaids of his clothing (at $40 for a pair of pillowcases); Calvin Klein sells pitchers ($90) that use the same stark, minimalist lines as his clothing; and high-end menswear designer Paul Smith offers a "retro" toothbrush and toothpaste set (for over $10) that echoes the look of his "men's-club-meets-downtown" style of clothing.

Source: Carlos Mota, "House of Style," *New York,* October 14, 1996, p. 60.

and equity to the organization. The challenge is to incorporate them successfully into a new style. The top-down approach is more strategic and systematic and better adapted for when a novel brand identity is created from scratch.

STRATEGIC ISSUES IN STYLE CREATION

Key strategic issues in style creation are:

- whether to juxtapose design elements;
- when styles should be adapted or abandoned.

Juxtaposition of Design Elements

There may be an inherent tension in a chosen design solution. In order to create a more interesting, unique look, a designer may consciously juxtapose different design elements in one or more identity elements. For example, within an ad there may be one visual element that stands out because its style is strikingly different from the rest of the ad. Within one interior space, there may be one piece of furniture that displays a different style. Juxtaposition in design can be as appealing as the occasional asymmetry in form; it is an asymmetry in style. The Gap, for example, uses black and white for its logo on signage, but blue and white for its logo on bags.

An interesting type of juxtaposition is eclecticism. An eclectic approach provides juxtaposition within the same corporate expression by using multiple sources of elements. Some international hotels use an eclectic approach by creating unique rooms that mix furniture and designs from different periods and styles. The decision to provide either variety or consistency rests on whether a particular aspect of design should be highlighted. High-awareness brands might want to highlight the logo, for example. Snapple's logo includes a frame and appears to jump out at the consumer due to the contrast with the underlying uniform color of the bottle.

Product lines often require juxtaposition. The Swatch brand of casual watches, which saved the Swiss watch industry from a years-long decline in the mid-1980s, represents a good example of this sort of style variety. While most watch manufacturers are concerned about protecting a unique look and therefore offer only small variations from year to year, the concept of a Swatch is build around the idea of fashions and fads.

Adapting or Abandoning Styles

Styles can appear outdated over time. We can easily identify numerous styles based on time periods. The trends of the 1920s, 50s, 60s, and 70s stand out as vivid reminders that styles can become quite dated. Overuse of styles, particularly unusual or otherwise vivid styles, can create permanent strong mental associations of those styles with the time period in which they arose. So too, a space dimension can be etched into our associations. Thus, constant monitoring of our environment and trends is essential in order to adapt and, if necessary, abandon styles when overall impressions have shifted. Dunkin' Donuts recently announced a change in identity in which the "outdated" pink-and-orange look will be supplanted with a drab mauve, termed "ripe raisin." The color will be placed in an expansion strategy (see Chapter 3) on roofs, signs, countertops, and walls. Brighter menu boards and backlit signs will add to the updated identity. Customer research alerted management to the outdated nature of the identity. Customers felt that the brand "was approachable and fun, and they did not want it to be upscale, but modern."[11]

MODIFYING A STYLE

The Case for Revolutionary Changes

Imagine one day you go to a business meeting. The room is full of team members dressed in dark business suits. Your eyes, however, are drawn to one person in khaki pants and a casual sweater. Why? Simply because, in contrast to all the others, the person in the sweater is dressed differently.

A few days later (let's say it's a casual Friday), you go to another business meeting. The same people are present and everybody wears casual clothing. Will you again be drawn to the same person? Clearly not. This example illustrates a basic fact about human attention. We notice things that stand out, things that are distinct.

A major factor contributing to distinctiveness is novelty. We tend to notice things that are novel, that we have never seen before. Moreover, we tend to be drawn to things that are loud, extreme, sometimes annoying. Finally, we pay attention to things that are different.

Thus, distinctive designs tend to be revolutionary as opposed to evolutionary. These principles are well known to advertisers. New Yorkers may still remember the Crazy Eddie ads in which "Crazy Eddie," the owner of a low-priced electronics chain, told customers about its "insane prices" by screaming at them. Lovers of upscale brands may remember the same approach for Chanel's worldwide campaign for the Egoïste fragrance for men. In these particular ads, numerous well-dressed women in evening gowns screamed the brand name while opening and slamming shut the shutters of their hotel-room windows. We may not like such ads, but we certainly notice them.

What applies to advertising also works in other contexts of identity image management. In business cards, a slightly larger rectangular shape, a vertical orientation, or a picture on the business card will be noticed. Quite appropriately, Kodak uses pictures. For colors, in the sea of the corporate dark blue, the Mary Kay pink and the Tiffany light blue are distinctive.

Unusual or revolutionary stylistic approaches may be compared to the adoption process that occurs as a result of diffusions of innovations. As with a new technology, a new look is liked first by the trendsetters before it is by the masses. The new look creates an *"avant-garde"* identity. Trendsetters, personality-wise, like to be different; they are variety seekers, and regarding image they are not at all averse to risk. While trendsetters tend to be in the minority, as opinion leaders they influence others. And since we often develop our own final opinions after comparing our opinions with those of others, trendsetters may make a powerful impact over time. Moreover, after experiencing things more than once, they become less new. And mere exposure over time seems to create liking. Did you instantly like the new minivan design in the mid-1980s when it first came out? More likely, it was love at second sight.

The Case for Evolutionary Changes

Being different, however, not only draws attention, it also involves risk because of another fact of human nature: noticeable, distinct things lead to more extreme evaluations—positive or negative. Middle-of-the-road approaches, while rarely catching our attention or arousing our emotions, are less risky.

DIMENSIONS OF STYLE

Managerial input in creating or modifying styles can be enhanced if managers are able to evaluate a design on major stylistic dimensions.

At the turn of the century, Heinrich Wölfflin, one of history's most renowned art critics, distinguished between two general opposite aesthetic styles: the classical and the baroque. According to Wölfflin, these two are the basic categories for the interpretation of the structure of artistic forms, not only works of art but anything made "with artistic and expressive ends." *Classical* and *baroque* indicate two general, opposite qualities and structures that artistic forms can have—regardless of their historical period. Five pairs of characteristics distinguish the classical from the baroque: the linear versus the pictorial; the closed versus the open form; the taste for depth versus the taste for surface; the taste for oneness versus the taste for multiplicity; the clear form versus the ambiguous form. This early aesthetic categorization may still be useful for managers. Each corporate element, whether it be a name, a logo, a corporate uniform, a product packaging, an advertisement or a building, can be analyzed using this simple bipolar dimension: whether the element is classical in style or baroque. As a result, different elements can be related to one another and the consistency of a collection of elements can be determined.

To define stylistic dimensions, we move beyond Wölfflin's broad categorization. In so doing, managers can isolate and adjust stylistic components that do not contribute to the desired style. Here, we identify four perceptual dimensions to evaluate corporate or brand identity-related styles: (1) complexity ("minimalism" vs. "ornamentalism"), (2) representation ("realism" vs. "abstraction"), (3) perceived movement ("dynamic" vs. "static"), and (4) potency ("loud/strong" vs. "soft/weak").

Style Dimension 1: Complexity

How ornate or complex do you want your organization or brand to appear? This dimension places style on a continuum that goes from simple

FIGURE 4.3

Dimensions of Style

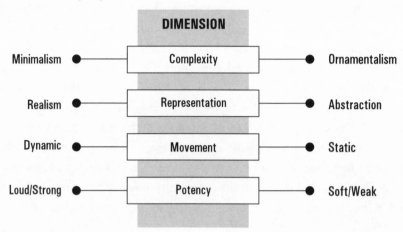

to complex or, from minimalism to ornamentalism. Minimalism strives for simplicity of structure and form, viewing decoration as unnecessary excess. Ornamentalism, on the other hand, loves complexity, variety of motifs, and multiple meanings. The Laura Ashley style—as seen on the company's line of clothing and home decorating products such as wall-paper and in the company's retail spaces—is an example of an ornamentalist aesthetics—small flower prints, stripes, plaids, and patterns adorn most Laura Ashley fabrics and surfaces; fabrics are often edged with ruffles and flounces or draped into dramatic folds. Often two or more patterns or decorative motifs are used together.

Trends Toward Minimalism. Old-time bathhouses and swimming pools used to be prime examples of ornamentalism. Inspired by Roman bathhouses or Turkish baths, they incorporated a complex symbolism in their architecture, tiling, and overall look. Today's gymnasiums, in contrast, are temples of minimalism. Reebok's new gymnasiums in Los Angeles, Irvine, and New York, part of its Planet Reebok campaign, are, according to *New York*'s Colin McGinn, "what a gym should be: a place of stark simplicity . . . it's all spaciousness and functionalism and unity of purpose, as if the concept of gym had been stripped to its most sublime and yet most American form."[12] The same can be said of contemporary fitness equipment. Today's single-station StairMaster brand and

Cybex machines are clearly more minimalist than their multistation Nautilus and Universal predecessors.

This trend toward minimalism can be observed in many other product categories as well. From automobiles to washing machines, stereos, and telephones, the broad trend in this century can be described as moving away from ornamentalist designs. Contrast old products from the early 1900s to the 1960s with those from the 1970s to the present day and a stark difference will be seen immediately. Virtually everything in the older group has a frame or is framed (chrome frames around automobiles and major appliances; wood frames around stereo or other electronic equipment; plastic frame around various household items), whereas the things in the new group have been slowly reducing and eliminating frames or have been using subdued colors to mask frames.

Bucking the Minimalist Trend. Like the other style dimensions, the complexity dimension applies to all corporate expressions from company uniforms, products and their packaging, to exteriors and interiors of buildings to communications. Style is a vehicle for differentiation that marketers often miss. The uniforms of most U.S. airlines are largely minimalist: simple, professional designs in corporate dark blue with straight lines. One of the airlines that breaks the rule is—quite appropriately—Southwest Airlines. Southwest Airlines has positioned itself as a maverick airline that challenges the stiff, professional image of the major players. Employees are encouraged to express their personalities and senses of humor, for example, when reciting the routine safety speech before each flight. In keeping with this identity, the ornamentalist Southwest uniform is colorful, playful, with complex Southwestern-inspired patterns.

Minimalism vs. Ornamentalism: The Example of Architecture. Minimalist corporate architecture has its roots in the Chicago School/Bauhaus type of corporate building. Ornamentalism has its origin in the neo-Gothic/Art Nouveau type of corporate building. Today's postmodern architecture and interior design is characterized by style pluralism and the absence of a unifying style. A wide variety of colors, shapes, and materials—sometimes in minimalist, other times in ornamentalist fashion—are used today.

Style Dimension 2: Representation

To what extent do you want to represent reality in your aesthetic elements? In the arts, the term *realism* is commonly used to refer to the (often life-like) depiction of the world of objects and human beings. In contrast, *abstraction* relies on the immediate impact of colors and forms; neither the work itself nor any of its parts represent or symbolize any objects in the real world. All corporate elements (logo, uniform, product and packaging, interior and exterior of buildings and forms of communication) can be viewed as realist if their forms make conscious use of associations to objects in the real world and abstract if they do not. In the past century, we can see a clear trend toward more abstract designs. The symbolism of Greek columns that incorporate figural representations belongs to the aesthetic of century-old universities but not to the modern corporation. But realism should not be discounted as a potentially powerful source of images. Cigna moved from the generic corporate look of its abstract "blue box" logo to one that depicts a stylized tree over the company name, a switch that better expresses Cigna's corporate identity as a family of "caring" businesses.

Merging Message with Style: the Case of Naturalism. A particular form of realism is *naturalism*, a style that does not refer to specific objects of nature but to nature as a whole. Naturalism is frequently found in products and marketing aimed at the environmentally conscious. Its primary color scheme uses hues found in or reminiscent of nature and organic materials. In retail environments it often uses soothing sounds and music that evoke natural associations such as water or wind. Unpolished woods, unbleached cotton, rough papers, and natural, recyclable materials are essential for an environmentally friendly, "green" style. All these elements (in conjunction with soothing New Age music, subtle fragrances, and soft light-brown colors) are found in the product line and retail outlets of Origins, the "green" brand from cosmetics firm Estee Lauder.

Using Realism to Create Identities. While abstraction has so dominated the corporate aesthetic that most organizations use abstract paintings and sculptures in the lobbies of their headquarters, some companies stand out by using their exteriors and interiors to refer to

FIGURE 4.4

Complexity and Representation in Visual Arts, Opera, Architecture, Fashion, and Culinary Design (each quadrant from top to bottom)

MINIMALIST REALISM	ORNAMENTALIST REALISM
Pop Art	Impressionism
Wagner	Verdi and Puccini
Functionalism	Art Nouveau
Yoji Yamamoto	Moschino and Versace
Californian and Italian	Chinese and Thai

MINIMALIST ABSTRACTION	ORNAMENTALIST ABSTRACTION
Constructivism	Abstract painting (Kandinsky)
R. Strauss, Glass	Stravinsky, Schoenberg
Bauhaus	Postmodernism
Armani and Montana	Valentino
Japanese	French

their product line or culture. The Disney buildings in Florida, designed by postmodern architect Michael Graves, are highly representational, even the corporate buildings and hotels for guests. The architect's drawings reveal that the animation building is mouse-shaped, and the building's entryway features a three-story version of the hat Mickey Mouse wore in the movie *Fantasia*. This is in line with Disney's corporate mission of creating fantasies and experiences and presenting itself to the public as actors and players.

Style Dimension 3: Perceived Movement

How dynamic do you want your organization or brand to appear? Most of the world is familiar with Nike's trademark and logo, the "swoosh." If one were to classify it in the stylistic dimensions above, its qualities suggest an abstract minimalist style. In contrast, its major competitor, Reebok, originally used a block-letter rendering of its name with a representation of the British flag, appearing to reflect a more representational but still minimalist style. Yet, the difference in the appeal of the two logos was evident. It is captured by a third relevant dimension, that of movement. The Nike logo seems "dynamic." The curving stripe depicts movement through its snapshot-like portrayal of wind in action. In contrast, the Reebok approach appeared static. One would expect an athletic-shoe designer to create a dynamic style, and in fact Reebok has added two swoosh-like marks to their logo, creating a more dynamic feel. When FedEx redesigned its name and logo in the early nineties, it also added dynamicism to it; the new logo has a secret arrow, created in the white space between the "E" and "x."

Creating Broadcast Identities. The perceived movement dimension is particularly relevant when corporate elements are depicted in motion or in action. For example, in TV advertising and other displays, some logos become moving images to show an organization's dynamic nature. The GE logo, for example, contains at the bottom a line that becomes a dynamic laser beam in TV ads. Similarly, the new logo for LG (Korea's Lucky Goldstar Group) shows the development of the letter strokes into a friendly face which then moves outward beyond its own boundaries to depict the "face change." Movements and their perceptions as slow or fast—static or dynamic—are also relevant in the context of service situations that require one or the other quality. Express mail carrier DHL's name on corporate materials has a pronounced slant to the right, creating the impression of haste and speed.

Style Dimension 4: Potency

How overwhelming do you want your brand or organization to appear? The degree of *potency* as applied to corporate or brand identity refers to whether an identity comes across as strong, aggressive, and loud or as weak, subdued, and quiet. The familiar package design for Procter & Gamble's Tide laundry detergent uses a bright shade of orange and features a bulls-eye design that expands off of the package, conveying a loud, powerful identity.

The approach of "bargain companies" is often on the aggressive and loud side of the spectrum. "Biggest sale ever!" and other hard-hitting selling techniques are typically announced in big letters in print ads or screamed at the customer in TV ads. Classy, upscale selling approaches are often subdued and quiet.

Lippincott & Margulies, an identity and image management firm, created a successful, quiet identity of understated elegance for Nissan's Infiniti automobile. Nissan faced the challenge of standing out against other, mostly European, luxury car makers when it entered the U.S. market in the early 1990s. The car was positioned as a distinctive piece of Japanese culture and craftsmanship and marketed separately from other Nissan products. "For this approach to succeed, we felt that a unique style, elegance and sophistication had to be projected in the name of the automobile, the layout and look of the showroom, and the advertising, promotional literatures and signs." The logo was derived from a symbol for infinity and was reminiscent of Japan's most revered mountain, Mount Fuji. Two-page ads showed pictures of water and rock (rather than the car itself) on the right side and, on the left, answered in a Zen-like fashion the question "What is luxury?" Special attention was paid to small details such as seasonal greeting cards, which were offered to buyers in beautiful, natural wrapping paper. The campaign was widely acknowledged for its clutter-breaking nature and established the brand as a unique luxury vehicle.

SUMMARY

Styles are visual (or auditory, olfactory, or tactile) expressions of an organization's or brand's identity. Styles are created by designers based on input provided by managers and strategic design consultants. Ideally, they reflect the private self of an organization or brand. The bright red colors of Coca-Cola's logo and the vibrant colors in its advertising express the youthfulness of the brand; the whimsical shapes and displays of a Swatch watch express its fashion-orientation; and the grandness of its music expresses United's positioning as a world-wide airline.

But styles alone are insufficient to express an identity. Style without content is *l'art pour l'art.* To be effective, styles must be combined with themes that express an organization's or brand's private self more succinctly and more directly. How managers can use themes for identity planning is the subject of the next chapter.

5

Themes

The $3.7 billion cookie market is dominated by Nabisco. Nabisco's share in supermarket sales is estimated at nearly 50% of the market, led by packaged brands such as SnackWells, Oreo, Chips Ahoy, and Fig Newtons. Thus far, Pepperidge Farm has never captured more than 10% of the market. But Pepperidge Farm's share has been increasing: to 4% in 1986, to 6% in 1989, to 8% in 1996. Pepperidge Farm cookies are labeled differently from Nabisco's. Nabisco's are cobranded (Chips Ahoy from Nabisco; Oreo from Nabisco; etc.); but in the public mind Pepperidge Farm is not linked with its well-known parent. (Pepperidge Farm, like Godiva, is owned by Campbell Soup Company.) Yet, even though it is a stand-alone brand, Pepperidge Farm has achieved recognition for four product lines, which they call collections.

Pepperidge Farm's "distinctive collection" is based on European imagery. Pulling in sales of 60 million dollars in 1994, it has offerings named "Lido," "Geneva," "Bordeaux," "Milano," and "Brussels," among others. The "collection" is reinforced by line extensions such as "Orange Milano," "Mint Milano," "Milk Chocolate Milano," and "Double Chocolate Milano." When they introduce line extensions, they use them to protect the core franchises.

EXHIBIT 5.1

Pepperidge Farm's Distinctive (top) and American Collection (bottom)

The themes of the "distinctive collection" are created by the cookie it-self, advertising, and, most importantly, at the point of purchase and consumption via the packaging. The packaging highlights a photograph of the cookie superimposed onto a map of Europe (see Exhibit 5.1). Each cookie is styled differently, as if it were the "home cookie" of the region named on the packaging. The packaging continues the distinctive Euro-pean theme with a narrative that incorporates a core text and variations that reflect the specifics of each cookie line. The package for Mint Brus-sels, for example, reads

> Imagine strolling down a cobblestone street to your favorite European bake shop. The aroma of Old World baking fills the air. . . . Pepperidge Farm brings that experience home with distinctive Mint Brussels, an exquisite combination of rich, dark chocolate and peppermint flavor sandwiched between two crisp cookies for a deliciously elegant eating experience. European heritage and Amer-ican ingenuity combine to create wonderful cookies you can enjoy every day.

The "Old Fashioned" collection plays on themes of tradition, security, and home goodness. It features cookie types such as shortbread, sugar, gingerman, hazelnut, Irish oatmeal, oatmeal raisin, molasses crisp, brownie chocolate nut, among others. "Remember the cookies in Grandma's cookie jar?" the packaging narrative begins.

> Simple, fresh-baked cookies made from timeless recipes with simple whole-some ingredients. Cookies that crackle and crunch when you bite into them. That's the kind of cookie Pepperidge Farm remembers and brings to you in our Old Fashioned cookies. Each with a healthy heaping of old fashioned taste and texture. Cookies that could have come right out of Grandma's cookie jar. Because Pepperidge Farm remembers.

Words like simple, wholesome, fresh, old-fashioned, vividly paint the theme. Cookie taste and texture are interlaced with the image of Grandma and the theme of memories. Reading the name (Old Fashioned) or the narrative immediately ties into the "Pepperidge Farm remembers" campaign, as if the grandfatherly voice from the TV ad is speaking to us as we read the label.

In the 1980s, when soft cookies were eating into Pepperidge Farm's share, "Pepperidge Farm was suffering," states the former vice president of marketing. "The cookie wars were on, and the giants were duking it out." Pepperidge Farm called in the New York consulting firm Brain Reserve Inc., which allayed their fears about the "soft" craze and suggested that they pursue the boutique cookie market.

Then, in 1985, Herbert Tolmich, manager of product development, worked with marketing to develop such a boutique cookie: a homemade-looking cookie, the lumpy large kind you find in the freshly baked-cookie section. Out of twelve prototypes, five were chosen by the marketing staff.

With this development, Pepperidge Farm struck another home run. It developed another hard-cookie line, this time with a new theme, the "American Collection." Playing on the old themes of regional motifs, the cookies were named after well-known geographic areas that have a resort identity or historical significance (or both) in American culture: "Sausalito," "Nantucket," "Chesapeake," "Santa Fe," and "Tahoe" (see Exhibit 5.1). Sales topped $50 million by 1994.

The success of Pepperidge Farm's collection themes was highlighted in late 1995 when Rob Kyff of the *Los Angeles Times/Washington Post News Service* sent it up in a piece on "word inflation."

> Add "collection" to this inflationary collection. From reading the package of Pepperidge Farm's "Nantucket" chocolate chip cookies, for instance, I learn these are no ordinary cookies; they're part of Pepperidge Farm's "American Collection," a line that includes other offerings like "Chesapeake," "Tahoe" and "Sausalito." I wonder whether this collection is displayed in a gallery at the Museum of Modern Art (perhaps near Cézanne's pears) or whether I'm going to turn on the TV someday and see high-fashion models in cookie bags striding down catwalks as Pepperidge Farm unveils its new autumn collection. I hear some of those models are tough cookies.

Pepperidge Farm's philosophy was succinctly stated in 1992 by General Manager Rydin:

> We do not think the baking industry is a mature industry. We believe there's a huge opportunity to grow the total category in bakery goods, and we want to take a proactive approach and be in a leadership position of communicating the advantages of breadstuffs to consumers. New products are the lifeblood of the category, and if you're not participating in new products, you aren't going to grow.

Consistent with this philosophy, Pepperidge Farm ultimately developed a Soft Baked Collection—and most recently, appropriated the reduced-free theme in its reduced fat Soft Baked Collection. The new variants play on established themes while changing the varieties to share in the continuing soft lure and booming sales of fat-free and reduced-fat products. Single-serving portions also account for a small but steady portion of the collection sales. They include offerings from the major collections: Distinctive Milanos, with four per package; American Collection Sausalito, Chesapeake, and Nantucket cookies, each with two cookies per package; and an Old Fashioned variety pack, which contains six individual serving pouches of sugar, chocolate chip, and Gingerman cookies.

EXPRESSIVE THEMES

As Pepperidge Farm has shown in the cookie market, a coherent, well-planned theme is a crucial component of an aesthetic. In this chapter we discuss themes in the context of corporate and brand identity. *Themes* refer to the content, the meaning, the projected image of an identity. Corporate and brand themes are cultural signs and symbols created by designers, advertisers, architects, and other identity creators to express corporate and brand characteristics.

Organizations use themes to provide mental anchors and reference points. These reference points allow the consumer to place an organization in a wider context and to distinguish its position. Themes can be expressed most pointedly if (a) they are used as prototypical expressions of an organization's core values or mission, or of a brand's character; (b) they are repeated and adapted over time; and (c) they are developed into a system of interrelated ideas.

Using Themes as Prototypical Images

Themes contain prototypical content. Psychologists define a prototype as "a hypothetical, most typical instance of a category." Prototypes have at their core particular features and characteristics. At the same time, they are idealizations of reality and not reality itself.

Consider the thematic image of Betty Crocker, used by General Mills for over 75 years. Hers is said to be the most famous face in American grocery stores and "a paragon of white middle America: a cheery housewife with blue eyes, creamy skin and June Cleaver features." Betty Crocker is a fictional character first portrayed in 1936 in a portrait by New York artist Neysa McMein. McMein combined the features of several women into a "motherly image." In Betty's most recent makeover in 1996, General Mills used a similar procedure. The faces of 75 real women were selected, then digitally "morphed" into one Betty Crocker prototype. "Betty Crocker has always reflected the faces of its consumers," a marketing manager at General Mills is quoted as saying. "We're using computer images to reflect faces from consumers across America."[2] In 1989, in a survey conducted by Donnelley Marketing Inc., Betty Crocker ranked first as the most trusted endorser of any product among the 25–49 and 50–64 age groups, even before real potential endorsers like Walter Cronkite, Bill Cosby, or Bob Hope.

U.S. supermarkets are full of prototypical images. Besides Betty Crocker, there is Aunt Jemima, Uncle Ben, and the Pillsbury Dough Boy, among others.

Sometimes prototypical images are based on real people. Over time, these real people (e.g., founders of companies) have become synonymous with a certain type of person (e.g., the independent entrepreneur) and are perceived as prototypes rather than individuals. Mary Kay (of Mary Kay Cosmetics), Lillian Vernon (of the successful home accessories company), Richard Branson (of the Virgin brand), Bill Gates, and Donald Trump come to mind. In the fashion industry, Coco Chanel is vividly present in CHANEL's identity (its fragrance, advertising, and its style). In the software industry, Dr. Norton (of Norton Anti-Virus Software) is on his way to becoming a similar prototype, especially since he blesses us with a picture of himself each time the virus software jumps into action on our computers.

Research conducted by the identity firm Gerstman+Meyers revealed the strong value of the figure of Sir Thomas Lipton (the founder of the Thomas Lipton Tea Company). As a result of the findings, the new packaging for Lipton Tea includes a bolder illustration of Sir Thomas in addition to his signature.

Strategically, using a prototypical figure to represent a company and/or its products has significant advantages over using real consumers or celebrity spokespeople for a thematic representation. The prototype is a generic symbol and thus has a broader appeal and a greater potential for identifiability among consumers than a spokesperson does. Moreover, the prototype/thematic figure does not have a life and does not do anything real; it is a myth, not subject to public scrutiny as a spokesperson inevitably is. The obvious example of the pitfalls of the real-life spokesperson is Hertz's Rent-a-Car's long-time use of O. J. Simpson; his murder trial put the company in an unenviable position.

Repeating and Adapting Themes

Themes require repetition in order to be imprinted in consumers' minds. Prototypical expressions often repeated can quickly become embedded in the customer's memory. The "spreading activation" theory is the leading theory of memory in psychological and consumer-behavior research. This theory views concepts as nodes of a network of associations in people's minds, with differing strengths of association represented by pathways. The model suggests that when a person thinks about one concept, the thought activates a node in the network which in turn invokes other nodes. With repetition, the pathways become well traversed, and one node (e.g., the brand name) activates other parts of the network and other thoughts easily, especially if it reflects a theme that invokes multiple associations.

Figure 5.1 illustrates the network of Absolut vodka. Among people who have seen lots of their ads, the Absolut brand is directly associated with the product category, "vodka," the bottle shape "trendy," and particular advertising. The product category "vodka," in turn, might be associated with lemon (because it is frequently served with a piece of lemon) and with pure, crystal-clear alcohol as well as other brands (e.g., U.S.-brand Smirnoff with a Russian name). When that consumer's memory is triggered, either directly (by the shape of the bottle) or indirectly (via the product category "vodka," e.g., "The Clear Choice," "Absolut Citron"), the associations spread through the whole network and constantly reinforce Absolut's core associations.

Notwithstanding repetition, themes are most effective if they are adapted over time so they do not appear dated. Betty Crocker has had

FIGURE 5.1

Network of Associations for Absolut

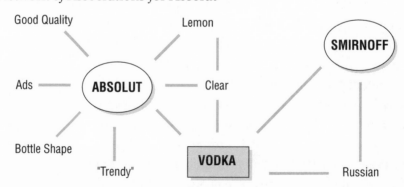

several makeovers to address changing fashions and the evolving roles of women in U.S. society. "In 1955, she cracked a smile. In 1965, she discarded her white collar for a pearl choker. In 1972, she put on business clothes. By 1986 she had become a bow-tied, dressed-for-success professional woman." Coca-Cola has always used a thematic approach, associating Coke with the ideas of happiness and fun. But it has also changed its approach from time to time while leaving the core message intact. In the 1960s and early 1970s, its advertising depicted hippie types from several nations singing "I'd like to buy the world a Coke" as part of a chorus that symbolized universal brotherhood. In the 1990s, no trace of the hippie connection remains; a "Coke and a smile" is the closest we find to the "peace, love and joy" theme of a generation ago.

Using Themes as Systems of Interrelated Ideas

Optimally, themes should be structured as systems of interrelated ideas so that the associational network is rich, thereby causing higher recall and elaboration. The Pepperidge Farm collections create a set of associations forming a set of related categories, with a set of items in each category.

EXHIBIT 5.2

Betty Crocker in 1965 and in 1996

Likewise, in Cathay Pacific's "Heart of Asia" theme (see Chapter 1), the brushstroke executions expressing the dynamism of the Asian region remain constant no matter what the message (e.g., destinations, smoke-free flights, connections, promotions, sponsorships). Absolut also uses this elaborate system of interrelated ideas. They have created a master theme: a hip vodka. Surrounding and related to the theme are subthemes—city themes, season themes, and many others. These themes are further broken down into more specific thematic categories that vary from year to year. For example, the Christmas theme, in the spirit of the season, varied from a disk playing Christmas carols to a pair of gloves with a Donna Karan promotion. The categorization becomes even more elaborate with sub-subthemes. Within the city theme, for example, there is an American cities campaign and a European cities campaign.

CREATING THEMES THROUGH AESTHETICS:
THREE STAGES

Executives ought to address three strategic questions concerning the creation of themes:

1. Which characteristics of an organization or brand should be portrayed?
2. Where can a set of rich themes be found?
3. How should the themes be represented in order to express corporate or brand traits?

These questions are illustrated in the framework presented in Figure 5.2. Three steps are required to answer these questions.

1. One needs to analyze the core elements in the internal and external marketing environments: the firm, its customers and competition. These analyses identify the company's constraints and opportunities in theme creation.
2. One should scan for rich thematic content from a variety of different domains within a culture. By analyzing specific domains (such as religion, politics, history, fashion), managers can more easily see appropriate thematic content emerge.
3. One should consider where the corporate themes should be embodied: in names, symbols, slogans/songs, narratives, concepts, or combinations thereof.

FIGURE 5.2

A Framework for Managing Themes

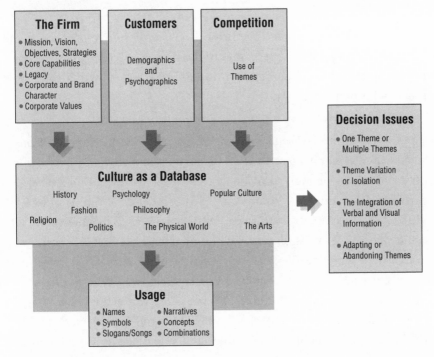

In the next three sections of the chapter, we focus on each of these three core stages of creating a theme. We conclude with strategic issues in theme selections.

ANALYZING THE ORGANIZATION, ITS CUSTOMERS, AND ITS COMPETITORS

The first and most complicated tasks for managers involved in creating themes is to perform a thorough analysis of these three realms.

Consider the Organization

When an organization selects themes, it must engage in some deep soul-searching (as described in Chapter 3). There are five general aspects of the organization to which a theme might relate.

- its mission, vision, objectives, and strategies
- its core capabilities

- its legacy
- its corporate or brand personality
- its values

Managers should carefully consider each of these five aspects of an organization as a source for themes that will be used to express the corporate identity. Except perhaps for mission, the aspects will also be applicable for brand identity.

The Organization's Mission, Vision, Objectives, and Strategies. A *mission statement* can be described as a statement of a company's core purpose; how the company provides value to its customers and how its existence is justified. A *vision*, on the other hand, is future oriented. Where does a company want to go? What does it want to achieve? What are its plans? Both missions and visions are intended to impart clarity, relevance, and direction. They are very general and difficult to convey in a theme—except, notably, through corporate advertising, where companies can specifically express their missions or visions through vivid aesthetics (both visuals and sounds). Archer Daniels Midland's "supermarket to the world" and GE's "We bring good things to life" campaigns use generalized messages of mission or vision.

Missions and visions are often linked to objectives and strategies that are more specific, often measurable, and usually achievable within a shorter time frame. Objectives and strategies add focus to the mission and vision and can more easily be expressed in corporate themes. For example, the Ford Motor Company has formulated the "Ford 2000" vision of becoming the world's leading automotive company. Corporate advertisements concluding with "Quality is Job 1" express different objectives. TV and print ads express the objectives with a "responsible employees theme" portraying Ford workers, designers, and engineers as the intellectual capital of the firm, next to the tagline "Quality is Job 1." Other ads use a "high-tech theme," portraying Ford as a world leader in using advanced technology that integrates design and manufacturing around the world.

The Organization's Core Capabilities. Core capabilities or competencies are strategic assets that may be difficult to imitate or copy. They include strengths in organization, culture, reputation, capital assets, employee productivity and morale, information systems, management,

R&D, manufacturing, intellectual property, marketing, or sales. They have been referred to as "sticky assets" that reflect an organization's history while potentially limiting its future opportunities. About Apple Computer's core capabilities, for example, it has been stated:

> Foremost . . . is that of innovation. Apple has been highly creative in product design, manufacturing, and the use of advertising. In product design, the mouse and icons were just the start. The look and feel of the Macintosh is only now being imitated by Microsoft's Windows. The do-it-yourself, simple start-up of Apple's products helped it greatly in the personal and home markets. And in the mid-1980s, it used award-winning television commercials to entice average consumers to take a "test drive" with the new Mac.[3]

In Apple Computer's case, the theme of "user-friendliness" appears in the rainbow-colored logo, in the friendly sound and smiling face displayed when the Macintosh is turned on, and in the nontechnical icon-based programs. Then there is the subtle allusion to a Biblical theme in the Apple logo, with its bite out, recalling Eve's biting of the apple from the Tree of Knowledge. Finally, Apple's original advertising caricatured the stiff but ineffective professionalism of big businesses that followed Big Blue blindly like zombies while flipping for hours through manuals filled with techno-lingo. Notwithstanding a viable theme or themes embodied in aesthetics, consumer preferences are notoriously difficult to predict, and Apple, some industry analysts claim, failed to appreciate the magnitude of the trend towards Microsoft's domination of operating systems. By 1995, Apple's core capabilities had been successfully imitated and the company seemed to have limited future opportunities. Ironically, this resulted in another theme, portrayed on the cover of *Business Week,* the theme of "The Fall of an American Icon" (see Exhibit 5.3).

The Organization's Legacy. Themes may be selected to express an organization's legacy—a positive part of the past that a company tries to preserve. Mercedes-Benz of North America used a thematic legacy approach in its recent introduction of the "next generation E-class." To place the new luxury vehicle into the context of the Mercedes legacy, it used visuals in two-page print spreads to display a series of six vintage cars on the left and the new car on the right. To reinforce its continuing association with luxury—a legacy in itself—the vintage cars were shown in black-and-white photos of famous actors and actresses from different time

EXHIBIT 5.3

Cover of Business Week *Magazine, February 5, 1996*

periods: Bing Crosby, Yul Brynner, Marlene Dietrich, Gary Cooper, Errol Flynn, and Clark Gable.

Westinghouse's subsidiary, Knoll, is an international office furniture company that offers everything from chairs, desks, and files to fabrics and wall coverings. In 1938, Hans and Florence Knoll founded the company with the idea of applying modern technology to create office signature pieces that help people and companies work better. Today the Knoll collection reflects the legacy of the minimalist Bauhaus movement and the tenets of modernism. (The Bauhaus movement was founded in Germany in the 1920s on the principle of creating simple, functional, and durable furniture for the masses, using the latest technology.) Knoll still follows the Bauhaus dictum that "Form follows function."

Knoll's legacy and commitment to timeless office masterpieces is expressed in its Bauhaus-designed logo (Monotype Bodoni), its minimalist, well-structured brochures in monochrome colors designed by Chermayeff & Geismar Inc., a leading design firm, and its trademarked corporate theme (simply called "commercial message" by Knoll): "Delivering intelligent workspaces worldwide." Knoll's theme promises "a space that satisfies people's diverse needs for an environment where they can do their best work and enjoy doing it." In other words, following the legacy of the Bauhaus movement, the intelligent workspace "adapts to companies and their people, supports the work process, integrates technology and is designed to endure."[4]

Corporate or Brand Personality. Brand personality has been defined as "the set of human characteristics associated with a given brand. In particular, a brand can be described by demographics (age, gender, social class, and race), lifestyle (activities, interest, and opinions) or human personality traits (such as extroversion, agreeableness, and dependability)."[5] Analogously, customers may associate certain human characteristics with organizations.

Recent research into brand personality suggests that there are five key perceived personality factors: sincerity, excitement, competence, sophistication, and ruggedness. For example, in one sample Campbell, Hallmark, and Kodak score high on sincerity; Porsche, Absolut, and Benetton score high on excitement; American Express, CNN, and IBM score high on competence; Lexus, Mercedes, and Revlon score high on sophistication; and Levi's, Marlboro, and Nike score high on ruggedness.

AT&T has established a uniform brand positioning for all its customer communications. It aspires to make each customer feel that AT&T is the most helpful company providing the most helpful service and the most useful technology—overall, a company worthy of trust. As a consequence, a set of AT&T personality attributes have been established "to guide the tone and manner of all communications with the public." AT&T wants itself and its services to be viewed as reliable, trustworthy, ethical, high quality, and high tech; to be thought of as providing value and being caring, knowledgeable, global, and responsive; and to be seen as competitive, contemporary, energetic, and innovative. AT&T positions itself to reflect two of the dimensions of personality discussed earlier: competence and sincerity.

Individual AT&T business units are free to emphasize certain attributes over others. But all communications must be within the framework of the overall positioning. The themes are related by various aesthetic elements. The globe symbol represents a three-dimensional sphere lit from above. The AT&T corporate theme line ("The right choice" or "Your true voice") reassures the customer of AT&T's quality and reliability. Trademarked slogans such as "Reach out and touch someone" reinforce the emotional and personal aspect of the image. Because the theme line and the slogan express the core theme of AT&T's identity, there are strict guidelines governing their usage. The theme line is the only phrase that can appear with the logo in print or TV ads, or as a tagline in a radio commercial. The slogan must always precede the logo and theme line in TV ads, whether it is spoken or visually displayed. The theme line or "AT&T" is the last information a listener hears in an ad.[6]

Values. Values are relatively stable (though not necessarily static) beliefs about what an organization should do, concerning both end goals (terminal values) and modes of conduct (instrumental values).[7] Organizational values often arise from a certain corporate culture. Merrill Lynch, for example, stands for the following principles: client focus, respect for the individual, teamwork, responsible citizenship, and integrity. Merrill Lynch claims that these principles guide its actions in 35 countries around the world.

Since organizational values are ultimately designed to deliver benefits to customers, it is useful to consider the characteristics that customers have been shown to value: efficiency, play, excellence, beauty, status, ethics, esteem, and spirituality. All eight of these traits may be converted into themes through common symbolism. A look at advertisements from the automobile industry makes this categorization and its attendant typology clear. Many small sedans, for example, use an efficiency theme, focusing on cost, gas mileage, and convenience; Volkswagen in its Beetle and later *"Fahrvergnuegen"* campaigns used a theme that emphasized playfulness and fun; Lexus uses excellence as a theme in its "the relentless pursuit of perfection" campaign; Jaguar uses beauty as a primary theme; Rolls-Royce, Lincoln, Cadillac, and Mercedes use status as a theme by marketing their cars as symbols of success; Volvo uses references to ethics and responsibility in their ads, which emphasize safety; Toyota and Ford use esteem as the basis of the theme of their good reputations; and Infiniti uses its spirituality as a theme.

To summarize, all of these elements of a company's internal and external environments—its mission, vision, objectives, and strategies; core capabilities; legacy; corporate or brand personality; and values—can form the backdrop of an effective theme. Managers must be able to pinpoint these aspects of corporate or brand identity in order to tailor themes to the customer, the next object of analysis in a theme-creating campaign.

Consider the Customers

When creating themes, executives must consider their customers' demographic characteristics, including age, sex, location, race, and national origin as well as psychographic characteristics including attitudes, values, personality, and lifestyles. Customers' age, for example, is a crucial category that can be used to rule out or in favor of a particular theme. Depending on whether an identity campaign is targeted toward teenagers, adults, or the elderly, different images are called for. Joe Camel may appeal to children; the Marlboro Man is intended for adults. The same applies to other categories such as sex, race, and nationality. Members of each category form subcultures with their own unique symbols as reference points.

Pertinent demographic characteristics in the business-to-business marketing of themes may include decision-makers' rank in the organization and the type of the organization itself. Many branded products help people of a certain rank to express their achievement or expertise. The same applies to different types of businesses (e.g., a "creative" vs. an "engineering" firm).

A lack of consideration of customers can backfire. Many end consumers and franchisers of Benetton were confused by that clothing company's series of politically and aesthetically controversial ad themes that featured AIDS patients, newborn babies, and multicolored condoms to express the "United Colors of Benetton." Customers were not sure what the disturbing or shocking images had to do with the clothing. In Germany, franchisers even sued Benetton in court for damaging their sales. Benetton, for its part, has begun producing a magazine, called *Colors*, that is devoted to photographic essays on politically oriented themes. As CEO Luciano Benetton explained in a lecture at Columbia Business School in November 1996, the company's striking ad campaigns are part of a unified strategy for marketing in several nations, which will be further demonstrated in the magazine.

EXHIBIT 5.4

Benetton Advertisements: Birth, Condoms, Angel/Devil

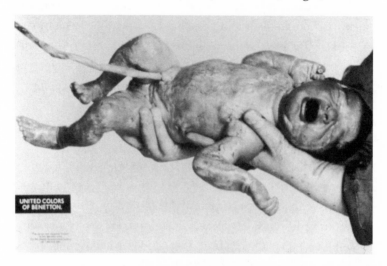

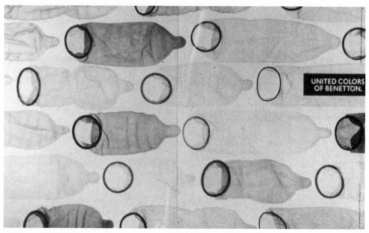

Consider the Competitors

A theme may be used to position your firm aggressively against the competition, e.g., by using similar symbolism, similar taglines, or similar messages in comparative ads. Over the years, this has happened in the Cola Wars, in the price wars in the telecommunications industry between AT&T and MCI as well as in the airlines, car rentals, headache medicines, and other industries.

To position a company's product effectively, it is essential to evaluate the themes used by the product's competitors. It is especially important to recognize themes that have been preempted by competitors. Studies have indicated that pioneers can enjoy tremendous advantages and gain a higher market share due to perceptual preemption. In these cases, competitors may imitate provided they do not violate laws of unfair competition (as we will discuss in Chapter 8). The prototypical theme may be embodied in a name or a symbol that is closely associated with the category. For example, Merrill Lynch's bull is one of the best possible symbols for the financial-markets industry, in which a "bull market" is a good market and words like "bullish" connote aggressive investment stances. In other words, by pioneering the use of one of the best possible symbols for its industry, Merrill Lynch has imposed a constraint on the visual symbolism that may be used by competitor firms. Only Dreyfus uses a similar symbol, namely a lion as part of its "Rule your Kingdom" campaign.

FINDING RICH THEMATIC CONTENT

Thus far we have discussed the organization's internal and external environment as sources of ideas that an organization may want to express in its theme. We now turn to the second question. Where do themes arise from? The surrounding culture contains a rich database from which to draw themes.

Consumer researchers who think of customers as part of an anthropological system describe the process by which new ideas reach individuals. According to these researchers, ideas are transferred from a culture to products/corporations and ultimately to the individual. Both individually and as a unit, designers, producers, advertisers, and consumers move cultural meanings between several locations in the social world. In the most typical scenario, a cultural meaning is drawn from a particular cultural setting and attached to a consumer. Then the meaning can be transferred from the object itself to an individual consumer.[8]

In general, the sources of themes can be divided into five cultural domains:

- the physical world
- philosophical/psychological concepts
- religion, politics, and history
- the arts
- fashion and popular culture

The physical world is the starting point of a rich repertory of images. These include everything we see around us: from animals and human beings to manmade objects such as buildings and roads. The Cross pen company's "lapis lazuli" theme, for example, is based on the history and physical qualities of the deep-blue lapis lazuli gemstone, which is featured on a line of Cross pens. "Once reserved for kings, Lapis now brings majesty to your writing," the ads read. "Known as Blue Gold during the Middle Ages, genuine Lapis is mined in small quantities in remote regions of the world." The ads use the gemstone to create an aura of rarity, beauty, exoticism, and historical importance.

Philosophy provides us with general concepts of time and space, logic, existence, and morality. Time and space can be the source of themes, as in the Pepperidge Farm cookie campaign, with its references to times past through images of Grandma's kitchen or old European cities. In the early 1990s, Swissair created a "Time is everything" theme. A "Time and Motion" ad campaign and art exhibitions featured avant-garde, highly abstract (mostly black-and-white) photography and art that made allusions to the passage of time, the present and the future, the preciousness of time, time as a resource. The theme was well selected for a carrier whose home country is associated with the invention and selling of watches and other time machines. It was also supposed to communicate a modern service concept as well as the futuristic positioning of the airline.

Religion, politics, and history provide myths, values, and habits, ideas about power, and historical examples that may be used as reference points to judge current situations: The Hebrew National meat-products company uses both a religious and a historical basis for its theme of high inspection standards in its commercials that picture Uncle Sam deferring to "a higher authority"—as he looks heavenward—

about whether to approve the ingredients for its kosher hot dogs. Philip Morris as well as the American Advertising Association have used "right-to-choose" appeals in their advertising.

The arts provide a visual and auditory database of images that are either created for their own sake and associated with certain styles and moods or reflective of well-known historical or mythical events.

Language is the mediator—the software—that we use to access information from the cultural database, and can often suggest the theme itself. For example, verbal and visual puzzles can express a theme, to such an extent that the puzzle virtually becomes a theme itself. For example, a few years ago Sabena Airlines, the national carrier of Belgium, won a creative-advertising prize for its destination ad showing a picture of Brussels sprouts and a big apple; the NYNEX Yellow Pages created a whole campaign around visual puns. As discussed in Chapter 3, the IBM Media Group in the 1980s presented a visual pun of its familiar logotype by Paul Rand: the abstract drawing of an eye, a bee, and the letter M. All three examples show that multiple domains may be involved in generating an idea. Language pulls them all together, becoming the source of a unique image capable of cleverly appealing to the different levels of our perceptions.

REPRESENTING THEMES THROUGH AESTHETICS

The final task involved in creating a theme is to decide how best to represent themes to convey corporate or brand identity. Themes can be expressed in a variety of ways (see Figure 5.3):

- as corporate or brand names
- as symbols
- as narratives
- as slogans or jingles
- as concepts
- as combinations of elements

Each type of theme expression elicits particular responses from the public and can be used to accomplish a range of objectives. Names may create identifying labels; symbols can transform into icons; slogans and songs may be remembered as mottoes; narratives may be told as stories; and combinations of these have the potential to represent complex concepts.

FIGURE 5.3

Expressions of Themes

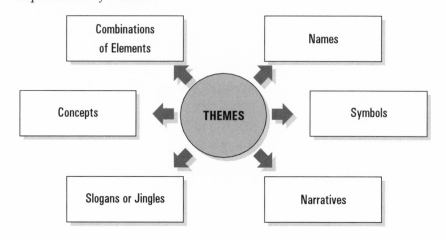

Themes as Names

Marketing researchers have identified the key characteristics of a good corporate or brand name by examining names across a wide range of product categories, industries, and languages. According to this research, a good name should be short and memorable; it should say something about the product (or company), and about key benefits; it should be easy to pronounce and easy to write; and, ideally, it should be usable worldwide. Though most actual company and brand names fail to possess all of these characteristics, they all need to be considered at the same time.

Some successful names violate nearly all of the above rules. Häagen-Dazs is neither short nor easy to remember at first; it appears to say nothing about the product category ice cream or how creamy the ice cream is; upon first encounter, it is not easy to pronounce. Even after several exposures, it is difficult to write. And it is questionable that it serves well in all its markets. Nonetheless the brand has been extremely successful. But is this success despite of or because of its name? Häagen-Dazs appears to be successful because its novel, unfamiliar name attracts attention and serves as the starting point of a unique theme somehow related to Nordic lands. Started as a company in the Bronx, then bought by Pillsbury, Häagen-Dazs sells the promise—and the fantasy—of a European ice cream associating itself with the cool, icy areas of northern Europe. The name creates curiosity and interest by its novelty. While it may not be recallable at first, it is recognizable and thus memorable, in part due to its novelty. It may appear that the name is unrelated to the product category, but it creates powerful associations with a cool, Nordic place.

One of the most important functions of names is their role as descriptors—as labels. Descriptive names say what a product does and what it is for (Dupont's "StainMaster" removes stains; Avon's "Skin-So-Soft" makes the skin soft). Names also often indicate a price point ("Budget," "EconoLodge," "Deluxe").

But names not only denote; they also connote. "Suggestive" names cause associations and trigger imagery. Even simple product category names, if used creatively, can be the beginning of a theme. When Sanofi, the holding company of Yves Saint-Laurent, introduced its Champagne brand fragrance in France in the early 1990s, the name was used not because the fragrance smelled like Champagne but because of the imagery, lifestyle, celebrity status, and aesthetics *associated* with champagne—in other words, the name was used as a theme. Naturally, the influential French "Comité Interprofessionel du Vin et Champagne" (CIVC) sued Sanofi because, as CIVC's president André Enders put it, "We lose our heritage, our worth, and we weaken and debase what is in the minds of the public that we have built up over three centuries." CIVC won the battle but lost the war. Sales of the fragrance were 40% higher than forecast. When Sanofi was asked to recall the perfume and delete the name in late 1993, few bottles were still in the warehouse to be returned. The thematic value of the fragrance had taken over. When Acura found that it was losing ground to other luxury car imports in the U.S. market, it changed its cars' names, losing Legend in favor of the seemingly nondescript letter-number combination names such as 2.5TL, 3.2TL, and 3.5RL. The names are less descriptive, but carry the connotation of imported luxury through their association with the naming system of competitor brands.

Other suggestive names include Armor-All, Hallmark, Sprint, Dove, SnackWell's, among so many others. The fragrance industry is full of examples of suggestive names that create themes. Poison, a Christian Dior brand name, creates the theme of magic, linking attraction with danger and the dark side of human nature. It uses dark colors to mesh the theme with aesthetic elements. Obsession, a Calvin Klein brand name, associates to the theme of passion and uncontrollable desire; it employs stark black-and-white photographic images. Safari, a Ralph Lauren brand name, thematically recalls hunting or other expeditions in Africa, and has green-brownish pastel colors to combine theme and style. In each case the theme is reinforced in print ads, but the name is the starting point, the hub for creating the theme.

Themes as Symbols

Conveying themes through symbols can enhance brand name evaluations or diminish them. In 1991, Interbrand Schechter conducted a survey of 900 consumers and asked them to judge twenty-two well-known logos. One group was shown only the visual symbol. Another group was shown only the company or brand name. A third group was shown the full logo, i.e., the company or brand name accompanied by the visual symbol. One brand that was evaluated significantly lower when picture and name were combined was Land O'Lakes. The brand name was evaluated positively by 59% of the respondents when shown alone but by only 52% when it was shown together with its Indian-squaw symbol. In contrast, the name KFC was viewed positively by 41%. The symbol of the colonel, however, was evaluated positively by 48%.[9]

Though popular symbols may attract attention, they rarely differentiate the product from competitors. Products offered nowadays include Mona Lisa liquid-soap dispensers, inflatable dolls based on Munch's "The Scream" and telephones that play the first few notes of Beethoven's Fifth Symphony when they ring. None of these pairings of product and symbol is particularly appropriate or memorable. Not surprisingly, Bill Gates, founder and CEO of Microsoft, recently bought the Bettmann Archive, the world's largest collection of historical photographs, and plans to digitize the inventory, making even more cultural icons available for use. But it is important to resist the temptation to use a well-known cultural symbol for its own sake, without clearly making a strong connection to your company or product.

Successful symbolism invites imitation. In the cigarette industry alone, companies in Russia, China, Indonesia, and elsewhere brandish cowboys, U.S presidential figures, the stars-and-stripes symbol, and the Statue of Liberty to sell their cigarettes. The famous symbol of a green crocodile used by French casual-clothing maker La Chemise Lacoste has found its imitator in Hong Kong-based Crocodile Garments, which uses a similar reptile snapping in the opposite direction. At one point, to protect its franchise, La Chemise Lacoste bought Crocodile Garments.

Symbolism is important not only for customers but for employees as well. It offers opportunities for positive or negative identification. Singa-

THE STUDY OF MEANING IN CONSUMER RESEARCH

Corporate symbols and meanings have been analyzed a lot recently by consumer researchers whose approach borrows anthropological and literary theory. Some titles from the *Journal of Consumer Research* (published between 1990 and 1997) should suffice to make the point that managers will get little help from much of the research coming out of these academic settings. Consider: "Consumer Myths: Frye's Taxonomy and the Structural Analysis of Consumption Text"; "Liberatory Postmodernism and the Reenchantment of Consumption"; "On Resonance: A Critical Pluralistic Inquiry Into Advertising Rhetoric"; "Selves in Transition: Symbolic Consumption in Personal Rites of Passage and Identity Reconstruction"; "The Lived Meaning of Free Choice: An Existential-Phenomenological Description of Everyday Consumer Experiences of Contemporary Married Women."

Source: Journal of Consumer Research

pore Airlines' Singapore Girl is one of the most successful, though controversial, commercial symbols ever. Indeed, most ads use the symbol prominently with the airline name in small print. All the women shown in the advertising campaign over the years have been actual staff flight attendants. From 1992 to 1994 a wax model of the Singapore Girl, modeled after a real flight attendant, was displayed in Madame Tussaud's world-famous wax museum in London as the museum's first commercial symbol. At the same time, the corporate icon was described as "a wildly successful, if unabashedly sexist, marketing tool."[10]

Themes as Narratives

The Walt Disney park architecture, designed at various places by world-renowned architects such as Michael Graves, Robert Stern, Frank Gehry, and Antoine Predock, tells the story of the Disney characters as visual narratives. As seen in Exhibit 5.5, Disney characters act as powerful symbols aiding in globalization of products and services.

Likewise, Iridium, a restaurant and jazz club in New York, uses striking fantasy designs to express the structure of jazz in visual terms. Similarly, thematic musical content (called "program music" by musicolo-

EXHIBIT 5.5

Mickey's Corner Store Front in Shanghai

gists) may be used as a narrative. As we saw in Chapter 4, background music (whether it be classical, jazz, blues, or rock) is often selected based on its general dimensions but not based on its specific content or meaning. Companies contact general retail background-music suppliers like Seattle-based Muzak but do not specify the pieces. Some companies, however, have started to use specific musical content to define or reinforce their identities. Starbucks is one of them. Starbucks plays carefully selected music at its coffee bars and in fact sells the music played in its stores as tapes and CD's, so that customers can take the store atmosphere to their homes. Pottery Barn's "A Cool Christmas" CD, sold at its stores, includes "Jingle Bells" performed by the Duke Ellington Orchestra and "Santa Claus Got Stuck in My Chimney" sung by Ella Fitzgerald—songs that will create a stylish Christmas environment in your home that matches the style of Pottery Barn home furnishings.

Themes as Slogans or Jingles

The Unilever brand name "I Can't Believe It's Not Butter" tells the story of the surprise that the consumer is supposed to experience when he or she encounters a margarine product that tastes like butter. The "uncola,"

7-Up, not only differentiated itself as not a cola; it created a theme, a motif of what "uncola" means: freedom from color along with excitement, clarity, and purity. The old Pepsi jingle "You've got a lot to live and Pepsi's got a lot to give," makes a connection between life's excitement and challenges and Pepsi's role in experiencing and achieving them. Recall the song "Aren't you glad you use Dial?" Surely we are, if we value dryness and odor protection, the logic goes. With one word borrowed from Carly Simon's song "Anticipation," Heinz created a theme that lasted for years; the image of the slow, thick ketchup refusing to pour remains to this day. The song "Plop, plop, fizz, fizz, oh what a relief it is," not only created a theme for Alka-Seltzer, but cued people to think that two plops are called for, thereby increasing sales. All of these are highly memorable themes, in major part because they were embodied in basic identity elements—a play on words, a catchy slogan, or a jingle.

The brochures for Ralph Lauren Paint, distributed through Home Depot stores and independent dealers, are full of rich narratives. The brochure for Duchesse Satin reads, "Rich and Sophisticated. The elegant lustre of a satin evening gown captured in paint. The uniquely formulated paint shimmers in a palette of silver and gold and precious hues like Aubusson Ivy and Ballgown. It is a perfect complement to the luxurious ambiance of a candlelit dining room."

Themes as Concepts

Saturn Corporation, a wholly owned subsidiary of General Motors, provides a good example of using a theme as a concept. The "Saturn" name echoes the name of the Saturn rocket that took Americans to the moon during the space race with the Soviet Union. In the case of Saturn Corporation, it became a theme for competing against Japanese auto manufacturers. Saturn is supposed to be "a different type of car. A different type of company." This overall concept includes several subconcepts such as quality, innovation, environmental consciousness, directness, and honesty. To express environmental consciousness aesthetically, the landscaping of Saturn facilities is unobtrusive and blends in with the surroundings. To express directness and honesty, straightforward names were used for colors (e.g., "red" instead of "raspberry"), and simple car-model names are used (e.g., Saturn SL1 and Saturn SL2). In line with these themes, the identity is all-American, contemporary, simple, and straightforward. The

THEMATIC EXPRESSIONS AT CARL ZEISS

Carl Zeiss and the Fine Art of Microsurgery

Prior to 1990, Carl Zeiss' marketing communications were no different from those of any other manufacturer of high-technology medical products. Zeiss' approach was cut and dried: use a flashy product photo and plenty of copy to back it up. This approach, however, failed to differentiate Zeiss from its competitors.

Zeiss made a bold departure from the norm in its industry with communications campaigns that used an aesthetic strategy: emphasizing the beauty and versatility of its product line. The first campaign of this type was the "Fine Art of Microsurgery" campaign. Incorporating fine-art and ballet themes, the campaign stressed the similarities between the intricate, disciplined design of the company's microscope and the art of ballet. The OMPI CS-NC microscope, mounted on a free-floating suspension system, is a well-regarded neurosurgeon's microscope package. Its virtues, maneuverability and balance, are key to the freedom of movement that surgeons demand. Likewise, ballet dancers must have perfect balance, be precise but highly maneuverable, and appear to defy gravity in their movements.

(continued)

(continued)

Both the fine art and ballet themes were used extensively in the marketing communications campaign, which incorporated medical magazine ads, trade shows, literature, and a calendar given to customers and prospects. Each ad used a "Fine Art of Microsurgery" headline, a minitheme subhead, a fine art-photography shot of a ballet scene and a smaller photo of a Zeiss product corresponding to the minitheme. The fine-art theme elevated the surgeon from craftsman to artist while raising both the corporate and the customer image—the buyer was now a connoisseur, someone with fine taste and an appreciation for the subtleties of artistic skills.

The image of Zeiss and its products grew immensely with the fine-art campaign. The Zeiss name has become very familiar in medical circles; sales jumped, and the number of sales leads increased substantially. The ad campaign won awards, with Polaroid even featuring photography from the campaign in its "Guide to Instant Imaging." "Our marketing communications campaign has done wonders for our selling efforts," states Joerg Schweitzer, marketing manager for the Surgical Products Division. "Salespeople now feel they are selling to a higher level, more than just a product. As a result, the fine-art and ballet themes are synonymous with Carl Zeiss."

Source: Courtesy Carl Zeiss, Inc., Thornwood, NY.
Materials supplied by Carl Zeiss.

Saturn logo and label are referred to as the Saturn Signature and the Woodmark. The identity is managed within strict guidelines. There are only a few ways in which the signature and woodmarks may appear.

Assisted by PAOS, a Japanese identity firm, Japan's INAX proceeded with a dramatic identity change from a ceramic-tiles and bathroom-fixtures producer to a bathroom-space designer and a major player in the soaring leisure-lifestyle sector in Japan. Central to this change was the re-creation of a traditional Japanese bathroom space into an experiential space. The business domain of "creating environments for beautiful living" included new marketing programs, ventures into new businesses, and new product development directions, all of which had important design and thematic implications. For example, INAX introduced computer

VICTORIA'S SECRET AND THE ROMANCE THEME

Throughout the 1980s and early 1990s Victoria's Secret Company Ltd. built its success in the lingerie market through a cleverly conceived theme of a romantic, aristocratic English lifestyle. This theme was carried through in every element of its corporate identity. Victoria's Secret is a thoroughly American venture—based in Ohio—but used a classical, thoroughbred English theme to convince women that it's classy, and not trashy, to spoil themselves with fancy undergarments. The garments themselves may be sexy, but the Victoria's Secret aesthetic used the English theme to package sexiness as romance, differentiating the company from more risqué, explicitly erotic undergarment lines like Frederick's of Hollywood or Italy's La Perla, which many women may shy away from. The Victoria's Secret catalog copy was written in a British-sounding prose style and used British spelling (such as "colour" and "favourite"). The voice on the toll-free number on which customers placed orders had an upper-class English accent. The catalog suggested that a London address was the main location of the company, although its corporate offices are located in decidedly less chic Ohio. In the catalog, scenes of leisurely English country life, complete with horses and ornate, richly decorated, aristocratic-looking interiors, were made to seem the perfect setting for sexy (but not too racy) romance. The copy invited the reader-consumer to picture herself living this cozy, attractive, romantic British life. The Victoria's Secret aesthetic has been extended to products that used the romantic English theme to create a total environment of romantic pampering: CDs featuring "the most romantic music ever" performed by the London Symphony Orchestra; a book of "favourite love poetry"; and, of course, scented body products such as perfumes, moisturizers, and bath products.

Source: The Victoria's Secret catalog.

technology into the toilets market through programmable toilets with adjustable water temperatures and spray devices, preheatable toilet seats and stereo units attached to toilets that allow the playing of classical music—"Bach and Mendelsohn for constipation and Wagner for diarrhea."[11]

Whether a theme is expressed in a name, in a symbol, in a narrative, in a slogan or jingle, in a concept, or, possibly, in some combination of these elements, the subject is not closed. Next comes a series of decisions relating to the strategic use of themes over time.

Which Theme Expression Should an Organization Use?

Under what circumstances and for what purposes should an organization use names, symbols, narratives, slogans or jingles, or concepts as part of its identity? An answer to this question requires a consideration of the functions and values of each type of theme expression and of its potential problems and disadvantages. Figure 5.4 lists advantages and disadvantages of each type of theme expression.

FIGURE 5.4

Advantages and Disadvantages of Theme Expressions

	ADVANTAGES	DISADVANTAGES
NAMES	• Provide Anchors • Short and Easy to Recall	• Difficult to Change • Difficult to Globalize
SYMBOLS	• Attention-Getting • Easy to Transfer to Other Cultures	• Can Get Outdated • Can Be Ambiguous
NARRATIVES	• Express Life Styles • Involving	• Take Time to Understand and Process • Can Easily Be Imitated
SLOGANS OR JINGLES	• Memorable Even After Years • Highly Involving • Catchy	• Slogans Are Difficult to Translate • Different Music Appeals to Different People
CONCEPTS	• Often Innovative • Grand and Encompassing	• Abstract • Difficult to Communicate • Not Legally Protectable
COMBINATIONS OF ELEMENTS	• Create Complex Themes • Provide Multiple Anchors and Cues	• Can Be Overwhelming • Can Contain Incongruency

STRATEGIC ISSUES IN THEME SELECTION

Beyond finding appropriate themes and the appropriate vehicles for these themes, there are four further strategic issues that managers must address when evaluating themes:

- whether to use one theme or multiple themes;
- whether to use theme variation or isolation;
- how to mesh verbal and visual elements to create a cohesive theme; and
- when themes should be adapted or abandoned.

One Theme or Multiple Themes?

A key strategic issue concerns the number of themes that a corporation wants to create for itself or for its products. A company may choose one powerful representational theme that summarizes its central positioning. Or it may create a multitude of themes that simultaneously represent different aspects of the organization. The strategic choice between a single and multiple themes often depends on the breadth of a company's product line and on how uniform the company wants to appear to its constituents (e.g., customers or end consumers).

The product range of Xerox Corporation is at least as broad as that of the McGraw-Hill Companies. But one firm decided to use a single theme and the other a multiple-theme approach.

Xerox, the inventor of the photocopier, dominated the copier market for almost a quarter of a century. In fact, the brand name was used synonymously with the category. In the 1970s, the company diversified. It invented the first personal computer (with a mouse and icon-based software), the laser printer and computer networking; it also diversified into insurance and financial services. By 1990, however, Xerox had decided to exit financial services and concentrate on its core business of document processing. Its first proof statement of this move was the introduction of the DocuTech Production Publisher, a revolutionary new multi-function product that employed digital technology to scan, copy, print, and bind documents that would traditionally have been prepared on offset presses.

Yet the company needed to create a unifying theme to reflect the breadth of its product array beyond copying. In 1994 assisted by Landor

Associates and Siegel & Gale, Xerox adopted the more energetic color red to replace its old corporate blue and restaged itself as "The Document Company" by elevating this former advertising tag line into prominence in the company's corporate signature (see Exhibit 5.6). A new marketing symbol, the "digital X," and communications campaign were launched to further express the company's vision of an increasingly digital future (see Exhibit 5.7). At its most literal level, the digital X actually represents the makeup of the company's revenue base. Three-fourths of the mark is solid, associated with traditional light lens and printing products. The upper right-hand arm of the letter is constructed of pixels, the small squares associated with digital technology, representing the 25% of revenues from digital products.

Today, Xerox uses its new corporate signature pervasively; it appears on all company materials, from stationery and product collaterals to vehicles and building signage. On promotional applications, which include product identification, packaging and presentation visuals, the digital X is featured boldly.

Like Xerox, McGraw-Hill had grown into a global information company serving business, finance, education, and consumer markets. However, few target markets were aware of the breadth of McGraw-Hill's products and services. The educational community knew it as a textbook publisher; the business community understood it as the publisher of *Business Week;* and the financial community associated it with Standard & Poor's. A core objective of the new identity, undertaken by Lippincott & Margulies, was to broaden the image of McGraw-Hill and communicate that it owns successful brands. This was accomplished by a name change from "McGraw-Hill" to "The McGraw-Hill Companies" and by a visual identity system with three interwoven themes: a "brand-rich" theme which communicated that the company has an array of multiple brands; a "principled" theme which underscored its legacy of intellectual leadership; and a "technologically sophisticated, dynamic and global" theme which communicated that its products and services meet worldwide standards and specifications.

Theme Variation or Isolation?

Thematic variation may occur either for a brand or for a corporation as a whole. The Coca-Cola company uses different themes for each target

EXHIBIT 5.6

Xerox Slogan (Logotype Reproduction Sheet)

Logotype Reproduction Sheet

THE DOCUMENT COMPANY
XEROX

THE DOCUMENT COMPANY
XEROX

THE DOCUMENT COMPANY
XEROX

THE DOCUMENT COMPANY
XEROX

THE DOCUMENT COMPANY
XEROX

THE DOCUMENT COMPANY
XEROX

THE DOCUMENT COMPANY
XEROX

THE DOCUMENT COMPANY
XEROX

THE DOCUMENT COMPANY
XEROX

THE DOCUMENT COMPANY
XEROX

THE DOCUMENT COMPANY
XEROX

THE DOCUMENT COMPANY
XEROX

THE DOCUMENT COMPANY
XEROX

THE DOCUMENT COMPANY
XEROX

Note: For Color Reproduction, use
Pantone® 032 Red for the Xerox logotype.

XEROX® and The Document Company® are trademarks of XEROX CORPORATION.

market. In the early 1990s, Coca-Cola laid out a multitheme strategy for its Fanta brand soft drink sold in three major markets: the Pacific, Latin America, and Europe. The objective was to capitalize on "deeply rooted regional identities (by creating) distinct marketing programs for each of the three regional strongholds for Fanta." In each target market, a distinctive imagery was created for Fanta. Across the Pacific region, an animated character was introduced who communicated through a television

EXHIBIT 5.7

Xerox Logo (Logotype Reproduction Sheet)

Logotype Reproduction Sheet

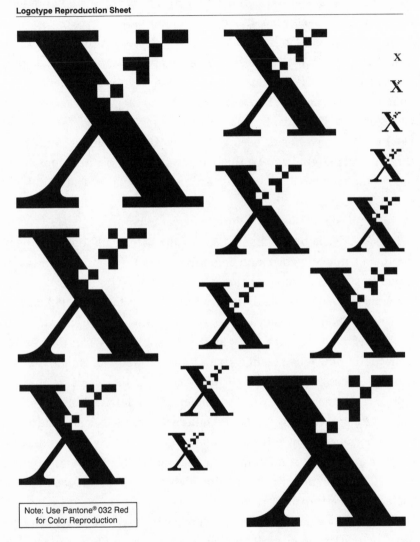

Note: Use Pantone® 032 Red
for Color Reproduction

XEROX® and the digital X are trademarks of XEROX CORPORATION.

screen on his T-shirt. In Latin America the Fanta Man was introduced, a funny character with an irresistible smile and a distinctive laugh. In Europe Elefanta was introduced, an adventurous mechanical elephant with a huge taste for Fanta. While the age target groups were the same across these markets, the theme characters used to reach the target groups differed depending on children's and teenagers' regional preference for high-tech, traditional cartoon, and music-video characters. The strategy reversed a negative trend in each of the three markets: in 1992, sales of Fanta were down 9% in the Pacific, 11% in Latin America and flat in Europe. But in 1993–94 sales grew by 7% in the Pacific; were flat in Latin America, and moved from -8% to +4% in Europe.

In contrast, most other Coca-Cola brands are positioned and promoted worldwide with consistent imagery. For example, Sprite is positioned worldwide as a clean, crisp refreshment around the theme "Obey your Thirst"; Coca-Cola is positioned as "taste the difference"; and Diet Coke (or Coca-Cola Light, as it is called in less calorie-conscious markets) as "You have never been refreshed like this before." And for all three brands around the world imagery of beach scenes, sports, and other situations in which people need refreshments are featured. Moreover, Coca-Cola views the trademark itself "as a remarkably resilient and multi-dimensional piece of cultural iconography."

The Coca-Cola brand thus possesses thematic isolation. One theme dominates in every corporate communication throughout all markets. In contrast, Fanta embodies thematic variation. Why is there no need for Fanta to create a single theme whereas there is for Coke? Put another way, when should we endeavor to use single themes as opposed to varied themes? The answer lies more in feasibility than in desire. The issue boils down to the question "Can we create a global theme?" Global themes provide strength of association that carry around the world. The images are easily transferred, and fewer resources are needed than in creating regionally tailored, varying themes. The global theme becomes a powerful icon. However, thematic variation has the distinct advantage of microtargeting various cultures. The message is tailored to them, potentially creating higher involvement, greater interest, and higher impact.

Thus, a choice needs to be made. A company can save money and employ a single theme or create higher involvement in local markets. Segmentation (variation) of themes carries costs; when the benefits are not clear, the optimal choice is to maintain a single theme. When are the benefits of thematic variation not evident? When a brand has attained such high recognition and esteem levels that its very presence is uniquely identified across markets. Coca-Cola has the ability to play on such thematic unity. A competitor, however, may benefit from employing thematic variation to compete with Coca-Cola in each market separately.

ORGANIZATIONS, BRANDS, AND THEIR SYMBOLS

Symbol	Meaning	Organization/Brand
Star	divine presence, enlightenment, wisdom	Texaco, Converse
Circle	unity, completeness, perfection, harmony	GE, AT&T
Triangle	aspiration	Delta Air Lines, Alcatel
Anchor	adventure, stability	Levis Dockers
Harp	Ireland, Celtic heritage	Guinness
Lion	leadership, power, royalty	MGM
Cross	relief of suffering, charity	Blue Cross
Cow	fertility, abundance, simplicity	Borden Ice Cream, Elmer's Glue
Diamond	clarity, perfection, rarity	Sprint

Source: Adapted from Claire Gibson, *Sign and Symbols: An Illustrated Guide to Their Meaning and Origins* (New York: Barnes & Noble, 1996).

The Integration of Verbal and Visual Information

Once strategists have determined whether to use one theme or several, they must turn their attention to the expression of the theme. Since themes often appear both in verbal form and in visual form, consistency between the verbal and the visual information becomes important.

Print ads often consist of several components, which are separated in the layout: (a) visual information in the form of a photo, sketch, or graphic illustration; (b) a headline; (c) extensive verbal information in the body of the copy; (d) a logo of the brand name and a visual symbol; and (e) a slogan.

The literature on verbal and visual processing in consumer research provides key insights that can guide decisions on meshing verbal and visual elements. Some propositions derived from research on visual and verbal information processing reveal the following about memory of, and attitudes to, ads with verbal and visual elements.

1. In terms of memorability, consistency among verbal and visual elements is critical. This applies to both logo and ad design. Brand names as well as other information are better remembered in ads when ads contain "framed pictures" in which the verbal message relates the picture to the brand.[12]

2. Taglines that allude to the brand name or are often derived from it (e.g., "Tantalizing women, they all wear TANTALUS," or "DYNAMO for dynamic men") make both the tagline and the brand name more memorable.[13]

3. Interactive imagery in logos (ROCKET delivery service, showing a cartoon with a carrier on a rocket) makes excellent mnemonics.[14]

4. In terms of inferences, too much consistency can be boring, unmotivating, and leave the impression of a lack of creativity. Allusion and moderate inconsistency, which provides opportunities for the consumer to elaborate, often works better.[15]

Adapting or Abandoning Themes

There are several reasons why a theme may need to be adapted or abandoned. Theme changes may become necessary because of changes in culture, the organization, its customers, or competitive actions.

Culture. Since themes are fed by cultural images, a theme can become tired and outdated. This may happen, for example, for brands that select themes related to sex roles. By the early 1980s, English Leather's tagline "All my men wear English leather or they wear nothing at all," used since 1967, had become tired. (The line itself seems to be have been an allusion to a classic Marilyn Monroe comment. When a reporter asked her what she wore to bed, she answered "Chanel No. 5"). In the late 1980s, Hanes Hosiery changed its slogan. The Hanes brand image had been built for twelve years on the slogan that women should buy Hanes because "Gentlemen prefer Hanes." Saatchi & Saatchi changed this sexist, outdated image to "Lady prefers Hanes." Sales, awareness, and trial of the brand experienced double-digit gains over the previous year.

Organization. Pressure for change can also occur because of changes within the organization. For example, a theme may no longer be in line with a firm's changed mission, vision, objectives, or strategies. The organization may also have diversified beyond its core business or beyond the business that its theme suggests. In the mid-1980s, General Electric had become the largest diversified multinational worldwide, with businesses ranging from appliances and light bulbs to financial services and aerospace. Research by Landor Associates indicated that neither its diversification nor its dynamism following Jack Welch's appointment as CEO were reflected in the name and logo. Landor proposed shortening the name into the acronym GE, shortening the name of its businesses (e.g., from General Electric Major Appliance Business Group to GE Appliances), and presented three final design solutions for the logo. It developed five levels of identification that GE could use to identify various businesses. The new identity meant a diminishment of the "Better living from electricity/technology" theme used formerly. On the other hand, it created a more contemporary identity that preserved certain key equities of the old one while adding new elements.

Customers. Customer demographics and lifestyles are constantly in flux. Changes in eating habits made it necessary for Kentucky Fried Chicken to shorten its name to KFC, Burger King to BK, Sugar Pops to Corn Pops. Although altering the theme, other visual aesthetics may remain the same to maintain the company style. As mentioned in Chapter 1, changes in clothing styles resulted in a change away from the "safari and rainforest" theme for The Gap's spin-off store, Banana Republic. Its product line, packaging, shopping bags, advertising, and retail environments now only convey the impression of a modern, upscale casual-clothes retailer. But the familiar name and the safari colors have remained to retain the aesthetic style.

Competitors. In the early 1990s, competition intensified for the Hyatt hotel chain in the U.S. and worldwide. On the one hand, there were threats at the top-luxury level due to the expansion by the Four Seasons and its association with the Regent chain (see the following chapter). The Hyatt touch in terms of luxury facilities, business centers, and fax machines in the rooms was no longer unique. On the other hand, by introducing new services such as automated check-ins and check-outs and superior frequent-stay programs, Marriott had made major inroads into the business-traveler market and was perceived as providing superior value.

How did Hyatt respond? Recently, in some of its advertising the Hyatt chain changed its theme from "Feel the Hyatt Touch" to "Discover the People with the Hyatt Touch." While it may seem trivial, this change amounts to a major shift in emphasis within the broader theme of exclusive service. Ads explain: "In the age of the virtual office . . . we're proud to introduce the actual person." The new theme is intended to introduce the personal touch into efficient business-hotel operations. The ad states: "At Hyatt, we offer our guests access to user-friendly business equipment. . . . All the tools you're sure to need when you're away from the office. Not to mention a friendly person who knows more than just how to use them." The revised theme is supposed to attract a broader range of business travelers by promising them a human connection along with convenience and efficiency.

SUMMARY

Themes are among the most powerful tools that managers have in creating and maintaining corporate or brand identities. With their ability to invoke associations and meanings, themes become etched in customers' memories in unique ways. But finding an appropriate theme and deciding on the best way to embody that theme in identity elements is a delicate task for managers, and a further effort is involved in deciding when it is time to modify or retire a theme. Managing the creation and implementation of a successful theme, however, is a key part of the task of creating an irresistible customer impression, the topic of the next chapter.

6

Overall Customer Impressions

THE FOUR SEASONS: UNDERSTATED ELEGANCE[1]

At the high end of the luxury hotel market, the Four Seasons + Regent Hotels and Resorts has managed to create and maintain an identity of timeless, understated elegance in the 37 hotels it manages in sixteen countries; once construction is completed on properties now in progress, Four Seasons + Regent will have 45 hotels in nineteen countries.

The company's hotels produce impressively consistent customer responses, despite variations in aspects of each property that keep each hotel sensitive to the culture and geography of its location. Indeed, one of the goals of the company is to have the finest hotel in each locale in which it operates, an objective that necessitates sensitivity to the particular features of each surrounding market. Research shows that, regardless of the location of a hotel, executive travelers' expectations of a luxury hotel do not vary. Thus, in order to establish itself at the top of this category, the company also needed to make staying in its hotels a dependable, consistent experience for guests.

History

Founded in 1961 with the Four Seasons Motor Hotel in Toronto, the company entered the U.S. market by acquiring the Chicago Ritz-Carlton.

The expansion continued into Washington D.C., San Francisco, New York, Seattle, Dallas, and Los Angeles. The company has now expanded outside North America, especially in Asia, with the acquisition of Regent International in 1992. This was a key acquisition: while Four Seasons had achieved its success in North America, Regent had a strong presence in Pacific Asia.

With the merger, customers familiar with one chain can be assured

EXHIBIT 6.1

Four Seasons Advertisement

"I've had to fly, sit in taxis, attend meetings and live on snacks for 24 hours straight. Now what?"

Now, you decompress at a Four Seasons Hotel, where the demands of business feel less demanding. A suit pressed in an hour? A plane ticket in minutes? A presentation with computer graphics? We're at your service 24 hours a day. Our menus offer selections from low-fat linguine with tomato and basil, to rack of lamb, to homemade chicken soup. And our health clubs and pools are equally irresistible after endless hours of travel. In this value-conscious era, the **FOUR SEASONS HOTELS** demands of business demand nothing less. For reservations, phone your travel counsellor or call us toll free.

Four Seasons · Regent. Defining the art of service at 40 hotels in 19 countries.

that they will find the same high standards at the other. Three properties opened in 1996: hotels in Istanbul and Berlin and a resort in Hualalai at Historic Ka'upulehu, on Hawaii's Kona Coast. In 1997, two resorts are scheduled to open, on Bali in Indonesia and at Aviara in Carlsbad. In 1998, a hotel will open in Las Vegas. The challenge for the company is to maintain its top-of-the-line standards for luxury at each of these locations—some of which do not bear the Four Seasons or Regent name. The venerable Pierre in New York and the Ritz-Carlton in Chicago kept their valuable names even when they were bought by the Four Seasons + Re-

EXHIBIT 6.2

Four Seasons Advertisement

"I'm arriving tonight and I have no time to pack. How much do I have to bring?"

How much would you like to bring? Our valets can press your suit—or a week's worth of them—in an hour. Our spacious rooms offer hairdryers and thick robes; our health clubs, gear from running shorts to aerobics shoes. And our 24-hour concierges are poised to provide anything you intended to bring, but didn't—from a sales presentation on a disk, to a best-seller. Hard cover or audiotape. In this value-conscious era, the demands of business demand nothing less. For reservations, please phone your travel counsellor or call Four Seasons Hotels toll free.

FOUR SEASONS HOTELS
FOUR SEASONS · REGENT
HOTELS AND RESORTS

Four Seasons · Regent. Defining the art of service at 40 hotels in 19 countries.

gent hotels. Marketing strategy is developed for each individual property, for local and regional room and food-and-beverage business, and
for promoting the hotel as a center of community activity, partly as a
means of developing local catering revenue.

In 1993, the Four Seasons opened its flagship hotel in New York.
Thought to be the most expensive hotel building ever built in the United
States, this 52-story building, designed by renowned architect I.M. Pei,
cost $360 million to build—a tab that comes to $1 million per room. The
only Pei-designed hotel in North America, the tower was constructed of
honey-colored French Magny limestone, the same material Pei used in
his famous extension of the Louvre in Paris. The look of the outside of
the building is grand and yet understated in the modernist style—the
building does not scream for attention on its crowded East 57th Street
block.

The focus of the design team was on the guest: The aim was to create
aesthetics based on the unique experience of staying at a luxury hotel.
"Architecturally, we designed the Four Seasons Hotel to continue the
grand tradition of a time when going to a hotel was an occasion," said
Pei. "Its emphasis is on celebrating the luxury hotel experience, with interiors designed around personal service and discreet ceremony." The
entrance to the hotel is done in spare, minimalist lines, yet dramatic
lighting and large smoky mirrors create an illusion of endless space. The
hushed yet energized feeling of the interior space of the hotel is often
compared to the feeling of being in a temple.

Customer Impressions of the New York Four Seasons

One guest's impressions tell an important story of the experience the
New York Four Seasons Hotel delivers. Writing in the *Asbury Park Press*,
Barbara Sturm tells the story of her weekend stay that emphasizes the
luxurious but understated, urban but unhurried experience of the hotel.
The time she takes to experience the many luxurious details and form
her impression of the hotel is noteworthy. "On the exterior, seven vertical setbacks start at street level and become progressively taller. The
cream-colored tower, which soars 682 feet into the sky, is so slender
that, at first glance, you do not realize that it's the tallest hotel in Manhattan. Pei has given the city something uniquely beautiful—a work of
art, as well as a building," she says. Once inside, her aesthetic experi-

ence involves many aspects of the hotel's features. "We were escorted in a fast-moving elevator to a soundproof, no-smoking suite on the 46th floor. I gasped with delight when the bellman opened the door. Facing us were 10-foot-high ceilings and a picture window framing the entire northern half of Manhattan." Ms. Sturm's experience was comfortable and unabashedly sensual—"The bed was outfitted with Frette sheets, goose-down-filled pillows, and a duvet. Floor linens and slippers arrived with the bed-turn-down service." She goes on to praise the "fluffy white towels" and "huge bathtub." All of her senses are engaged by the room; on the way out the door to the restaurant, for example, she writes, "I couldn't resist nibbling on red cherries from the fruit basket."

The next morning, this guest continues her visit in the hotel's beauty center. "The three-hour 'Executive Recharger' elevated my mood," she writes. "Treatments included a one-hour massage, European cleansing facial, aroma therapy, manicure and pedicure." Her experience of total relaxation in the midst of the bustling city stands out. "One of the best features of the weekend was having no schedule. We allowed ourselves the freedom to lounge, rest and recuperate." When she decides to go the fitness center to work out, she describes the space as "large and uncluttered," and notes the headphones and individual television attached to each treadmill. "For stretching, I had a spacious, mirrored aerobics room all to myself. Then, I used the sauna, steam room, and whirlpool." She ends her piece by quoting Mae West: "Too much of a good thing is wonderful."[2]

The Aesthetics of the Interior Design

Comfort was paramount in the designers' plan. The hotel set itself apart from competitors by making sure that the guestrooms were the largest in the city while still charging rates comparable to the competition's. Each room features a foyer, separate dressing room, and a living/sleeping area with cable television, radio, complimentary videos, window blinds that can be operated from bedside switches, and a two-line telephone with a speaker and computer modem. In the all-marble bathrooms, the tubs fill in one minute and another television, radio, and telephone are found. In the interior decoration, by Don Siembada and Jay Leff of Chada, Siembada & Partners, consideration for comfort and aesthetic pleasure continued. The modernist style of the hotel's architecture was continued in the decor, with a color scheme of caramel or copper in each room, built-in cabinetry, and custom-designed English sycamore furniture. Paintings are also modern, with cubist and abstract works dominating.

Food as Part of the Luxury Experience

The hotel restaurant, called Fifty-Seven Fifty-Seven, for the address of the hotel, was also planned to continue the themes of the hotel in its decor and in its cuisine. The cool and elegant decor is continued, and the room is as spacious as the rest of the property, lending it a restful but nonetheless urban atmosphere. Like the rest of the hotel, the restaurant seems to be at once an organic part of the city and a luxurious retreat from it. *New York Times* restaurant critic Ruth Reichl praised the experience of eating in the restaurant, calling it "one of the city's stateliest dining rooms," "a memorable public space" and "an elegant refuge." The menu is innovative and up-to-date, a departure from the traditional menus of most hotel restaurants. The elaborate but refined cuisine is contemporary American, with a regional and Mediterranean emphasis. "Today, Fifty-Seven Fifty-Seven seems like a wonderful luxury; it is not just another hotel restaurant but one that is setting a new standard for an old tradition," sums up Reichl.[3] Room service from the restaurant is delivered to guestrooms according to a brisk standard: eggs should arrive in ten minutes, according to procedure.

The Four Seasons + Regent on the Web

The Four Seasons + Regent Web site is one of the ways in which the company promotes a uniform aesthetics without compromising the brands of the individual hotels. It is tailored to the needs of both affluent business travelers and travel professionals who book deluxe business and leisure travel. Research found that 40% of the Four Seasons + Regent clientele used the Internet. The home page of the site opens with a crisp fine-art photo of a flower that fades out on the top and bottom. Visitors to the site can choose where to go among four areas labeled Find by Location, Choose by Amenities, Select Package, and How to Reach Us. Each hotel's individual site contains its own elegant Regent or Four Seasons (or in some cases, like the Pierre in New York, its own name) logo at the top, with the words "A Four Seasons Regent Hotel" underneath. Each hotel's site opens with a stunning photo of some aspect of the hotel, faded at the top and bottom like the home page. The first impression you have is of the experience of being there. Words scroll underneath each hotel photo that describe the experience: "Just blocks from Rodeo Drive. . . . After a day of tough negotiations watch the sunset over Beverly Hills," reads the page at the Beverly Hills Four Seasons; "Visit La Scala and Il Duomo, so close. . . . Steps from the most celebrated fashion houses." For the Ritz-Carlton Chicago, which does not sport the Four Seasons name, only the words on the page link the hotel to the chain: "The only Ritz-Carlton that deserves the name of a Four Seasons." Visitors to the Web site can "tour" each hotel to take in all its features, viewing guest rooms, lobby, physical fitness facilities, and so on with one click each.

Besides touting the benefits of the location and the experience of the hotel, the words for each hotel appeal to the sensuous side of potential guests: "A chilled towel and misted spray service poolside" in Hawaii; "Lose yourself in the sensuous villa accommodations"; "tranquil courtyards and idyllic gardens"; "pamper yourself with a fireside massage." The vocabulary varies, but the connotations are all the same: comfort, indulgence, luxury, pampering, top-flight service, understated elegance with no detail or sensory realm ignored.

THE IMPORTANCE OF OVERALL IMPRESSIONS

The overall impression of the Four Seasons Hotels as a refuge of contemporary understated elegance is created through the comprehensive and systematic management of individual style attributes, and styles and themes inherent in identity elements. These elements together produce a coherent overall impression and image of an understated luxury hotel.

Overall customer impressions are the ultimate test of the quality of the identity management process. They must therefore be the major concern of any identity management. Corporate resources are wasted if corporate expressions, embodied in styles and themes, do not produce the desired customer impressions.

Managing overall customer impressions calls for an appreciation of the impression-formation process and its outcome. Yet designers, identity consultants, and managers often focus primarily on corporate and brand expressions, often at the exclusion of customer impressions. They perform identity audits with senior management and, on the basis of this input, proceed to change a company logo and its signage. Packaging consultants and advertising agents speak with brand managers and advise them to change the packaging or ad slogan without ever consulting the customers.

This is reflected in attitudes like "the design was great! Too bad the audience did not appreciate it"—often expressed by designers—which is counterproductive in the realm of aesthetics management. It only serves as a painful reminder that the product or service was designed without a solid consideration of customer behavior.

MINIMIZING GAPS BETWEEN
EXPRESSIONS AND IMPRESSIONS

A lack of consideration of overall impressions may result in customer misinterpretations of corporate or brand expressions. Expressions might not make sense when scrutinized by the customer, or they may be seen as inconsistent, or as unattractive. Confusion could ensue ("What are they trying to say?") and negative impressions might arise ("I do not like it").

Japanese retailer Takashimaya confused consumers with its style and "art" theme when it first entered the U.S. market with its flagship store on Fifth Avenue in New York. Instead of clothing accessories or fragrances the ground floor consisted of an upscale flower shop and an art gallery—an unusual approach for Takashimaya compared to its stores in Japan. Clothing merchandise was nowhere to be seen, and customers felt lost. Perhaps Takashimaya's approach was too esoteric. Since then, the company has gradually changed the store's layout and merchandise display to become a more conventional upscale department store.

Closing the interpretation gap requires that a company assist the customer in the desired interpretation. Takashimaya, for example, could have supported its unusual retailing approach with an ad campaign and brochures explaining why the store has a flower shop and art gallery on the ground floor. The campaign could have stated, for example, that a lot of inspirations for the colors and shapes in clothing, furniture and porcelain design, which constitute Takashimaya's key merchandise, come from nature and art.

MONITORING UNEXPECTED CUSTOMER IMPRESSIONS

Corporations sometimes have to deal with customer impressions that are outrageous or completely at odds with reality. For example, customer impressions can be formed from strange sources such as contemporary legends, those spider-eggs-in-the-Bubble-Yum rumors that circulate at lightning speed through popular culture. For over a decade, Procter & Gamble has faced swirling accusations that it is linked to satanism, for example, that its CEO donates large shares of the company's profits to his satanic church, and that a ram's-horn symbol will soon start appearing on all P&G products. The claims were supported by reference to the symbolism embodied in the aesthetics of the logo. But in 1995 P&G finally found the source of the rumors, suing an Amway distributor for making false and defamatory statements about the company. This unusual customer-impression problem is likely to continue to require monitoring and strong management by P&G.

On a far less dramatic scale, Timberland faced a media firestorm in 1993, when its brand of boots and outerwear began to be adopted, not by the rural, outdoorsy customer base it sought, but by inner-city youth. The company tried to disassociate itself from its new urban, hip-hop fashionableness, and then was charged with racism for reacting negatively to a huge new source of sales. Timberland maintained that it was merely trying to keep its corporate and brand image stable, not associated with a fad of any sort. The company's ads continued to portray a distinctly antiurban aesthetic. But Timberland could have identified the new situation earlier and responded with a less divisive message while still keeping the integrity of its original identity.

Sources: Newsweek, October 24, 1995; *New York Times,* November 7, 1993.

OVERALL IMPRESSIONS: PROCESS AND CONTENT

Overall impressions are formed from mental representations of an organization's or a brand's aesthetic through a mental process of interpretation. In this chapter we first discuss the process that occurs in customers'

FIGURE 6.1

The Nature of Overall Impressions

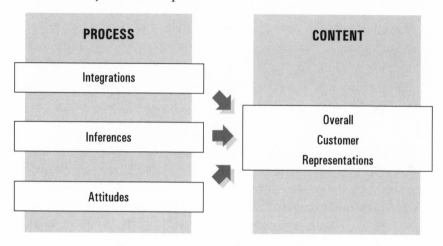

minds when they are exposed to the forms, the styles, and the themes embodied in identity elements. We then discuss the content of their mental representations by detailing several key dimensions that are used to judge any corporate or brand aesthetics.

PROCESS: HOW CUSTOMERS ARRIVE AT OVERALL IMPRESSIONS

Customers are not passive recipients of an organization's aesthetic output. They are active information processors of the numerous identity elements they experience each day. They edit and interpret the primary elements, styles, and themes to form an overall impression of the organization or its brands. Some processing, however, may occur nonconsciously while others may occur deliberately. Deliberate processing is most likely when customers have an intrinsic interest in a particular firm or product or when they are confused by a campaign and try to make sense of it ("What does Benetton want to say when it uses pictures of AIDS patients, multicolored condoms and newborn babies in its clothes advertising?")

Overall customer impressions are based on three types of processes that consumers regularly engage in when they process information: (1) integrations, (2) inferences, and (3) attitudes.[4]

1. Integrations

Information integration is an area of extensive research in person perception. An important question is: How do individuals integrate the many pieces of information about a person into a coherent impression? Two effects are key in suggesting an answer. Research on the "centrality effect" and the "primacy effect" shows that certain pieces of information weigh more heavily than others. As a result, they produce profound differences in the overall perception of a person.

The Centrality Effect. Please try to form an impression of a person based on the following traits: "intelligent — skillful — industrious — warm — determined — practical — cautious." When presented with this list, many respondents have imagined a hard-working scientist with a strong desire to accomplish something of great benefit. The impression changes entirely when we substitute the trait "warm" with the trait "cold." Now he or she is seen as snobbish, arrogant, and calculating. Experimental research has found, however, that the difference between traits like "blunt" and "polite" do not have the same impact as those of "warm" and "cold." "Warm" and "cold" are *central traits* that pervade our entire judgment of the person.[5]

The same principle applies to perception of organizations or brands. Certain identity elements have a central position in determining customer impressions. Imagine a bank with identity elements of the following colors: a gray building, a pastel-pink building, staff in dark blue uniforms, light gray counters, and light blue bank cards. The pastel-pink building stands out. (There are, in fact, banks with this color scheme in Japan.) The impact would not be as strong had we chosen pastel-colored vehicles. For a bank, the building is a central identity element. Thus, it is critical for any corporation to identify its central identity elements because they drive customer impressions to a disproportionate extent.

The Primacy Effect. First impressions give a stronger impression than later impressions. First impressions last; they stay with a person—or company—for a long time. It took British Airways many years to get rid of its "bloody awful" image even after service and its aesthetic had tremendously improved. The big lift came finally by means of a successful visual identity campaign by Landor that entirely changed the airline's public face, combined with an advertising campaign by Saatchi & Saatchi using the (at the time) provocative theme "The World's Favourite Airline." Nowadays, British Airways consistently rates among the world's top carriers, and updates its identity and image on a regular basis.

Due to the primacy effect, managers also need to pay close attention to the sequencing of identity changes in the roll-out of a new campaign. A worthwhile approach is to implement the new identity first in a central identity element that may provide a halo effect for other identity elements.

2. Inferences

Inferences are conclusions that customers draw based on the identity elements that they perceive. Inference is a process whereby customers make sense of something by filling in missing information based on their experiences and commonsense knowledge.

Consumer researchers have studied inferences primarily in an advertising context. When watching ads and going beyond the information given in the ad, consumers spontaneously create support arguments for product claims, counterarguments against product claims, and thoughts about the source (e.g., the celebrity or expert in the ad, the advertiser, etc.). Similarly, when consumers are exposed to the public face of a corporation, they draw inferences about the color ("Red is exciting"), shapes ("This angularity suggests tension"), styles, symbols, and themes ("They value tradition") of the organization. As in advertising, some of these inferences will be consistent with the expressed corporate or brand self; others might not be.

3. Attitudes

Attitudes are effective evaluations of customer impressions. They can be positive, neutral, or negative.[6] They also vary in strength, from neutral over mildly positive to enthusiastic. If a company tackles a sensitive issue, evaluations will be stronger and more intense (either positively or negatively). Opinions are often split about an identity. As Tom Peters has written, "Design is about LOVE and HATE, not like and dislike."[7] A lukewarm reaction is ineffective for producing an image, motivating employees or customers, catching attention, or selling a product.

Direct experiences lead to strong, stable attitudes. Customers are sure of their tastes and how they feel. Indirect experiences lead to vaguer attitudes with less strength. In contrast to product attribute/benefit advertising and image advertising, attitudes about a company's identity often result from direct exposure. Thus, if an organization is not absolutely sure that its identity is a winner, it should avoid direct contacts between customers and identity elements. It should first test out the identity, e.g., through identity elements that allow for indirect exposures, like announcements in the press and identity-explanatory ad campaigns in order to shape customer interpretation.

CONTENT: DIMENSIONS OF OVERALL IMPRESSIONS

Every year, Eugene and Nina Zagat publish a guidebook called the *"Zagat Survey"* that provides restaurant ratings for cities and regions in the United States: Atlanta, Boston, Chicago, Dallas/Fort Worth, Hawaii, Los Angeles, Minneapolis, New Orleans, New York, Philadelphia, the Southwest Region, Washington, and others. By now, the *Zagat Survey* also covers selected cities abroad such as Montreal and London. The *Zagat Survey* is a democratic approach to restaurant ratings: several thousand people participate, eating about 5,000 meals per day. The Zagat team tallies the results and reports them as averages on scales from 0 to 30 for four categories: food, service, cost, and decor. In addition, verbal summaries (with verbatim quotes) are presented for each restaurant.

Consider some of the phrases used in the booklet: "a lively young downtown coterie," "this garagelike Dixie dive," "casual, eclectic dining in the treetops," "posh and gracious hotel dining," "hip and funky diner," "a woody and warm room," "held together by nostalgia," "airy European decor," "utilitarian swank decor with a sleek, settle-in bar," "noisy, hippie-ish," "a dark, slap-dash Arab bazaar decor," "cooly [*sic!*] elegant."

Over the course of a single restaurant visit, as well as before and after the visit (through ads and reviews, through the matches that they collect and the photos they might take), customers are exposed to many different identity elements with inherent styles and themes, which they integrate into an overall summary representation. These overall representations of the restaurants are complex and evaluative, as we would expect based on the customer impression-forming process that we discussed earlier.

Thus, occasionally visitors are split in their impressions about the decor, and the Zagat description reflects it. What is "a charming townhouse" to some, is "cramped elegance" to others. What some call a place "full of nostalgia," others call "dining with the deceased."

Certain descriptions that are related to several major perceptual dimensions occur time and again. Descriptions of the Four Seasons hotel chain and those of restaurants in the Zagat guides sound remarkably similar. As part of a research project on international hotels, one of us (Schmitt) has collected qualitative and quantitative customer impressions of several hotel chains with U.S. and Asian consumers in order to isolate key impression dimensions. There are key perceptual dimensions of overall representations of identity elements, not just for hotels and restaurants but for any aesthetic object that we might encounter, such as cars, appliances, retail spaces, even public spaces and entire cities. These include: impressions related to time and time movements, space, technology, authenticity, sophistication and scale (see Figure 6.2).

Time Representations

With the present as the anchor point, a time dimension may refer to the past, the present, or the future, resulting in "traditional," "contemporary," or "futuristic" representations.

Traditional. Customers often judge an identity to be traditional if it uses elements, styles, and themes that are strongly identified with past periods. Individuals and (as we will see in Chapter 9) cultures differ in their

FIGURE 6.2

Dimensions of Overall Impressions

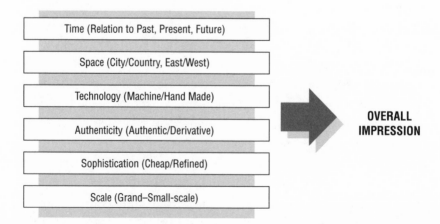

Time (Relation to Past, Present, Future)

Space (City/Country, East/West)

Technology (Machine/Hand Made)

Authenticity (Authentic/Derivative)

Sophistication (Cheap/Refined)

Scale (Grand–Small-scale)

OVERALL IMPRESSION

FIGURE 6.3

Impressions Related to Time

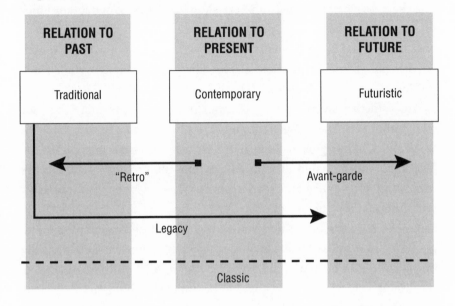

time orientations, i.e., in the degree to which they value the past, the present, or the future. If the customer considers tradition to be a value that is worth preserving, then his or her attitude toward traditional aesthetics will be positive; the impression may be termed "conservative." If the customer opposes the past, he or she may call traditional aesthetics "old-fashioned," "outdated," or even "reactionary."

From an aesthetics management perspective, it is difficult to use individual style elements to convey a traditional aesthetic. Colors as such are not unambiguously associated with the past. Yet, an overall representation of "traditional" can be achieved by using black-and-white photography and soft lenses. Shapes and materials are also reminiscent of the past: Roman brick columns, vertical or horizontal orientations in buildings, and patina-green roofs call to mind the past.

Asbach Uralt, a cognac and one of the most traditional trademarks in Germany, uses a traditional shape, a traditional typeface and a name reminiscent of tradition ("uralt" means "ancient"). The Swiss watch manufacturer Patek Philippe also uses a traditional aesthetic. The company still has a family name as its corporate name (it's not Seiko or Swatch!). Each watch is hand crafted, another sign of the past. Gold watches are displayed with a dark brown watchband. The traditional aesthetic is also evident in its 1996 "Begin your own tradition" advertising campaign. The campaign includes black-and-white photography and motives that suggest the passage of time, e.g., a photo showing the back of a father holding a young child who practices playing piano. The ad uses a conservative italicized typeface. The copy ends with the words, "Which is perhaps why some people feel that you never actually own a Patek Philippe. You merely look after it for the next generation."

An aesthetic that strives for a traditional impression is appropriate for many products. "Traditional" connotes quality, customer loyalty, security. In a traditional approach there is the risk, however, of appearing old-fashioned and outdated. It is therefore important to track whether the traditional appearance and symbolism is still attractive and approaches the sentimental value of a classic.

Brooks Brothers, a traditional menswear brand, seemed to be past the point of no return in the late 1980s. In the eyes of most customers below the age of senior citizen, it did not offer the value of tradition any more, nor was it a classic: it just seemed to be hopelessly outdated. Since the brand has been acquired by Marks and Spencer, the U.K. department store group, as part of its U.S. expansion, the Brooks Brothers brand identity has been successfully revived through aesthetics. It now claims the terrain of traditionalism very successfully with a clothing line that sticks to its core "mature gentleman" image, expressed by its button-down oxford shirts, casual and formal menswear, redesigned stores, and such accessory items as hand-bound cocktail and cigar books.

Contemporary. A contemporary overall impression is created by using the styles and themes of the present. According to Peter Levine, an identity consultant with Desgrippes Gobé & Associates who is a keen observer of cultural trends, in the late 1990s trends include: symbolism of the digital world (pixels, flows of information, connectedness), globalism, a new honesty, spirituality, and purity.

The wild success of the CK ONE® fragrance (shown before in Exhibit 4.3), launched in 1994 by a Unilever subsidiary, Calvin Klein Cosmetics Company, is due to an astute observation of contemporary cultural trends. This breakthrough new fragrance, for use by both men and women, achieved record sales in months without cannibalizing sales of the preexisting Calvin Klein brand fragrance line, consisting of Escape, Eternity, and Obsession. The product, which comes in a pure, no-frills, minimalist flacon, was sold in department stores as well as record stores on stand-alone shelves to give it a mass market appeal for youth. This strategy resulted in an appealing impression of a contemporary fragrance.

Futuristic. A futuristic overall representation, with its focal point in the future, can be achieved in several ways: through an avant-garde design, the use of new materials, a new typeface, new printing techniques, through the unusual or unprecedented combinations of existing elements. Futuristic impressions can be groundbreaking and avant-garde or "science-fiction-like" and "weird." Pirelli, the Italian tire maker, uses a futuristic approach in its advertising with photos by Richard Avedon.

Time Movement Representations

"Retro." Sometimes, the goal of an overall representation is to recreate a period, i.e., to create in the here-and-now an overall representation of a particular period in history. The "retro" approach to expressions often strives for a nostalgic impression. Nostalgia is a sentimental yearning for the past, a wish to recover some past period or feeling. Nostalgia often focuses on certain target segments, e.g., aging baby boomers. A powerful way to achieve it is through music (the "sounds of their youth"), narrative and symbols, and other theme elements.

Retro trends are difficult to launch. They often start in an unplanned fashion (e.g., because of a successful movie) and are often entirely based on word of mouth. Their appearance in a culture is hard to predict, and they are often short-lived. They are temporary steps backward on the way to the future. They are appropriate for fashion products but better avoided for other identities or reserved for identity elements that can be changed fast (e.g., ads rather than logos). They may, however, provide a spark to a struggling brand by reminding consumers of its aesthetic and cultural leadership in the past.

Some restaurants in U.S. cities use this approach in recreating the atmosphere of a fifties supper club through vintage photos of the period, dim lighting, a glittering ballroom-evoking space design—and by serving lots of martinis. Fashion and fragrance lines invoke certain periods and then playfully reinterpret them (e.g., an ad of a Chanel No. 5 flacon rendered by Andy Warhol). Interestingly, though colors as such are timeless, certain color combinations seem to be associated with certain historical periods (e.g., primary "pop" colors with the Sixties, naturalistic colors like brown and green with the hippie culture of the Seventies).

In 1995, the athletic-shoe market experienced a retro trend. Retro successes included a Converse canvas sneaker called the One Star, designed in the 1970s; Adidas' 1960s-era sneakers with trademark stripes on the sides; and Puma basketball sneakers new in the 1990s but dubbed "Clyde" after 1970s New York Knicks star Walt "Clyde" Frazier. Retro trends benefit companies that were successful in the past but may have become second-tier over the years—such as Adidas, Converse, and Puma, which were leading brands in the 1960s and 1970s but had less than 5% market share in the U.S. in the early 1990s.[8]

Avant-garde. The opposite time movement to "retro" is avant-garde. Avant-garde impressions result from cutting-edge, iconoclastic design and identity approaches. French interior designer Philippe Starck is known for his avant-garde approach to hotel and restaurant designs in Europe, Asia, and America. He designed, for example, the interiors of the Royalton and Paramount hotels in New York, Hotel Manin in Tokyo, and (now-closed) Café Coste in Paris. One of his latest creations is the large restaurant and bar space atop Hong Kong's Peninsula Hotel, one of the most traditional grand hotels of the world. The design includes a computer-controlled projection of light that simulates a waterfall behind the major bar area, dramatic lighting, and minimalist rest rooms (all chrome and glass) that allow both men and women a spectacular view of Hong Kong harbor and Kowloon from this unusual venue.

APPLICATION: DIESEL

Diesel is Europe's hottest marketer of jeans. Diesel sales worldwide grew from $9 million in 1985 to $350 million ten years later. Its goal is to push U.S. sales ($15 million in 1995) to $100 million by 1999.[9] Diesel uses a hybrid approach of avant-garde and "retro" that is evident throughout its entire identity.

The quirky and satirical Successful Living advertising campaign, a product of Swedish ad firm Paradiset, was started in 1991 and has been run internationally ever since. The fall 1997 campaign takes a look back at significant moments in history. The campaign, shot in Miami, takes actual historical situations and transforms them in a witty way, using the latest computer technology to generate new images on older material (see Exhibit 6.3). Diesel's retail stores in Berlin, London, Paris, New York, Washington, Chicago, and San Francisco create an atmosphere that is "futuristic with quirky retro accents—brightly lacquered fixtures, fake-wood paneling, space-age metal and vintage furniture from the sixties and seventies." The clothing itself is also a hybrid of avant-garde and "retro." The fall/winter 1997 men's collection includes "gothic-inspired," "punk," and a "motor" theme. The women's collection incorporates a variety of classic materials of this century, such as tweed, nylon, angora wool, cotton, satin, and velvet as well as new materials such as "super-soft stretch ultrasuede," "striped gabardine," and "techno vinyl."

Legacy. A *legacy* impression is created when the company or brand is endowed with a sense of history or a sense of past time that is projected into the future. The customer should be familiar enough with the company history to find the historical approach plausible and persuasive. In 1996, Siemens, a German supplier of over 700 systems and products from fuel injectors and microprocessors to halogen headlamps, ran legacy ads, spreading over two pages, that stressed the history of the company and its future. ("1908. That was then. 1996. This is now.")

Sonae, a company in Portugal, used an interesting legacy approach to launch its new logo and corporate identity. Sonae was founded in 1959 and pioneered the production of decorative laminates. It soon broadened its range of wood products, and in the 1980s expanded into supermarkets, real estate, information technology, leisure, and tourism. Its average annual growth rate in the 1980s was 38%. In the early 1990s it chose a new logo that symbolizes growth and energy. The logo represents the nurturing and development of new businesses and is accompanied by the slogan "from the smallest seed into the largest tree." Sonae thus makes appropriate reference to its beginnings in wood products and uses this symbolic representation to lead itself to the future.[10]

Classic. A classic impression implies that something lasts, endures, and is of permanent value. The judgment of whether an identity is classic or timeless changes over time. To put it differently, the impression of being classic is created at a certain point in time. An organization can only achieve a classic impression over time if it updates parts of its aesthetic

EXHIBIT 6.3

Advertisements for Diesel Brand Jeans

occasionally. Especially if it claims to be, as the Reverso watch brand does, "Avant-garde since 1925"!

Many product categories have their "classic" brands; Chanel No. 5, Johnnie Walker, Porsche Carrera, the Ritz-Carlton and many others come to mind. Brands become classics by using a consistent approach in styles and themes over the years. A classic brand and its aesthetic representation are untouchable, from a different world, in their own league. Marketers of a classic brand stick to its core, even in the face of competition.

Budweiser, "The King of Beers," is more than 120 years old. Its traditional message contains a mixture of pride and self-confidence ("This Bud's for You," "Proud to Be Your Bud," and "When You Say Budweiser, You've Said It All"—surrounded by blue-collar imagery) and has worked

EXHIBIT 6.4

Budweiser Advertisement

for decades. In November 1994, however, marketing professor Philip Kotler commented: "They may need a really fresh, new, powerful image that appeals to those they are losing." Clive Chajet, chairman of Lippincott & Margulies, disagreed: "I would not be pushing the panic button," he said. Chajet seemed to be right. Kotler may have failed to consider the value of a classic, which can extend its value into the future with minor updating. Budweiser's advertising has featured frogs in a pond under a moonlit sky, as well as ads showing the classic Clydesdales playing football in a field (see Exhibit 6.4). The visuals are as blue-collar as always, and the message remains one of pride and self-confidence.

Space Representations

Like time, overall representations of space take managers to where they want their organizations or brand to be. Space representations appear in multiple forms.

City/Country. One general aspect of space representation is the city/country dichotomy. City/country is a powerful aesthetic-segmentation variable. Preferences for a city or country aesthetic are linked to lifestyles. City people and country folk do not mix a lot. The city dweller stays at home on the weekends, when the country folk swarm into the cities. Country folk sniff at city folk who arrive on the weekend to inhale fresh air in their designer country outfits.

A city/country identity is created easily. A country impression on supermarket shelves is created by stereotypical images of cows and grass, the elements, mountains, and rural dressing of the French Realist type. A city impression is created by many people, more cars, loudness, skyscrapers, and black dress.

There are also impressions of specific cities that may be alluded to as part of an identity. DKNY uses the impressions of New York City to its benefit. Ben & Jerry's ice cream employs a grass-root community Vermont imagery (e.g., symbolized in the spotted cow as its primary visual icon). Beijing Jelly, a popular Chinese life elixir, uses Chinese medicine associations favorably and the perfume "Paris," in its advertising logo, alludes to the city of elegance.

East/West. The Cathay Pacific campaign (discussed in Chapter 1) strives for an impression of "East and West." Sophisticated integration of East and West is a trend also found in restaurants around the world (in Hong Kong, Tokyo, London, New York, Los Angeles). The TOT ("Talk of Town") restaurant in Hong Kong has perfected this chopstick-and-cutlery aesthetic down to the last detail.

The trend was started by Gray Kunz, a Swiss-born chef who worked for years in the Peninsula in Hong Kong and who is now at Lespinasse in New York. He is an expert in innovative "East meets West cooking," mixing classical French with Oriental spices. Examples of his menu: sautéed perch with fava beans (spiced with lemon grass and knob ginger) and espresso cardamom soufflé as a dessert. The ambiance at the restaurant, however, does not match the food concept. The room, with a Louis XV-style salon look, is entirely French. The name symbolism is also entirely French, referring to Mlle. Julie-Jeanne-Eléonore de Lespinasse, who ran a salon for the intelligentsia in Paris during the 1760s and had a heartbreaking affair with the Comte de Guibert. As a result, customer impressions are described in the *Zagat Survey* as "ornate," "stuffy," and "pompous."[11]

Other Aspects of Space. Forms, styles, and themes can be played on to create other various overall impressions related to space. For example, a homelike identity vs. businesslike, and indoor vs. outdoor. The subway systems of Europe give one an impression of being indoors, while many in the United States, because of the choice of flooring, walls, etc., give us an impression of being outdoors. Some retail identities appear like home, while others feel as though one is in a business setting of some sort. Specific place impressions can also be managed, for example, to create an overall impression of nations like Spain, Italy, Mexico, or regions like New England, California, or the Southwest. Kleenex Tissues' "expressions" use visuals tied to specific spaces on various identity elements. Their tissue boxes use style and theme to create various space-related overall impressions. Print advertisements name the impressions, like "South WoWstern" (*sic!*), with visuals of American Indian style and red-desert colors, and thematic symbols of bulls, and "Thai-riffic," with Eastern style and pictures of arched curved roofs and a person from Thailand in traditional garb.

Technology Representations

Another pervasive overall representation concerns the degree to which a company's aesthetics reflects the use of technology. Identity elements may appear to be produced by technology or to be handmade. They may have a high-tech look or a natural look, an artificial or natural feel or taste; they may sound synthesized or produced by traditional musical instruments.

Attitudes concerning this impression depend on individuals' attitudes toward technology and on the type of company or product category. Individuals who are environmentally sensitive, for example, prefer the natural look. To appeal to these consumers, Estée Lauder created the Origins brand, which is not linked to the Estée Lauder identity and name. Like the Body Shop, the Origins store interior and product design evoke nature.

Authenticity Representations

Impressions of an identity are also based on whether the identity seems authentic and original or derivative and imitative. Authenticity and originality draw people's attention and are clutter-breaking. Authenticity often means breaking with the norm of an industry in order to stand out—a process that Wells Rich Greene BDDP Inc., a New York-based advertising agency, calls "disruption."

Identities are judged as derivative when they borrow the core identity elements or symbol of another identity. They may also be judged as derivative when the actual execution is different but produces the same perceptions of styles and themes. Typically, impressions of derivation are negative because customers value originality.[12] However, if the company quotes its own style, the impression may not be that of derivative. Customers may notice the allusion (as discussed in Chapter 4) and appreciate it. But extreme derivative identities cause legal concerns, as we introduce in Chapter 8.

Sophistication Representation

Depending in major part on aesthetics planning, some aesthetics strike us as "unsophisticated," "unrefined," or "cheap." Others are "sophisticated," "refined," and "luxurious." Baci brand chocolates uses a series of descriptions and visuals to create such an impression of sophistication (see Exhibit 6.5). We have already seen that the Four Seasons has managed an impression of sophistication. In contrast some hotels, like the Watergate Hotel in Washington, in all its styles and themes, look "cheap." Law firms typically use aesthetics to create an overall impression combining sophistication with power. The entrances, signage, lobbies, offices, and other space aesthetics are reminiscent of large corporate-American boardrooms. While various styles may prevail, depending on, and symbolizing, the law firm's culture, the consistent impression that they all strive for is that of powerful sophistication.

Sometimes, entire countries are associated with an image of sophisticated or unsophisticated aesthetics. France, Italy, and Japan are associated with sophistication in a variety of aesthetic domains. In contrast,

EXHIBIT 6.6

Baci Advertisement

EXHIBIT 6.6

Airline Sales Counter in Shanghai

both Russia and China have rich cultures, magnificent buildings, and art work from a glorious past. Yet, for the large part of the twentieth century, both countries have neglected the entire management field of corporate and brand aesthetics. In the Soviet Union, and in China under Mao, anything beautiful and aesthetic was considered bourgeois and antirevolutionary. This ideology peaked during the Cultural Revolution in the late 1960s and 1970s in China, when art works, personal belongings, and anything else aesthetic and of value was publicly destroyed by the Red Guards. Exhibit 6.6 shows the sales counter of a major Chinese airline. Aesthetics and identity management in both countries are still in poor shape, although the Chinese government tries to address the issue in its new "famous brands" campaign. Unless both countries change, they will have serious problems competing in international markets.

Scale Representations

A prevalent representation consists of the perceived scale of the business (grand vs. small-scale). An overall impression of grandness starts with the name: "Grand Hyatt," for Hyatt's upper-end brand of hotels; "Virgin Megastores" for Richard Branson's Virgin retail complexes that sell music, movies, books, and multimedia; "Millennium Tower," for a planned skyscraper, designed by Norman Foster, to be completed in Japan in the early 21st century. It continues in the styles and themes of the Grand Hyatt's entrances and lobby areas, with oversized flower arrangements and sculptures; in the oversized neon signs in the Virgin Megastores in Burbank, Costa Mesa, Los Angeles, Sacramento, San Francisco, and New York; and in the actual height of the Millennium Tower: 750 meters high, 335 meters higher than the Sears Tower in Chicago. For the Grand Hyatt, it is further enhanced with an ad campaign: "Entering the Grand Lobby was like walking into another world. Ascending the marble staircase merely heightened the sensation" says an ad for the Grant Hyatt in Hong Kong. And a television commercial for "Virgin Megastores" superimposes the Virgin logo atop the Acropolis and the Eiffel Tower. As Christos Garkinos, vice president of marketing of the Virgin Retail Group, explains: "We think we offer a great environment with huge selection that's fun to hang out in. It's a way to experience pop culture in one setting. And we definitely have a personality, a lot of which comes down from what Richard is all about: outward-looking, hip, irreverent."[13]

SUMMARY

Overall impressions result from customer processes that create overall representations of a company's or brand's identity. Company and brand

FIGURE 6.4

Summary of the CE/CI Framework

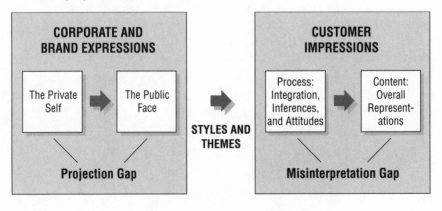

expressions are only meaningful as they transform into impressions. The interpretation process means that one expression might create vastly different impressions; and thus impressions of your company and its brands require research and monitoring. The representations themselves and the resulting impressions tend to be of a few major sorts that highlight the directions managers might want to take in creating expressions through aesthetics.

Current trends as well as your organization's or your brand's image should first be assessed to create new impressions. Aesthetics strategies need to be judged on whether they create desired impressions. In the next chapter, we discuss research for assessing, creating, and monitoring impressions.

PART III

MEASURING AND PROTECTING AESTHETICS

7

Assessment and Research Tools for Aesthetics Management

RESEARCHING AND MEASURING CORPORATE AND BRAND LOGOS

In this book, we have provided numerous examples of aesthetic elements and of styles and themes that seem to have a positive effect on consumers' perceptions of a company and its products. Most of our examples have been illustrative. Is there a way to move beyond the conceptual, analytical, and often intuitive understanding of aesthetics? Is there a research methodology that provides more precise data on which types of aesthetics work and which ones don't?

Professors Pamela W. Henderson and Joseph A. Cote of Washington State University and Alvin Schechter, Chairman and CEO of Interbrand Schechter, an identity firm, have studied the impact of logos on consumer perceptions. Henderson and Cote have approached the issue using correlational analyses (via multiple regressions) in order to study general logo characteristics. Mr. Schechter has used an applied experimental approach to study the impact of the name and visual components of a logo in terms of their image value. Both approaches are valuable and may be used in conjunction with techniques discussed in this chapter to study other identity elements besides logos as well.

The Henderson and Cote Study

In Henderson and Cote's work,[1] three experts first selected a total of 195 logos (i.e., visuals without names) of foreign companies and products to be included in the study. Foreign logos were selected to eliminate the confounding effects of familiarity, reputation, or prior repeated exposure to the logo. That is, somebody might be inclined to rate the logo of AT&T very positively—not because he or she likes the logo itself, but maybe because of satisfaction with AT&T service.

Next, a large group of consumers was asked to rate each logo on twelve design characteristics: complexity, organicity, activeness, roundness, horizontality, depth, symmetry, cohesiveness, representativeness, durability, meaning, and perceived familiarity. These ratings were used to determine the key perceptual dimensions along which logos are perceived. To do so, the researchers first computed correlations (statistical relationships) between each of the design characteristics. Clearly, those design characteristics that are highly interrelated seem to be measuring (roughly) the same characteristics. This procedure, in conjunction with another procedure called factor analysis, thus allowed the researchers to identify the key perceptual dimensions underlying the design characteristics of the logos employed. They were what they called (1) elaborativeness; (2) naturalness; (3) association; and (4) symmetry. The first two dimensions are almost identical to what we have called "complexity" and "representation" in Chapter 4 on styles. *Association* refers to the degree to which respondents reported to understand the logo, and *symmetry* to the degree to which the subelements of the logo were symmetrical. Thus, when designers, based on managerial input, create new logos they should pay attention to these key logo dimensions, i.e., whether they want an elaborate or simple logo, an abstract or natural one, whether it should be symmetrical or asymmetrical, and how to make consumers understand the logo.

So, now that we know how people perceive logos, the question arises, which ones do they like? In their research, Professors Henderson and Cote also obtained ratings on five affective evaluations: dislike/like; bad/good, low quality/high quality, uninteresting/interesting, not distinctive/distinctive. They then used multiple regression analyses to determine which design characteristics best predict whether or not consumers like a logo. Their results: (1) consumers preferred relatively elaborate logos over simple ones; (2) they liked logos that evoked clear associations; (3) they liked natural logos; and (4) they liked symmetrical logos.

The procedures used by Professors Henderson and Cote can be used easily by any company to test its existing logos as well as new ones. In fact, it may be used to do rigorous testing of any identity element (signage, stationery, packaging, store interiors, etc.). What is required is a number of stimuli of these identity elements, relevant measurement scales, and an appropriate sample of respondents. Then the research consists of the following steps:

(1) Ask respondents to rate the given identity element on a number of design characteristics; (2) perform a correlation or factor analysis among these characteristics to identify key dimensions; (3) elicit attitude ratings of the identity element; (4) perform a multiple regression analysis to identify which dimensions determine attitudes toward the identity element.

The Schechter Study

Alvin Schechter[2] was interested in the image contribution of logos, i.e., to what degree consumers infer from the logo that the company or brand is trustworthy, offers high quality, is a product for today's lifestyles and a product consumers would want to use. Using an experimental design, a national sample of 1,800 consumers was randomly assigned to one of three groups: (1) a baseline "name only" condition in which participants were shown a series of index cards containing the company or brand name; (2) an "icon only" condition in which participants were shown the visual part of the logo in color without the company or brand name; and (3) a "full logo" condition with the name and logo. (Random assignment is a critical procedure in any experiment in order to control for systematic individual differences: some people may, in general, like logos better than others, and without random assignment may all end up in one experimental condition.)

Schechter reasoned that the difference in scores between the "full logo" and the "name only" conditions determined the image contribution of the logo design. For 45% of the logos, the difference score was close to zero, i.e., the icon neither enhanced nor diminished the image value of the names. For the remainder, there was an image impact of the visual. The six best image contributions occurred for the following companies or brands: Motorola, Buick, US West, Mercury, Cadillac, and Nike. The worst image contributions (i.e., negative scores that indicate that the name alone was better than the full logo) were observed for Continental Insurance, Minolta, Infiniti, Land O' Lakes, Fuji, and Texas Instruments.

The study also revealed interesting differences among logo categories. Overall, pictorial and letter symbolism in the visual icon enhanced the image more than characters, abstract depictions, or wordmarks.

The experimental procedure used by Schechter can be used by any company to determine the image value of subcomponents (name vs. visual icon) of existing logos or new ones. Alternatively, it may be used to examine multiple subcomponents of any other identity element (e.g., of names and text and visuals in packaging; of names, taglines, headlines, and visuals in advertising, etc.).

The Schechter study, however, has two key methodological problems. First, computing a difference score to measure image impact is dubious in comparisons across groups (i.e., between-subjects comparisons). Second, the differences between experimental groups and the differences among logo categories were not tested for statistical significance. We therefore recommend the following revised procedure:

(1) Determine relevant subcomponents of a given identity element; (2) randomly assign respondents to experimental conditions representing these subcomponents; (3) have respondents rate the subcomponents given to them; (4) analyze mean differences between the experimental groups via Analysis of Variance (ANOVA).

More detailed analyses on the value of subcomponents and how certain subcomponents might interact with each other to create better or worse combinations can be assessed through a procedure used often in new product development called "conjoint analysis," which also uses experimental design procedures.

THE ROLE OF RESEARCH IN
AESTHETICS MANAGEMENT

We have seen two potentially useful methods to assess identity through aesthetics. In this chapter, we discuss the major methods that can be used to analyze identity and perhaps predict its success. Before that discussion, however, we introduce the controversy regarding the effectiveness and the role of research as applied to design and identity.

Unlike most business decision making, identity and image management has a strong artistic component. The end product of identity and image planning—the product that the customer sees (in the form of logos, brochures, buildings and offices, advertisements, or Web sites), or hears, or touches—is the outcome of the creativity of graphic designers, architects, and interior designers, copywriters and art directors in ad agencies, and other aesthetics experts.

These aesthetics experts are correct when they tell managers that skill, training, and experience in addition to creativity are integral parts of the design process. Yet, as in other areas of managerial decision making, and perhaps more, design is often conducted with too heavy a reliance on intuition. Anecdotal evidence is often the only evidence used when asking someone to justify intuitive judgments.

THE PERILS OF ANECDOTAL EVIDENCE
IN AESTHETICS MANAGEMENT

If asked why a darker rather than a lighter color was used as part of a logo design, the designer may respond that the darker color in this context will represent a more powerful image consistent with the organization's strategy. If asked again, "Why," meaning, "Why do you think that this would be the effect of the darker color?" a typical response might be that in other examples where the designer has worked and through his/her experience, this was likely to occur. This invocation of personal experience functions as anecdotal evidence. The designer has a number of experiences and stories on which to draw, and does so.

This kind of hypothetical dialogue represents both the benefits and the drawbacks of anecdotal evidence. Such evidence helps people hone their intuition; it supports and shapes intuition. But it can lead to poor decisions for three reasons.

1. It is limited and therefore often skewed. Anecdotal evidence is not broad and representative. It usually entails some (not many) instances drawn upon to bolster a particular position. These instances may or may not be typical or representative of the overall state of affairs in the world.

2. It is self-supporting and therefore of questionable reliability. Anecdotal evidence often is recalled selectively with the result that supporting anecdotes are more readily used than nonsupporting ones. This leads to potential biases in analyses and decisions.
3. It is highly subjective. Anecdotal evidence often represents the intuition and opinion of a sample of one. The degree of consensus is not assessed, let alone considered.

As a result, a strong reliance on anecdotal evidence results in biases and errors in decision making. Over the years, decision researchers have identified a myriad of biases and errors, which are largely due to insufficient sampling and an overreliance on anecdotal evidence. Here are two examples:

- Ignoring base rate and probabilities. Based on a "success story," decision makers (e.g., designers) may rely again on an element that produced success in the past even though the probability of repeating the success may be extremely low. They are unduly impressed by the availability of the success story in memory.
- Insufficient adjustment. Designers may become focused on a preferred design solution. Although it perhaps ought to be rethought due to overwhelming research evidence, they continue with the same idea and only slightly vary the execution. They insufficiently adjust to the "arbitrary anchor" provided by the first design idea.

Thus, though anecdotal evidence is a key tool for designers in shaping and guiding intuitive senses, it should be bolstered by more representative and objective research.

SUSPICIOUS VIEWS OF RESEARCH IN THE DESIGN PROCESS

Unfortunately, many design and identity firms approach research with suspicion. "Design and reactions to design can't be measured!" the argument goes. Only the creative mind can produce superior results. Customer input, if anything, does harm to the design process by producing mediocre, middle-of-the-road solutions that may lead the designer astray. Thus, research is useless, a waste of money and, in the worst case, damaging to the design process.

This view is expressed, for example, by design luminary Ivan Chermayeff, founder of Chermayeff & Geismar Associates, who believes that consumers are often unable to predict reactions to design; they are usually unable to "lead" designers.[3]

This view is shared by others, such as the late quality guru W. Edwards Deming, who opined that innovations are never derived from consumers.[4] True, many breakthrough designs and identities were developed by creative, illuminated minds without any cut-and-dried research. But there are as many examples of designs that failed because of the shortsightedness of those responsible for developing the design, who, out of skepticism, or worse, out of ignorance, failed to employ the even simplest research and assessment techniques.

Most design firms lack the skills necessary to perform adequate research. Landor has put emphasis on research and continues to do so with one of the largest research departments of any identity firm. But many identity firms simply do not have an in-house research department. Yet, aware of management's desire for some kind of back-up justification for design solutions, they do offer the focus group, the proverbial hammer which they bang for all questions. The focus-group interview, however, is only one research tool among many and it has serious limitations. Therefore it needs to be used with caution.

The lack of adequate research performed by design and consulting firms has led to a niche in the market that is filled by a few research firms that specialize in design and identity. Cheskin + Masten, a firm in San Francisco, is an example of a well-established research-and-strategic-planning firm geared almost solely to the issues of identity and design. Moreover, although most design firms have added to their names "strategic planners" or "strategic communications consultants," few have carved out a niche by positioning themselves as focusing on research and strategic planning as paramount for development of design. Most firms are scrambling to bridge the gap, but often limit themselves by not understanding either the marketing world or the research world.

RESEARCH FOR IDENTITY PLANNING

Research and design go hand-in-hand. In order to design aesthetics (using styles and themes) that express the corporation's identity and create the right impression in consumers' minds, research is needed throughout the

FIGURE 7.1

Steps in Identity Research

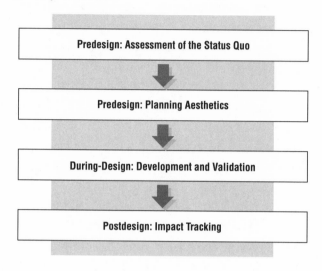

process—in assessing the status quo, in planning the aesthetics strategy through styles and themes, during the design development process, and in the postdesign process (see Figure 7.1). Research is often conducted in only one or two stages, i.e., by employing "postdesign" disaster checks using "qualitative" research (described later), or in a predesign positioning phase or a during-design phase. We present below a more comprehensive view of the research steps amenable to the process.

1. Predesign Step: Assessment of the Status Quo

The identity-management process typically starts with an assessment of corporate expressions and customer impressions. In this context, managers usually want an assessment of the current state of aesthetics or identity in their own company relative to its competition. This assessment entails discovering "who we are" in terms of our aesthetic presence. While this kind of inquiry might sound mystical or hokey, it can actually be quite rigorous and systematic. It involves a straightforward company, customer, and competitive analysis and a consideration of broader cultural factors that impact customer tastes and preferences. In addition, it may define the scope of an identity project, its objectives, and the problem to be focused on.

2. Predesign Step: Planning Aesthetics

After assessment, research is useful in developing strategies for positioning through aesthetics (e.g., the new styles and themes). Positioning an entire organization is more difficult than positioning a company's products or services. The research involved, therefore, requires greater resources and integration in order to be useful.

3. During-Design Step: Developing and Validating Design

The implementation phase of a new aesthetics positioning includes design development, a function performed by the various design firms. It is a multistage creative process resulting in new designs and identities. Research in design development is needed to pretest designs (e.g., logos, signage, packaging, spatial designs) just as advertising agencies use copy tests before they place the ads in the media.

4. Postdesign Step: Tracking the Impact of Corporate Aesthetics

Postdesign research assesses the degree of success of a design project. Success or failure should be assessed with respect to the objectives, specified in predesign step 2 above. Even a successful identity and image requires fine-tuning over time. The corporation's aesthetic needs to be upgraded and updated as societal tastes change. Otherwise, it loses its impact over time. Therefore, customer impressions of an aesthetic need to be tracked over time. Again, the analogy to advertising applies: just as advertising agencies track brand awareness, comprehension and image, it is necessary to examine how color and shape perceptions, and broader perceptions of styles and themes, may vary over time.

BASIC TOOLS FOR USEFUL RESEARCH

What are the relevant research tools in the design planning process? Most research techniques used by design firms, research firms specializing in design, and strategic identity consultants are general research tools of the social sciences. Most of them are of a verbal nature. Any general research or marketing research textbook provides a good overview. However, when applied to the design management process, these tools must often be adjusted to serve the intended objective of identity and image planning.

We first discuss three types of general research methodologies that are important for identity management: (1) secondary research, (2) primary qualitative research, and (3) primary quantitative research (see Figure 7.2). After discussing each briefly, we will discuss particular methods in the context of the four steps of the identity-planning process (assessing status quo, planning aesthetics, design testing, and postdesign tracking).

Secondary Research

Secondary research entails collection of already published materials. News reports, polls, trade-press articles, scholarly articles, general business-press articles, public-relations releases, news wires, transcripts of TV and radio shows—all comprise secondary research. These sources are readily available at libraries. Managers can conduct secondary research in-house without the need for expensive secondary-research suppliers or public relations agencies. Without the resources of vast library holdings, a company can collect great amounts of relevant information from two major pay services: (1) LEXIS/NEXIS and (2) DIALOG. These are two comprehensive databases comprising a wealth of secondary research including all the types mentioned earlier. Another useful though more unwieldy source is of course the Internet (to be discussed in Chapter 11).

FIGURE 7.2

Research Methods

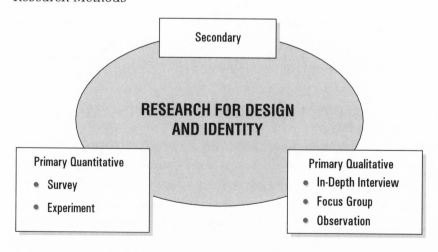

Primary Qualitative Research

Primary research implies that the research is being conducted by collecting new (unpublished) data. *Qualitative* research indicates that we are deriving information without quantifying it. Qualitative data are useful in both generating and evaluating new ideas, design concepts, and mockups. Qualitative data are used because some very important information is inherently nonquantifiable, or better analyzed through conceptual analyses as opposed to numerical analyses. Explaining emotional responses, for example, is quite difficult through quantification. Instead, in-depth discussions tend to elicit more useful information.

Nowhere else in research for design is there a greater need for creative insights. In studying corporate expressions, research subjects may be employees of the company. In studying customer impressions, the subjects of the research are end consumers (or sometimes business customers).

Standard qualitative settings include (a) in-depth interviews, (b) focus groups, and (c) locations from which to observe certain behaviors.

In-Depth Interviews. In-depth interviews are one-on-one interactions of interviewer with interviewee. The interviews typically last between 45 minutes and one hour and the interviewer follows guidelines, albeit the approach is often fairly flexible, allowing for deeper inquiries than could occur with a set-in-stone questionnaire.

Focus Groups. Focus groups are usually conducted with about eight to ten participants at a time and last from one to two hours. The setting is usually some sort of conference room, with a "moderator" (the interviewer) at the head of the table. The moderator works out of a discussion guide that leads him or her through the necessary inquiries.[5]

Locations From Which to Observe Certain Behaviors. Observational studies may occur anywhere and under a variety of circumstances. The data are typically collected by monitoring and recording one's interpretation of the observed person's behavior.

The first two research settings entail interaction with respondents while the last may or may not. The kinds of interactions with participants vary. We may, for example, feel comfortable directly questioning participants about likes or dislikes, but require indirect techniques (like associational tasks, matching tasks, drawing tasks, among others) when we feel that people would be unable to answer a question meaningfully.[6]

In-depth interviews and focus groups are best used at the early stages of the identity-management process. For the purpose of identity management, they are ideal techniques for assessing the personality and values of the companies through internal interviews with managers. Managers often have a wealth of information and views on their own corporation, which can be easily brought out into the open via open-ended verbal techniques like questionnaires and focus groups. These techniques are also useful for measuring general customer impressions. For example, to find out whether the "look" of a company seems in general to be "out of fashion" or still "contemporary," or whether the company has an environmental "feel," a focus group with consumers may be used. These general impressions may then be followed by quantitative research, in which specific impressions of visual elements are rated.

Observational techniques are most relevant whenever identity elements affect behavior. This is the case, for example, for spatial design. Observation is also important when self-reported data would be inadequate to learn about some phenomenon. Self-reports are often unreliable (1) when we call on people's memory, (2) where they would not ordinarily pay enough attention to something to be able to respond meaningfully, or (3) where we desire sensitive information. Moreover, generally, self-reports of attitude or even intention are not correlated completely with behavior; thus it is often wise to measure behavior itself. Observation is useful, therefore, in determining the impact of a point-of-purchase display on retail shopping patterns, how a design of a self-service island for a gasoline chain is affecting consumers, how various lighting designs affect purchasing patterns, or whether packages attract or repel, among others.

Primary Quantitative Research

Quantitative research implies that we analyze the data quantitatively. Here, interactions with participants vary from direct questioning to observing certain behaviors (eye tracking, for example). Direct questioning can elicit immediate quantitative judgments (like/dislike on a five-point scale, for example) or verbal responses ("How would you describe the product contained in the package I just showed you?") that are subsequently coded. Whatever kind of information is obtained, however, it is all converted to quantitative data for analysis.

In order to generate sufficient confidence in its reliability, quantitative research typically requires large samples; in practice we want information from usually more than 100 respondents for each defined group. As with qualitative research, these respondents may be consumers or employees as well as competitors, stockholders, or any other relevant group.

Standard quantitative settings include locations from which to observe behaviors (as with qualitative research), as well as two other techniques: surveys (whether by telephone, mail, computer, or mall or street intercept), and experiments.

Surveys. Surveys tend to be large-scale collections of useful data. The data can be quantitative or qualitative, meaning that we can gather either numerical responses or other types of information (verbal information, for example). The analysis, however, is quantitative in nature. The data are generally collected in questionnaire form, most typically by telephone, but also via intercepts (mall or street, face to face), and through the mail. When visual stimuli need review, intercepts enhanced with computer graphics and guided computer questioning are often desirable.[7]

Experiments. In experiments, we manipulate identity variables in a controlled setting and study how they affect a response in a causal manner. For example, if we wanted to test a new color (blue) for the name Sony to see if it elicits positive attitudes and behavior for Sony products, we could show the blue logo and ask a question about subjects' like/dislike of the logo, or monitor facial expressions, etc., as behavioral observations. Yet since we would be trying to establish cause and effect (color causing a reaction), we need to be sure that the cause of the reaction is color. Here the color may be causing the reaction or, instead, the shape of the logo without the blue color may be eliciting the reaction. We could ask people the reason for the responses, but this is self-reporting and is not as reliable as actually being sure what the cause is. The way to extract out the reactions based on the color is to isolate the effect of the color. One easy way to do this is to set up a control group, to whom the similar logo is shown with the standard black color. The difference between the reactions for the two groups would indicate the effect of the blue color in comparison to the existing black color. All experiments, however elaborate, are based on the "control group" reasoning above, to ensure that any effects are indeed caused by what we want to test.

With these kinds of tools in mind, we describe now a comprehensive assessment of a company's aesthetics strategy. The research discussed applies as well to focusing on one product category or brand as well as any other management-driven restrictions on the scope of a project.

ASSESSING THE STATUS QUO

As discussed in Chapter 3 on corporate and brand expressions, a corporate-identity audit requires a complete understanding of what kinds of information are needed to understand the current state of an organization's identity. Usually information is needed about (1) the industry as a whole, (2) specific competitors, (3) customers, and (4) cultural trends.

Industry Analysis

In any potential project, it is vital to begin with an industry-wide analysis of design. Just as margins, cost structures, and new product development vary across industries, so do aesthetics and design.

The analysis entails a research phase that provides a detailed inventory of what an industry is doing concerning aesthetics and design. What logos are being used? What colors are used? What product configurations are used? How often do design changes occur on average in this industry? Are there particular aesthetic elements that are noteworthy or distinctive for this industry? What styles and themes are prevalent, if any? What are the styles and themes currently being used? What overall impressions prevail? What are the overall impressions being used? An analysis of aesthetic approaches in a variety of different industries is needed if a company has a brand that has offerings in different industries.

The industry analysis may point to opportunities for distinctiveness. The new logo for the Korean electronics conglomerate LG (Lucky Goldstar) stands out as a playful alternative among rather dull professional logos among other firms. The Union Bank of Switzerland's advertising, with its corporate executives reciting Shakespeare's poems, is distinct in its style and theme from other banks. Similarly, PAOS, a Japanese identity firm, convinced TriBank, a merger of three Japanese banks, to use Disney characters and pictures of birds and other elements to gain clout as a friendly retail bank within the conservative corporate look of the Japanese banking industry. Thus, an analysis of the industry as a whole can form the basis for an entirely novel approach.

Competitor Analysis

Competitor analysis offers your company's management a look into the breadth and depth of your immediate competitors' approach to identity and design. This, in turn, can provide insights into competitors' future identity approach and tell your management how to position itself vis-à-vis the competitors in terms of your company's visual presence. In Chapter 2, we described how Lucent Technologies chose an innovative name and logo based on competitor analysis.

The data are often secondary, derived from news stories, trade press articles, annual reports, or 10(k)s. Data are easily obtainable from companies, which often provide brochures, concise histories of their brands, and pictures of changes over the years. For historical changes, as a last resort old advertisements, print or broadcast, can be perused. The most relevant output of competitive analysis is the perception of the competition in the eyes of potential customers. The methodology for understanding potential customers' perceptions of competitors' aesthetics is equivalent to the methodology used for understanding our customers' perceptions of our own company's aesthetics, which we discuss next.

Customer Analysis

Customer impressions (discussed in Chapter 6) refers to actual beliefs that relevant publics have about a company, its products, or its services. Analyzing customer impressions of a company's aesthetics is at the heart of identity management. It is the prime task for research at the first stage of assessing the status quo.

Customer impressions can be assessed on various levels, from the broadest test of a company's image to isolating specific aesthetic elements and testing perceptions of those elements. We believe that where primary attributes (such as colors, shapes, or textures) can be isolated, there is usefulness in doing so.

Quantitative Customer Analysis

Quantitative customer analysis is usually performed for three types of variables or concepts: (1) awareness, (2) attitudes and beliefs, and (3) usage and behavior.

1. *Awareness.* Customer awareness is measured via recall (unaided or aided) and recognition tests. Can customers spontaneously describe a logo, a packaging, the interior of a building? If not, can they recognize it when shown pictures or graphic displays? General Electric used awareness data to decide about the redesign of the GE logo. Experimental research using recall and recognition tests revealed that the oval shape of the logo and other elements were instantly recognized as belonging to GE even when the name was removed from the logo. As a result, GE rejected a radical redesign because it perceived that it had immense equity in the existing logo.

2. *Attitudes and Beliefs.* A second group of variables concerns attitudes—beliefs and inferences—of the company or its products based on visual information. What meaning does a certain color convey to consumers if a company in a certain industry is associated with that color? Consider cars. What do the colors "red," "black," and "blue" connote as colors of automobiles? Research on beliefs is conducted best in a comparative (i.e., experimental) setting, e.g., by showing packaging of the same shape with different colors.

3. *Measurement of Behavior.* Finally, there is the measurement of behavior. Consumers may be shown pictures of spatial settings, for example, and be asked how they might behave in this or that setting. Alternatively, their behavior may be directly observed (video or photo ethnographic research, for example) and then analyzed with further qualitative data such as in-depth interviews.

Quantitative information (awareness, beliefs and inferences, intentions and behavior) should be collected for the company and for at least one major competitor. The competitor is best defined as "aesthetic competition" and not necessarily in terms of highest sales or market share. The purpose of research in the "status quo" phase is not only to assess but also to plan. Therefore benchmarking against a formidable "aesthetic competitor" is more useful for future planning than benchmarking against the highest-sales or highest-share competitor—unless sales and market share are driven by the competitor's unique aesthetic approach.

Qualitative Customer Analysis

What does the company's/brand's aesthetic and identity mean to customers? How does the company's/brand's aesthetic fit into people's lives? These questions are extremely important for understanding consumer brands, from cosmetics and running shoes to fountain pens and mobile phones. All these products are not only utilitarian goods but image products that fit or do not fit a user's lifestyle.

Mass surveys of quantitative information provided as syndicated data are only useful as general barometers of lifestyles and habits of customers. Simmons and MRI provide such data, as well as Claritas and many other research firms. The drawback is that these data do not focus directly on design preferences and the research firms do not supplement the data with in-depth explanations of any sort.

A more useful tool is qualitative ethnographic research. Cheskin & Masten ask potential target consumers to take photos of themselves at home doing various routine activities. These photos are then categorized and analyzed using content analysis. This analysis is bolstered by in-depth interviews and interviews with experts on the groups in question. These data are useful for determining people's lifestyles and may contain hints for designing an aesthetic.

This research, however, still begs the question: How do corporations or brands and their aesthetics fit into these lifestyles? The Cheskin & Masten approach could easily be expanded, however, to explore the aesthetics of a company and brand in more depth. In advertising research, Young & Rubicam, to assess a brand's personality, asks consumers, "If the brand was an animal, what animal would it be?" By the same token, the aesthetic of a company or brand may be explored by asking consumers to take photos of people, places, spaces, landscapes, city views, activities, etc., that would fit with the brand. These photos might then be rated and coded by independent coders to determine the colors and shapes, styles and themes, and overall impressions that are associated with the company or brand.

Qualitative-Quantitative Approaches

A mixture of a qualitative and quantitative approach is often used in the assessment of styles and themes inherent in designs. For example, if a luxury-hotel chain like Hyatt were to assess its image across the world, it should try to ascertain what styles or themes people perceive in the name Hyatt and the Hyatt logo, and more, what styles and themes people perceive in the lobby or the rooms. Separate studies should be conducted for each unique collection of identity elements (rooms, lobbies, etc.) to determine reactions. Visual testing can be conducted thorough photographs. The idea is to test styles and themes for a variety of locations as well as consistency within and across these elements. A wealth of useful information can be created from perceptions of styles and themes, to intentions to go (to one or more of the locations shown). The research is partly qualitative and partly quantitative. Separate samples of respondents would address the different kinds of stimuli to be tested. To test consistency across stimuli, one group would compare all stimuli.

Trend Analysis

Trend analysis refers to research focusing on forecasts of micro- and macro-changes. For aesthetics management, the cultural environment is of particular importance. Wallace Church Associates Inc., a cutting-edge strategic-design and communications firm in New York, prides itself on having someone on staff who worked for the famous prognosticator Faith Popcorn. This kind of research has its usefulness. It ushers those who can predict correctly and first into a leading role, whether for trends of societal behavior or values, competitive forces, customer lifestyles, perceptions, values, or aesthetic tastes. Solid trend analysis rests on secondary research as well as on primary qualitative research and is often conducted in the form of observation or interviews.

Trend analysis is key to gain a competitive edge but is often highly subjective. Take the current trend in the United States toward casualness and comfort in dressing, a trend that has finally reached corporate America with the institution of "casual Friday." This trend, if it lasts, certainly has implications for the look and design of office furniture (from colors that suggest a more relaxed approach to shapes and fabrics), as well as for the aesthetics of clothing accessories (pens, personal organizers, mobile phones). But is it likely to last? Or will we be seeing a backlash to more formal corporate styles (even on Friday)? What type of data would help us forecast this long-term development?

In trend forecasting, it is critical to have a longer time horizon. If one has a shorter one (say, 3–5 years), then one might mistake a fad for a trend. With a long time horizon, it is often possible to analyze current developments in terms of their long-term societal and cultural significance. Using this type of long-term analysis, we predict that "casual Friday" is likely to stay because we would find clear evidence for (1) decreased formality in dressing over the century; (2) an increase in the readiness with which informal forms of social behavior are adopted in the office ("Call me Tom") and (3) an increased need to express one's individuality.

DETERMINING WHERE TO GO

After the assessment of the status quo, the company decides on an aesthetics strategy, which specifies where to go next. A key element of the aesthetics strategy is positioning the company through its aesthetic manifestations. Thus, in determining where to go, companies need to conduct further customer research as another "predesign" step.

Managers need to understand how customers might envision the company's aesthetic positioning. Qualitative research is useful here to derive meanings. Focus groups or in-depth interviews can supply the means by which people can respond directly to the positions. Creative techniques can follow that can lend guidance to the choice of aesthetics in creating the positioning. Participants in a group can be asked to create visual collages that depict the ideas in the positioning statement. This can create a useful visual vocabulary for the designers. This research can be extended to create other aesthetic elements such as music, texture, shape, etc.

This kind of predesign research is not usually conducted, but it can provide tremendous insights. For example, design attributes can be tested qualitatively to determine what impressions they give. What associations people have with various colors, shapes, etc., can help in the positioning and predesign criteria. How people respond to visual themes can be tested with an experimental design.

This is similar to the customer analysis discussed earlier, except that here we have moved beyond the point of initial assessments and are focusing directly on positioning for change. The results of earlier research may be combined with a separate research endeavor here. For example, in ethnographic research it was found that Pepsi-Cola is associated with blue as much as it is with red. With this equity assessment, we can determine what blue means to people in order to decide how to position Pepsi aesthetically. Pepsi also assessed corporate expressions to see how to differentiate itself from the leader Coca-Cola (red by association). As a result of its research, Pepsi determined to begin marketing an all-blue can.[8]

Beyond specific attributes, styles and themes can be tested. For each identity element managers in collaboration with designers and consultants identify and, through customer research and managerial judgment, evaluate styles and themes of their own company or products and services and those of the competition. Guidelines (and later profile options) can be created and compared to each other on the basis of (1) expression of positioning, (2) distinctiveness from competitors ("shelf" impact), and (3) sensitivity and appeal to customers' needs.

From these research findings, planners can help guide the design brief that guides their creative designers in their processes. The design brief is akin to the creative strategy found in advertising agencies. These documents are instruments of translation, from the world of positioning and marketing to the world of art and creativity. As such, they require delicate balance, between overspecifying (acting as designer) and underspecifying (not acting as marketer). For example, a design brief stating that a product needs to be "of higher quality and more contemporary" is too vague. Adding a number of specific attributes to focus on gives designers the direction necessary to do their jobs well and facilitates conversation with management.

DEVELOPING A DESIGN

Through a design brief, designers may create a number of alternative designs, be they packages, logos, spaces, or any combination of elements. "During-design" research can aid in the process.

Current vs. Proposed Design

Once a number of alternatives have been created, quantitative testing of reactions to the designs can be conducted. With package designs, it is relatively straightforward to show packages and ask a variety of questions relating to the alternatives. Monadic testing is desirable if costs allow, since in the real world, people do not make side-by-side comparisons of the sort required in a comparison test. Communications value, including perceptions and purchase intent, can be collected and related. Since this is an experimental design, one can associate various levels of purchase intent with the different designs shown and determine which design causes higher purchase intents. The method of collecting responses can be enhanced by incorporating "dial" methodology, a handheld device that records reactions. The reactions can be of the entire package or design or of particular attributes inquired about.

It is also possible to use photos, or even simulations. Professor Ray Burke at Indiana University has developed a computer simulation of the shopping experience that helps in the assessment of package-design strength. Many firms use eye tracking as well. Perception Research is a firm specializing in simulations where eye tracking is monitored. Their idea is that shelf impact is key to determining choice—not a completely accurate assumption.

Real-Life Experiences

Complex designs incorporating logos, spaces, i.e., entire environmental complexities are difficult to test without mock-ups. One can test each individual element and even certain combinations. But without the full sensory experience, it is difficult to rely on the findings.

An interesting method to test "whole" reactions (consistency between identity elements) in addition to underlying attributes is the "building-block" method. This is a large-scale study incorporating hundreds of respondents, in which they are taken step by step through a series of alternatives from the most basic elements to ever more creative strategies for persuasive appeals. This kind of step-by-step research amounts to a large-scale survey, but in the context of sensory stimuli well suited to testing design.

MONITORING AND TRACKING

Monitoring and tracking research is of two types: short-term and long-term. *Short-term research* involves the assessment of whether an undertaken identity creation or change was successful. Like advertising-impact research, it typically occurs right after the implementation of the new identity and then onward for a few months. Long-term research involves the constant tracking of an identity over time in order to fine-tune (upgrade and update) the company's aesthetics as customer tastes change.

What exactly should be tracked? Tracking variables typically include the key quantitative variables discussed above in the status-quo phase: awareness of the new identity or recent changes; beliefs and inferences; intentions and behavior. In addition, it is useful to assess the public relations as well as the sales impact. (A good proxy is sales inquiries related to the identity.) Publicity value of an identity (in terms of media coverage) is important because it saves advertising costs when announcing the identity change and because it may draw customers to the identity.

SUMMARY

We have advocated a systematic research approach to identity planning in any phase of the planning process. This is not to diminish the value of creativity and originality and the often insightful intuition of designers and other aesthetics experts. Quite the contrary. Research itself can provide valuable input to the creative process. Psychologists divide the creative process into four phases: analysis of the problem, immersion into the problem to be solved, illumination, and synthesis. Especially in the first two phases (analysis and immersion), when the designer looks at the problem from any angle, research can provide valuable input. Research is less useful for the actual creation of the groundbreaking idea, the illumination phase, but has a role to play in the final "synthesis" phase in terms of testing the effectiveness of the ground-breaking idea.

Research is also valuable as a communication and coordination device. It brings to the table of experts (managers, consultants, and designers), the person who ultimately makes or breaks a design solution, the person who must be the ultimate judge of the success of an aesthetic—the customer.

8

Protecting Aesthetics and Identity

In 1978 two brothers, Felix and Mike Stehling, opened a restaurant called Taco Cabana in San Antonio—the first of what would be a series of fast-food restaurants in Texas. The cuisine was Mexican, and so was the "trade dress," the legal term for corporate identity. Taco Cabana described its identity as follows: "A festive eating atmosphere having interior dining and patio areas decorated with artifacts, bright colors, paintings, and murals. The patio includes interior and exterior areas with the interior patio capable of being sealed off from the outside patio by overhead garage doors. The stepped exterior of the building is a festive and vivid color scheme using top border paint and neon stripes. Bright awnings and umbrellas continue the theme."

By 1985 Taco Cabana had opened five more of its Mexican fast-food restaurants, all with the same identity. In that year, Marno McDermott and Jim Blacketer opened a Two Pesos restaurant in the Houston area, using an identity similar to that of Taco Cabana. In the words of the developer of the Fuddruckers restaurant chain, "[Taco Cabana and Two Pesos] are shaped the same. They look the same. When you're inside they feel the same. They have the same product." Two Pesos expanded rapidly in and out of Texas, but avoided the San Antonio area. By 1989, 29 restaurants had opened.

EXHIBIT 8.1

A Taco Cabana Restaurant (top); a Two Pesos Restaurant (bottom)

The Action Against Two Pesos

In 1986, Taco Cabana expanded into new markets, Houston and Austin—as well as Dallas and El Paso, where Two Pesos was also doing business. Having been the first to employ the identity that the two businesses shared, Taco Cabana sued Two Pesos for trade dress infringement, among other related charges (such as theft of trade secrets). The case went to trial, and the jury found that Taco Cabana had an inherently distinctive trade dress, that this trade dress was nonfunctional—that is, it was aesthetic in nature and not related to the functioning of the product itself—and the identity of Two Pesos would cause a likelihood of confusion on the part of ordinary customers as to the source or association of the restaurant's goods or services. Therefore, Two Pesos could not legally maintain its "borrowed" aesthetics and identity.

The Appeal and the Supreme Court Opinion

Not surprisingly, Two Pesos appealed the decision. They conceded that protecting identities might be critical to the successful establishment of a new product or service. Yet, they argued, if the identity were found not to have created a so-called "secondary meaning," a special association in the minds of consumers linking the identity directly to a particular source, it should not be protectable.

But the appeals court and the U.S. Supreme Court affirmed the original decision. The Supreme Court stated that, as with trademarks, corporate identities are protectable not only if they have attained the status of "secondary meaning," but also if they have not attained secondary meaning but are "inherently distinctive." The Court relied on the policy underlying the federal trademark laws, which, it affirmed, serves to protect trade dress no less than trademarks. Two Pesos was ordered to change its offending identity in its entirety.

The opinion established that protecting trade dress was in the interests of both business owners and consumers—business owners must be able to benefit from the goodwill and reputation generated by their business, while consumers should be able to distinguish among competing producers. As the Senate had summed up the matter in passing the Lanham Act, the public should know that when they choose a product bearing a particular trademark, "it will get the product which it asks for and wants to get," while the owner of a trademark must be protected from "pirates and cheats" who try to profit from the energy, time, and money he has invested in presenting his product to the public. The Court quoted this language approvingly, along with the words of Congressman Fritz G. Lanham of Texas, sponsor of the Lanham Act: "The purpose of [the Act] is to protect legitimate business and the consumers of the country."[2]

Not Unduly Limiting Competition

In the *Taco Cabana* case, the Supreme Court made it clear that trade dress is inherently valuable and must be protected. But the Court also used the case to establish some limits to the protection of corporate identity. In particular, the Court took into account the question of the range of identities that are available for a particular kind of product or service. Where there is only a limited range of available identities, the issue becomes the protection of fair competition. Previously, legal protection had often been denied to trade dress under the assumption that there are only a finite number of identities available. In the name of protecting fair competition, the *Taco Cabana* decision assured that identity was not protectable in circumstances in which doing so would lead to an unfair monopoly. As a concurring opinion on the case stated, a design is considered "legally functional, and thus unprotectable, if it is one of a limited number of equally efficient options available to competitors and free competition would be unduly hindered by according the design trademark protection." Competition is thus assured in cases where there are a limited number of trade dresses, which might be exhausted if protection were granted.

LEGAL ISSUES IN IDENTITY

As the *Taco Cabana* case shows, the concept of corporate identity has important legal dimensions. An appreciation of the legal issues involved in establishing and protecting identity is a great asset to managers as they work with a design team. Can we borrow the stainless-steel look that The Gap uses? Can we use descriptors like "Plus" or "Ultra" without concern? Should we be concerned about copying or adapting shapes or colors for our product? How do we know when to be concerned about "me-too" products—our own or competitors'? How and when should we deal with a situation in which a competitor appears to be copying our identity?

Managers tend to view legal concerns as nuisances. As you develop a brand, for example, what might appear to be the innocent borrowing of a look or a trend in boardroom talk should raise concerns. A sensitivity to the legal landscape allows managers to grow antennae for legal pitfalls that are neither too sensitive nor too dull. For larger companies with in-house counsel, this chapter will help the manager to interact with the legal department in forming designs or identities. For smaller companies without in-house legal staff, this chapter will give managers a better sense of when counsel's advice is essential. While there is no substitute for legal advice and the guidance of an attorney in particular cases, managers need to have a basic understanding of the requirements that make elements of corporate and brand identity protectable under U.S. law. Even in cases that involve protection outside the United States, the information and ideas we will outline are crucial, since most countries' laws in this area are based on the same concepts.

IDENTITIES AS LEGALLY SANCTIONED BARRIERS TO COMPETITION

Brand and corporate identities help companies create barriers to competition. To some degree, a company or brand can obtain a legally sanctioned monopoly over certain aspects of the identity so as to create these barriers. Executives need to be aware of the extent and limits of the barriers to competition that they and their competitors can legally rely on. These potential monopoly rights are the province of what is loosely referred to as intellectual-property law, an area that includes trademark law, copyright, and patent law (see Figure 8.1). Before turning to the tricky notion of trade dress, which we introduced in the *Taco Cabana* case, we'll begin by exploring the most basic objects of legal protection: the brand name and the logo.

PROTECTING BRANDS FROM CONFUSION

The essential purpose of brands is to identify products. A brand tells the user that a product comes from a particular source, regardless of whether that source is known or unknown. Names or marks that function to identify a source can be protected as trademarks and can enjoy monopoly status. These monopolies are unlimited in time, but are often limited in their scope to particular product categories.

FIGURE 8.1

Laws Affecting Identity

Freedom from Potential Confusion

Federal trademark law is embodied in the Lanham Act. An important Section of the Act, Section 43(a), is worth reviewing in full, since it is the main source of current federal trademark law:

> Any person who, on or in connection with any goods or services, or any container for goods, uses in commerce any word, term, name, symbol, or device, or any combination thereof, or any false designation of origin, false or misleading description of fact, or false or misleading representation of fact, which—
>
> (A) is likely to cause confusion, or to cause mistake, or to deceive as to the affiliation, connection, or association of such person with another person, or as to the origin, sponsorship, or approval of his or her goods, services, or commercial activities by another person, or
>
> (B) in commercial advertising or promotion, misrepresents the nature, characteristics, qualities, or geographic origin of his or her or another person's goods, services, or commercial activities,
>
> shall be liable in a civil action by any person who believes that he or she is or is likely to be damaged by such act.[3]

What this legislation says is basically this: Company B may not use certain identity elements (colors, names, symbols, etc.) already in use by company A if such use would be likely to cause confusion or mistake in the marketplace concerning the relationship between companies A and B, or if such use would misrepresent company A's or company B's products or services. The protection afforded by trademark law is substantial and valid for as long as the product is sold. It is a virtual perpetual monopoly.

The first section of the Act is relevant for basic identity protection.

The second section is relevant primarily for protecting attacks to one's identity in false advertising claims. According to the first section, for example, calling a new camera "Kodak" would probably be a prohibited marketing strategy as likely to create confusion with the already established brand Kodak. According to the second section, depicting any recognizable aspect of the existing Kodak's identity in a false light would be a prohibited marketing strategy as being a misrepresentation.

Extreme Derivative Identities: Appropriation and Confusion. Planned derivative styles can be considered a fair method of competition to a certain extent. But they may also become brand appropriations that confuse customers. Recall that Starbucks brought an action against a competitor in the Canadian market for copying its "look."

There have been many cases in which a company appears to have copied or capitalized on another's name. Valentino cookies appeared to try to capture part of the Valentino fashion identity and Silver Toe socks probably had Gold Toe socks in mind. Many of these instances of alleged identity-snatching have been litigated by trademark owners (Dunhill scotch whisky vs. Dunhill pipes and tobacco products; Blue Cross health clinic vs. Blue Cross medical insurance; Trump's Palace casino vs. Caesar's Palace casino; AAA insurance vs. AAA automobile services; VISA promotional services for hotels vs. VISA bankcard company; Scott's furniture polish vs. Scott household plastic and paper products, and on and on).

This sort of copying happens not only with names but also with logos, corporate colors, patented shapes, and other identity elements.

Fair Copying. Certain copying is allowed, however. Marketers may use derivative identities to cue customers about similarities to the original identity. (Yet along with this inference may come the inference of being a "me-too" product or service.) The solution for derivative identities may be to emulate, to come close, but not to "confuse." To come up to this fence without crossing over it, the question becomes, "What are the legal criteria for assessing whether there is confusion?"

What Is Confusion?

There are three kinds of confusion that a brand can cause in a consumer's mind: (1) general-knowledge confusion, (2) sensory-perception

FIGURE 8.2

Types of Confusion

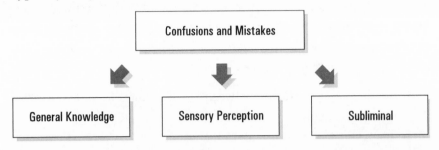

confusion, and (3) subliminal confusion (see Figure 8.2). We will discuss general-knowledge and sensory-perception confusion here; subliminal confusion comes up later on in this chapter.

General-knowledge confusion ("GK") refers to confusion as to the meaning of the marks—whether the new company appears to be sponsored by the existing one, or whether the companies appear associated or somehow connected or related. Sensory-perception confusion ("SP") amounts to a perceptual mistake. For example, a brand named "Panaosonic" has been sold in a variety of New York City electronic and appliance stores. Looking quickly, or not having paid sufficient attention, a buyer could well purchase this brand thinking he or she was purchasing the well-known Panasonic brand of electronic equipment. This mistake would be sensory-perception confusion. Causing either type of confusion is prohibited by law.

Likelihood of Confusion

Companies vigilantly try to protect their brands, identity, and image. In 1986, a bagel bakery that decided to call itself "McBagel" was sued by McDonald's. In 1980, an auto supply store and gas station operating under the name "Texon" was sued by Exxon. The maker of Domino sugar sued Domino's Pizza in 1980. The list goes on and on. Do these new brand names run afoul of the Lanham Act?

Defining confusion and ascertaining when it occurs are two different tasks. Determining whether confusion is likely to occur depends on numerous factors. It can be a tough call. For example, Coby brand headphones have emerged on the market in the past few years, competing with the Sony brand. Each name consists of a four-letter word, and the two are quite close phonetically. The federal courts across the United States have focused on similar bodies of factors to decide these cases. How can a manager be guided in attempting to predict whether or not a court is liable to decide that there is a likelihood of confusion or mistake? Managers can look at seven major issues:

1. the degree of similarity between the two names, marks, or other identity elements
2. the degree of similarity in product categories
3. the similarity of advertising media and trade channels
4. the degree of care and sophistication of the buyers
5. the evidence of actual buyer confusion
6. the strength of the name, mark, or other identity elements
7. the intent of the newcomer.

The greater the similarities in mark and product categories, presentation in media and trade channels, and the less care consumers would take in evaluating the product or service offerings, the more likely it is that confusion will occur. Evidence of actual consumer confusion clearly helps, and surveys demonstrating such confusion are used frequently in these cases. Strength of the identity elements is often tested simultaneously with confusion, for the confusion test often requires a secondary showing of strength. Since the final two factors, strength of the identity elements and intent to cause confusion, will come up repeatedly throughout this chapter, they are examined in greater detail below.

Strength of the Name: Distinctiveness or Secondary Meaning

From a legal standpoint, brand names come in four general varieties, representing differences in the strength of the name:

1. arbitrary or fanciful names
2. suggestive names
3. descriptive names
4. generic or common names

Arbitrary Names. The most protectable names—the strongest marks— fall toward the arbitrary or fanciful end of the spectrum. A name is deemed "arbitrary" if it bears no relation to the product category at hand. Among numerous others, Kodak for film, Xerox for copiers, *George* for a magazine, and Colgate for toothpaste might be considered arbitrary names. Arbitrary names are afforded the most protection because they are deemed highly distinctive.

Suggestive Names. Suggestive names allude to the qualities of the product or surrounding associations people make with the product. Examples are Puffs facial tissues, Mr. Clean household cleaner, and Velveeta cheese product. Arbitrary and suggestive names (presumed at common law to be "inherently distinctive") are also afforded greater protection than the next two categories.

Descriptive Names. Descriptive names tell about the product category. A name like Softsoap or Sportschannel might be considered descriptive. These sorts of names are not protectable as *inherently* distinctive. Microsoft's Windows, for example, was denied a trademark registration as Windows because it was not seen as inherently distinctive. Microsoft believes that, while the name is not registered, it is still protectable because it has acquired secondary meaning—consumers associate the name with Microsoft's product alone. In other words, it has achieved acquired distinctiveness. Descriptive terms with secondary meaning are protectable (and also registerable). Once a marketer moves toward using descriptive names, protection is more difficult to ensure, and can only be obtained after repeated exclusive use.

Generic Names. Finally, generic names are those that tell us what the product category is; a brand name "Catsup" for catsup would be viewed as generic. Generic names are not protectable because of the need to preserve competition; providing a monopoly for a generic term would prevent other products or services from bearing that generic term. But even generic names can sometimes acquire a secondary meaning. In a recent case that one of us (Simonson) worked on, the Patent and Trademark Office had initially denied registration of the mark Sportschannel for cable network services providing sports programming. The rationale was that "sports channel" is a generic term for a type of service and that Sportschannel is identical to this generic term. Survey evidence, however, determined that a majority of people considered the term Sports-channel to be a trade name and not a category or generic name. The case was later settled out of court.

Strength of Marks and Other Identity Elements. What is a "distinctive" icon? A distinctive restaurant motif? A distinctive color? How can managers assess the potential legal strength of a proposed icon? It is much more difficult to classify icons or other identity elements. Thus, the distinctiveness of these is usually decided not on its classification but on the "uniqueness" of the identity. For example, in a recent case, Starter, a maker of sports clothing that uses a star icon, brought an action against Converse, which had long used a white star on its sneakers, to allow Starter to enter the athletic-footwear market. One argument made for the newcomer was that the star icon of Converse is not a "strong" icon because it is a common geometric form. Unfortunately, such arguments run afoul of the fact that for any particular category, such as footwear, a common icon might have become quite strong as an identifier of one company in the minds of consumers. Thus, concerning gasoline the star means Texaco; concerning cars it means Dodge. When creating identity elements, managers need to focus on the uniqueness and complexity of their identity elements. But even common icons can be unique for particular product or service categories—if they are the first to reach the marketplace.

Bad Intent Is Damaging

The intent on the part of a new brand to confuse consumers is the black sheep here, and deserves special attention. The question of intent is really a question of equity or fairness. Courts have an easier time prohibiting some act of imitation or copying if they deem it to be intentional. As some courts have claimed, we can presume that if a company attempts to copy an existing brand in order to deceive the public, it will succeed. "As soon as we see that a second comer in a market has, for no reason that he can assign, plagiarized the make-up of an earlier comer, we need no more; for he at any rate thinks that any differentia that he adds will not, or at least may not, prevent the diversion and we are content to accept his forecast that he is likely to succeed."[4]

Thus, when the Opium fragrance brand of Yves Saint-Laurent brought an action against the makers of a brand of perfume called Omni, a sufficient finding of likelihood of confusion was established by the lower court and appeals court to force Omni to stop marketing the perfume in its present form. On appeal by Omni, the appeals court noted that Opium's trade dress was copied by Omni and that Omni included a direct reference to Opium in a slogan appearing on a tab which rose from the top of the box. The lower court did not find that the trade dress was confusingly similar, but did find that the slogan was: "If you love Opium, you'll love Omni." A second slogan was also disallowed by the lower court: "If you like OPIUM, a fragrance by Yves Saint Laurent, you'll love OMNI, a fragrance by Deborah Int'l Beauty." Finally, a third slogan, the subject of the appeal, was "If You Like OPIUM, a fragrance by Yves Saint Laurent, You'll Love OMNI, a fragrance by Deborah Int'l Beauty. Yves Saint Laurent and Opium are not related in any manner to Deborah Int'l Beauty and Omni." The appeals court rejected the appeal. Their analysis focused on the tremendous investment by Yves Saint-Laurent in Opium and on the intentional copying.[5] The decision clearly sends a cease-and-desist message to intentional copiers.

PROTECTING IDENTITY FROM CONFUSION

The trademark is the most basic identity element that is protectable as a source indicator. Other identity elements with their aesthetic styles and themes, however, may also be protected as an outgrowth. Trade dress is a rapidly expanding area of law. The term has grown to include the shape and appearance of a product as well as that of all the elements making up the total visual image by which the product is presented to consumers.

With the move from protecting mere names to protecting other identity elements, the focus on the visual is understandable. But not only visual elements are protectable. Scents, sounds, textures—indeed, an entire corporate aesthetic as we have defined it in this book—may be protectable as trade dress as long as the requirements are met. (Even themes may be protected, in the realm of copyrights, which we will discuss later.) Broadening the scope to all identity elements, the definition of trade dress can read this way:

Any aesthetic element (color, scent, melody, style, etc.) or aesthetic style embodied in any identity element or collections thereof that is capable of acquiring exclusive rights as a type of trademark or identifying symbol of origin.

While the protection of trade dress depends on whether the elements can have such exclusive rights, at the core of trade-dress protection is the issue of corporate aesthetics. The overall impression made by a product or service is what determines whether there is a likelihood of confusion. When Merriam Webster brought an action against Random House for confusion as to Webster's dictionary, referring to the similar book cover design, the lower court found that there was a likelihood of confusion; they based their reasoning on a piecemeal dissection of each aesthetic element and found that many were similar. But the appeals court overturned the decision, saying that taken as a whole, as a style, the impressions conveyed by the logo, the color, and the different marks did not suggest the likelihood of confusion.

Trade dress cases come in all varieties. Slogans have merited attention, as in the Opium case. Package design and bottle design cases are plentiful. The Revlon hair bottle, the Dom Perignon Champagne bottle shape and label design, and the Listerine bottle shape, among many others, have fought for their aesthetic rights. The outcomes of such cases are mixed depending on the evaluation of all the factors, but the overall customer impression of the identity is a key focus. In the early 1990s McNeil, the maker of Tylenol PM, brought an action against Bristol-Myers Squibb for its Excedrin PM packaging. The PM was similar; moreover, the look of the package was similar. Again, though, the overall customer impression was at issue, and the prominence of the two different names weighed heavily against finding a likelihood of confusion.

Protection is thus afforded to many single elements as well. Where the design is simply a small part of an identity element, the overall impression cannot be considered. Thus, Levi's specific pocket stitching design was successfully defended against imitation even though the difference between brands of jeans as a whole might also be discernable. As a recent Supreme Court decision stated, "The courts and the Patent and Trademark Office have authorized for use as a mark a particular shape (of a Coca-Cola bottle), a particular sound (of NBC's three chimes), and even a particular scent (of plumeria blossoms on sewing thread)." The court went on to afford protection to specific colors as well.[6]

USING REMARKABLY SIMILAR AESTHETIC ELEMENTS

A battle in the wine industry over the use of similar bottle-label designs has moved to the legal front. The Kendall-Jackson winery established itself as a leader in the premium varietal wine market. Its Vintner's Reserve Chardonnay sells for about $10 a bottle. When Ernest & Julio Gallo, Inc., the nation's biggest winemaker, started marketing its Turning Leaf Chardonnay, they used a visual identity that was almost identical to Kendall-Jackson's. Both feature labels with a prominent downward-turned leaf changing to fall colors, both have leaf-stamped corks, and both have similar bottle shapes.

Kendall-Jackson sued for trade-dress infringement, alleging that Gallo is trying to benefit from the work Kendall-Jackson has done to develop the premium varietal market. The suit also charges that Gallo has used unfair means to commandeer shelf space right next to Kendall-Jackson, in a further attempt to snare Kendall-Jackson customers and confuse them as to the products' identities. Kendall-Jackson claims that Gallo's sales have been declining precipitously for years, and that the company now wants to move away from its jug-wine image to a more upscale image as a maker of higher-quality varietals. The question for the courts to decide is whether Gallo is infringing on the distinctive trade dress that established Kendall-Jackson as a player in the premium-varietal-wine market.

Sources: Business Week, April 15, 1996; *Corporate Legal Times,* December 1996.

SPECIAL REQUIREMENTS FOR
PROTECTING AESTHETIC IDENTITY

Functionality in Aesthetics: Protecting Product Designs

To be most protectable under trademark law, a product design must be conceived first and foremost in order to convey the identity of the product. In legal terms, it must be established that *the trade dress is not functional.* There have been many cases in which similarity of product design has been litigated, and the outcomes have hinged on the functionality of the design: Coach vs. Ann Taylor on handbag design; LA Gear vs. Thom

McAn on shoe design; Kohler vs. Moen on faucet design; Tyco vs. Lego on block design; and Schwinn vs. Ross on exercise-bike design, to name just a few.

Individual cases may be hard to predict, because the various federal courts have applied at least four different tests for functionality. A well-respected definition of a functional feature is "one that is essential to the use or purpose of the article or affects the cost or quality of the article."[7] It is sometimes hard to disentangle the utilitarian function of a design from the purely identification-oriented aspects, but the more a design can be shown to be intended to convey identity, the stronger the argument will be for protecting that design against competitors' similar designs. When Ferrari brought an action in 1990 concerning the external shape of its vehicle, the court followed a test used by many of the courts and stated that the design is nonfunctional if it represents "a mere arbitrary embellishment, a form of dress for the goods primarily adopted for purposes of identification and individuality."[8] The Ferrari's shape was found to be nonfunctional, and the company was granted a trademark in the shape.

Can an Aesthetic Be Functional?

Given that aesthetic value serves an important function, it might seem as though a product's aesthetics could easily be considered functional, and thus not be protectable as a distinguishing aspect of identity. Until recently, courts distinguished between the identifying aspects of an identity and the aesthetically pleasing aspects; only aspects identifying the product were considered protectable. But within the past few years, most federal courts have rejected this notion. The standard that appears to be emerging is that a "design is functional because of its aesthetic value only if it confers a significant benefit that cannot practically be duplicated by the use of alternative designs."[9] The standard is ambiguous, and no doubt this is an area of potentially rapid change; managers should consult counsel about such matters.

Distinctiveness in Identity and Aesthetic Elements

The Case of Color. The requirement that an aesthetic or identity have either distinctiveness or secondary meaning raises the important question of whether simple aesthetic elements alone can rise to that level and become protectable. This issue is applicable to a variety of aesthetic elements, but it comes into play primarily when it comes to protecting colors.

When the Campbell Soup Company wanted to register its red-and-white color scheme, the application was rejected on the grounds that monopolies in colors cannot be issued due to the limited number of colors and what has been termed the "color depletion rule"—competition would be stifled by removing individual colors from the public domain. But decisions in these cases have gone both ways. In 1985, Owens Corning Fiberglas's use of a pink color for its insulation products was permitted as a trademark; a federal court stated that colors alone can be eligible for trademark protection. Yet when, in another federal circuit in 1990, Equal NutraSweet attempted to gain protection for its Equal brand's blue packaging, its application was denied. NutraSweet's Equal brand depended heavily on color to stand out from its major competitor, Sweet'n Low. The brand plays on the external cue of package color to differentiate itself at the point of purchase: Equal's ad campaign refers to the "blue stuff" and the "pink stuff," attempting to make color the most salient aspect of the product and a cue as to what is right or good or preferable. The NutraSweet company attempted to protect this valuable asset, to no avail.[10]

The Supreme Court, however, did resolve this dispute. In 1995 the Court finally settled the issue by stating that color alone indeed can be protected, as long as it is distinctive or has acquired secondary meaning. The requirements for establishing that secondary meaning has been achieved, however, are difficult to meet.[11]

Tests for Distinctiveness. While brand names can be categorized into four types, with differing levels of protectability corresponding to the degree of distinctiveness of the name, it is not so simple for other aesthetic elements. Generally, two tests for distinctiveness have been applied for these other aesthetic elements or combinations thereof: (a) The *Chevron* test requires that the trade dress be "arbitrary or fanciful" as well as nonfunctional, and (b) the *Seabrook* test rests on determining whether the trade dress is of "common basic shape or design, whether it is unique or unusual in a particular field, or whether it is a mere refinement of commonly adopted and well-known forms of ornamentation for

a particular class of goods . . . [viewed by the public as a dress or ornamentation of the goods]." The crux is the uniqueness of the design.
Looking at the identity as a whole—the "overall customer impression"—
is the preferred approach to determining uniqueness, as opposed to dis-
secting identity elements.

PROTECTING IMAGE

Associational Confusion or Misappropriation

"Misappropriation" is the term used for enhancing the image of a new
product by using some aspect of an existing product. This action is considered to be theft of an intangible property right. The idea is that there is
a moral duty to protect companies in their investments. In 1980, *Playmen*
magazine was sued by *Playboy* concerning the newcomer's suspiciously
similar name. The federal court stated that it was considered confusion
"to capitalize on the special attention a new magazine would obtain because its name, having no other meaning, conjures up the *Playboy* name
and all it represents."[12] *Playmen* was stopped from doing business.

Misappropriation is prohibited even if the new product is not in direct competition with the existing product. In 1993, in another federal
case, when MiracleGro plant food was faced with another company
using the name "Miracle Gro," it did not matter that the new company
was using it on a completely noncompeting product line, hair-care products. None of the traditional factors used to show likelihood of confusion were really relevant. The court focused not on the notion of SP or
GK confusion, but rather on what has been termed "subliminal confusion," or "associational confusion." The court stated that "even if consumers do not consciously assume that the defendant's product [the hair
care product] is somehow affiliated with plaintiff's product [MiracleGro
plant food], there is the likelihood that consumers will be attracted to
defendant's product on the strength of the goodwill and positive image
established by plaintiff with respect to the MiracleGro mark. The trademark laws are designed to protect this type of subtle, associational confusion, even if it can be dispelled by the consumer upon further
investigation of the defendant's product."[13]

The notion of "subliminal confusion" was also used in the case of Kids
R Us, which appeared to copy Toys R Us. Kids R Us was found to dilute

the Toys R Us name. While some courts have been reluctant to accept this type of argument in the absence of "real" confusion, marketers should know that such subliminal confusion has indeed been found to be in violation of the Lanham Act; it is one more weapon that can be used to combat identity proliferation or copying. Perhaps most important in these cases is the intent, often admitted, by the offending party to have gained an advantage from echoing the original brand's name or appearance.

Even if a federal court fails to accept the "subliminal confusion" argument in protecting trademarks or trade, state remedies may exist for the same exact issue. The Lanham Act specifically states that it does not preempt other remedies in state law. Thus, even if no case is made based on federal trademark law, state law may protect a marketer's trade dress in actions based on misappropriation. In this context, misappropriation is characterized as a type of unfair competition under common law. By contrast with the case of confusion, trademark appropriation is a developing area of state law that can severely curtail even those brand strategies that do not "confuse" consumers. The typical assumption in the law is that, even in the absence of confusion, a weaker brand will tend to benefit by using a preexisting brand name. Thus, while the conditions under which this benefit to the new brand may occur remain vague, marketers should bear the concept of misappropriation in mind as another powerful tool to stop copying.

The Right to Maintain Image

Misrepresentation and dilution are two areas of the law that protect a company's right to maintain its image. First, companies have the right to be free from misrepresentation that causes them harm. The second paragraph of the Lanham Act's Section 43(a) alludes to this type of action. Second, a body of law called *dilution* law protects companies from two types of dilution. One of us (Simonson) has termed these (1) evaluation dilution (or tarnishment) and (2) typicality dilution (or reduction in distinctiveness).[14]

Misrepresentation. According to Section 43(a) of the Lanham Act (second paragraph), one may not "in commercial advertising or promotion, misrepresent the nature, characteristics, qualities, or geographic origin of his or her or another person's goods, services, or commercial activities." Usually these cases relate to product claims. But in parodies the aesthetic elements and the identity of the company are often depicted and satirized. A recent television spot by Polar Corp. typifies the type of cases brought under this rationale. Starting in 1993, Coca-Cola ran advertisements with a computer-generated polar bear drinking and enjoying Coca-Cola. Soon thereafter, Polar Corp., a marketer of Polar brand seltzer, ran a humorous campaign where an animated bear, similar in appearance to Coca-Cola's, walks across the frozen tundra. He breaks the ice beneath him and fishes out a can of Coca-Cola. He makes a dissatisfied grunt and tosses the can into a trash receptacle labeled "Keep the Arctic Pure." Then he fishes again and gets a Polar Seltzer. He smiles and drinks the soda. The court stated that:

> by causing the polar bear to throw the can of Coke into a trash bin labeled "Keep the Arctic Pure," Polar has implied that Coke is not pure. Because there is no evidence suggesting that Coke is not pure, the Court concludes that Polar has misrepresented the nature and quality of Coke.[15]

Dilution. Dilution is an area of the law that attempts to protect a brand's image and distinctiveness. The concept declares that "once a mark has come to indicate to the public a constant and uniform source of satisfaction, its owner should be allowed the broadest scope possible for 'the natural expansion of his trade' to other lines or fields of enterprise."[16] From this, two rights for brands followed: the right to preempt and preserve areas for brand extensions, and the right to stop the introduction of identical brand names even in the absence of consumer confusion. By the end of 1996, over half the states had already adopted so-called "antidilution" statutes, modeled after these two points. These laws typically prohibit branding that has the "likelihood" of "diluting" the original brand or of causing "injury to business reputation." Thus, for example, when Jordache came out with their Basics 101, they brought an action in 1993 against Levis for the court to declare that there would be no confusion with or dilution of the Levis 501 mark. Levi Strauss' idea was that the "01" ending would lose its distinctiveness, and the three-digit numbering (Levi's 505, 501, 550, etc.) would also be diluted. The court dismissed both motions for summary judgment leaving it to the parties to pursue more litigation or settle.[17]

Most recently, Congress passed the federal antidilution statute, which now prohibits dilution anywhere in the United States. That law maintains the current limitation of the dilution doctrine to protect only "distinctive" brands that are generally protected.[18]

Evaluation Dilution. Evaluation dilution refers to injury to business reputation. It occurs often with parody products and with advertising. With advertising, an evaluation dilution (tarnishment) action is usually also accompanied by an action based on the second part of Section 43(a) of the Lanham Act. When Lardashe Jeans entered the market for large women's jeans, the play on Jordache's name was potentially injurious to Jordache's reputation. Here, however, the Court found that people wouldn't make the association, but it might easily have found otherwise.[19] Any play on one's brand that might "tarnish" its image may be actionable. In advertising, parodies abound.

Typicality Dilution. Typicality dilution has been described mainly with reference to brands as "blurring of the distinctiveness of a brand," "whittling away of the identity and hold upon the public mind of the mark," or "diminishing or destroying the distinguishing quality of the mark." A "cancer-like" growth of new brands has been viewed as a culprit, potentially destroying the distinctiveness of names (or other identity elements) of first comers. Here, dilution refers to a reduction in a brand's (or other aesthetic element's or combination of elements') typicality. Typicality refers to the power the element has to conjure up a particular product category. For example, in 1988, a new entrant in hotels entered and called itself "McSleep" and the question arose whether over time, McSleep would "dilute" the distinctiveness of McDonald's. In other words, would the syllable "Mc" lose its quick associational strength with the hamburger-making source and acquire associations with the hotel source? In other words, connections with other product categories might destroy the distinctiveness that the first brand (McDonald's) has created. Even concerning auditory stimuli, dilution can be claimed. In the early 1990s a new car was to be marketed by Toyota Motors. The car was to be named Lexus. But Lexis, a data service known well to lawyers and accountants, brought an action against Lexus claiming that the Lexis name would be diluted, that when hearing the word "Lexis," people would attribute it to the cars and not to the data service, which would lose its distinctive name. They lost the lawsuit not because dilution is not a viable claim, but because the court distinguished the sound of "lexus" from that of "lexis." (In this case, since the names were identical, dilution was one part of it, but there was also an implicit claim of SP confusion, that is, people might not know which name they were being exposed to.)

The Right of Originality and Invention

Copyright. Copyright law protects original ideas embodied in tangible mediums. Authors, whether individuals or companies, are protected from others freely copying or otherwise using these embodiments. Copyrights can exist in designs as long as the creativity in the design causes it to be considered "original." The rationale here is to protect authors, and to protect their original works.

Thus, the most obvious use of copyright is in protecting themes embodied in narratives, melodies, label design, etc. The numerous identity elements and combinations within a theme can be protected, including musical compositions, package designs, business-card designs, bag designs, sculptures, painting, photographs, among many others. Even a modicum of originality can suffice, as long as the idea is embodied in a medium. For example, directions on the labels of beauty products have been held copyrightable. But typically, short slogans, names, and the like are held not to embody sufficient "originality" for protection. Finally, the design must not be functional or utilitarian.

Design Patent. A final area of protection relating to identity is the design patent. The federal statute provides that

> whoever invents any new, original or ornamental design for an article of manufacture may obtain a design patent therefor.

The design must be different from what is called prior art, meaning that it must be "new" and it must be "nonobvious." If it possesses such novelty, a design patent would protect a product configuration, i.e., the aesthetic design of a product. The patent protects the owner from competing designs with resemblances that would be so close as to deceive ordinary observers.

MANAGING THE PROTECTION PROCESS

In corporate planning of any scope, from a name change to a full-blown organizational-identity plan, managers will be well advised to work proactively to prevent legal challenges of any sort and to work offensively upon discovering any potential infringement. Three areas must be managed. Two are preemptive in nature: interacting with designers and preventing infringement from others. The third is reactive, dealing with infringement if it appears to be occurring.

Working with Designers

Managers may work with a variety of designers in identity management, such as various kinds of product designers, graphic designers, interior designers, scent specialists, even software designers, to name but a few. These designers will be creating intellectual property for your organization. To protect the organization, the following are the key issues that need to be considered.

Own the Intellectual Property. Your organization should own the copyrights for its designs, design patents, and trademarks. Written agreements should be drafted and used for all independent contractors or employees involved in design work to ensure that the organization owns the intellectual property that they produce for its use.

Ensure Confidentiality. Every effort should be made to maintain confidentiality. This entails creating confidentiality agreements to ensure that designers do not reveal what they are working on or leak other information obtained from the organization in the course of the identity-creating project. (This need not be a separate document; it should be part of the employment or independent-contractor contract, in which you ensure your ownership of your intellectual property.)

Create Original Designs. Any designs created for your organization should be original, in order to be conservative in avoiding infringing on others' intellectual property. At a most conservative level, the designs should not be copied from existing designs. If any such borrowing or modeling is occurring, designers need to know up front that managers must be made aware of this and must see the source designs around which any new design is being modeled. Since it is often easy for designers to present examples of identities containing the styles, themes, or overall impressions that managers appear to seek, managers should be careful to monitor designers' use of examples. They should carefully compare (or give to counsel to compare) these similar designs with the designs created for your organization. Indemnification agreements and insurance should also be considered, to avoid the potential pitfalls of infringement.

Designers Can Compete. It is important to have designers warrant in their independent-contractor or employment agreement with you that they are under no legal restriction that would prevent them from designing for your organization. If a designer had signed a noncompete clause for a former employer, you will need to know this up front.

Inform Designers. Managers should inform designers, as team members, of the various particular needs of the project concerning protection. Many of the designers that we have interviewed have told us that when they understand the strategic ramifications, they design better. For example, Intel had come out with the 86 series of chips in the mid-1980s: the 8086, then the 286, the 386, and the 486. The 586 was the next chip to be marketed. Intel, however, had a strategic problem since these number designators were not considered sufficiently distinctive to provide adequate legal protection. Other companies used the same terms as though they were no one's intellectual property. To remedy this for its next line of chips, Intel hired Lexicon to come up with a series name that would reflect the number 5, yet be protectable as being suggestive or arbitrary. The name the designers created was Pentium, which is not only one of the most powerfully recognized names in the computer industry, but also fully protected as a trademark. Intel had preempted its competition from acting as "me-too's" one more time. Designers had to understand the kind of mark Intel needed in order to create a strategically powerful name that was also readily protectable.[20]

Working to Prevent Infringement

Beyond the manager-designer interface, managers should be concerned with protecting their investments from infringement. Below are guidelines that will help to protect intellectual property. (The last two are discussed in greater depth when we talk about surveys in the following section.) Create a policy of not copying the property of others; learn how to deal with potential infringement; and join trade associations to protect yourself from infringement.

Educate Staff. Education of product specialists, marketers, and other communications professionals can help them understand how to create strong identities and what to look for in spotting infringement. Have counsel create educational seminars/workshops to raise staff awareness of intellectual-property-protection procedures.

Incentivize. Create employee incentives for spotting infringement. Many infringement cases begin when someone in the organization sees an infringing product, an ad, or a story about prospective marketing plans that might be infringing. Your organization has many sets of eyes and ears to spot potential infringement. Without these, it is much more difficult to keep a vigilant watch to protect your intellectual property.

Tell the World. Indicate your product trademarks with ™, service marks with ℠, and registered product or service marks with ®. While a © copyright notice is optional, it is best to warn potential innocent infringers of your rights by posting copyright notices on copy and designs. For design patents pending, post a notice to that effect clearly, and for design patents granted, post that notice with the patent number(s). Notifying the public in this way helps to stop innocent infringement, warns potential intentional infringers of your vigilance, and helps to ensure better legal protection. Registering trademarks and copyrights, while not required, also affords added legal benefits in the form of certain presumptions in your favor and in the form of varying available remedies.

Act Quickly. Intellectual property is best protected when infringement is found and addressed early. Infringing products or services can be stopped; negotiation can be more productive before the infringer has spent much money developing its identity, and more time will be available to find appropriate experts and to conduct needed studies. Managers should never forget that trademarks can be "abandoned." Recently, Xerox mounted a print advertising campaign: "You can't Xerox a Xerox on a Xerox." In other words, Xerox wanted to ensure that its name would continue being protected. If Xerox were to allow others to use the term generically, it could lose this valuable asset. Remember that Aspirin was once a trademark. Imagine the power of that brand had it been protected.

Invest in Ammunition. Conduct routine preemptive surveys for the files. For virtually all kinds of potential trademark infringement (confusion, dilution, appropriation), a "strength of the mark" survey for the record can help more than one could ever imagine. As Simonson[21] discusses, once a competitor acts in the marketplace, it is difficult to compare pre-levels of mark power to post-levels. Pure periodic tests can be strong evidence of changes based on competitors' actions. Strength surveys can also be used early in a litigation to mount a motion for a preliminary injunction and provide fodder to show the power of your identity and prove that it could be harmed without the injunction you are seeking.

HOW TO HANDLE INFRINGEMENT
AGAINST YOUR IDENTITY

Once a potentially infringing act by a competitor is brought to the attention of a manager, there are several steps to be taken in order to determine whether legal action is necessary and to prepare for that possibility.

Maintain Records and Have Them Ready

An employee comes to work with an ad, a trademark, a story, a photo, a news article, or any other piece of information reflecting potential infringement of the intellectual property of your organization or brand. Typically, an initial panic sets in characterized by the feeling that it's too late, we need immediately to rush or we're in trouble! This panic, which sets in for fear of not acting quickly enough, can be mitigated by having thought out in advance what kinds of steps will be necessary to take in such a circumstance, how to take them, and who is designated to authorize taking them.

Contacting intellectual-property counsel is an early step to take. Counsel will have checklists of the information that they will need now and in the future if the dispute goes to court. Counsel will also probably end up conducting a variety of searches, such as a trademark search, and/or searches for other usage of the name or design at issue. Your job is to have that information ready and available. For many kinds of trade-mark or trade dress infringement cases, it will often help to have the following data for both your organization or brand and theirs:

1. target market characteristics
2. description and copies of the designs that are potentially infringing and being infringed
3. marketing plans or reports including reports, memos, and the like relating to how the designs were created or planned
4. past and expected sales in units and dollars
5. past and expected locations of expansion
6. past and expected market share penetration
7. planned launch ad and promotional budget
8. planned future advertising and promotion budget
9. media of ads and method of promotions
10. any surveys ever conducted on the brand or the organization and the results of them

For infringing advertising or brochures, some of the above information is irrelevant. For products and services, however, virtually all of the above information may be useful to assess infringement and potential damages.

Demand to Cease and Desist

Potential infringers should be informed of their potential infringement and told in writing to cease and desist. These letters are usually short, to the point, and often drafted by counsel. They provide a strong paper trail to document your vigilance and they also suggest the potential offender's posture, helping you to plan further actions. An example of such a letter is set forth on the next page.

Line Up Experts

To assess infringement and damages, experts for trade-dress litigation purposes run the gamut from nonacademic practitioners expert in a particular industry to academics expert on the cognitive processes of consumers. Counsel virtually always chooses and hires the experts, with the consent of the client. However, managers should be involved in the

---

EXAMPLE OF CEASE AND DESIST REQUEST

Fast Track Corporation
63 Main Street
Tracy, NM 75220

Dear Fast Track Corporation:

We have learned that you recently started to sell multicolored microwaveable pans and bowls in a self-storage container packaged in a multicolored carton bearing a rainbow design. We understand that you entered the marketplace in New Mexico and in three weeks plan your national introduction through retail outlets in cities and suburban malls.

As we are certain you know, for many years Rainbow Corporation has been selling cookware, including colored pans and bowls for microwave cooking, under its well-known RAINBOW trademark and has three U.S. trademark registrations, one of which includes a rainbow design. These products are advertised extensively on television and radio and are sold through our catalogs by mail and at our catalog counters in suburban malls. As a result, the rainbow design and the RAINBOW work mark are widely recognized by purchasers and prospective purchasers as source identifiers of products of our company.

Your use of a rainbow design on the cartons containing your microwaveable pans and bowls is an infringement of our RAINBOW and RAINBOW and design trademarks. Confusion is likely because purchasers and consumers will believe that these are our products now selling directly at retail.

If you do not notify us within two days of the facsimile transmission of this letter that you are immediately discontinuing distribution and sales of your products in multicolored cartons bearing a rainbow design, we will refer this matter to counsel for legal action to protect our valuable trademark rights.

Very truly yours,

RAINBOW Corporation

Source: Reprinted from Robert C. Dorr and Christopher H. Munch, *Protecting Trade Dress* (New York: John Wiley & Sons, Inc., 1992, plus 1996 supplement), p. 406. Copyright © 1992, 1996 by John Wiley & Sons, Inc. Reprinted by permission of John Wiley & Sons, Inc.

process, for managers are often better able to determine proper marketing or business expertise than counsel is. Five particular groups of experts should be identified, and it should be determined whether an expert from one or more of these categories will be useful.

1. *Various Nonacademic Practitioner Experts in an Industry.* For a case about restaurant design, it would be best to have someone who knows how designs are created in the industry, the history of restaurant design, the major players—all of which information is best obtained from an experienced expert in the field. So too, for any industry. Such practitioners can best give insider opinions about customs and practices in the industry.

2. *Academic Experts in Consumer Behavior.* Many cases revolve around general processes (false advertising or trademark confusion, for example), where generalists who study and research consumer behavior should be offered to explain and comment on the processes that are likely to occur in a given case. Academics, typically in marketing but sometimes in psychology, are usually used for this purpose.

3. *Academic Experts in Particular Specialties.* Academics, even if qualified to speak on a topic like consumer behavior concerning brand confusion, may have particular specialties that can be tapped for additional probative value. Experts on "new product development," "design," "identity," and "branding," are those publishing in the field, participating in conferences, known in the field, and generally focusing on particular issues within these fields. They are often found by perusing the academic literature or by networking or word of mouth.

4. *Survey Experts.* Survey experts are usually, but not necessarily, academics. It has become well known that a few academics gear themselves solely to this kind of consulting. Training is often through experience, as survey design per se is hardly ever taught in Ph.D. programs in marketing or psychology. In sociology, while there is more emphasis on survey design, the statistical training is often less advanced than in marketing or psychology. These are general stereotypes but they hold much truth. Survey experts should be analytical, understand the legal and marketing issues, have experience in conducting surveys, and be detail-oriented individuals.

5. Pilot Survey Experts. Attorneys often choose one expert to create a questionnaire, then have another expert (unknown to the first expert) conduct a pilot study to determine potential pitfalls in the questioning and potential ways to avoid them. Then, after suggestions from the attorney on changes, and some discussion, the first expert can conduct the main study. In this way, the main survey expert is not tarnished at all by any of the findings in the pilot study.

Managers should be aware that there is a danger here of an expert becoming a hired gun as opposed to an objective researcher. Your attorney will naturally place pressure to "win" on the expert; you should monitor the process to avoid this. Experts are not counsel; they are not obligated to, nor should they, advocate for their clients. It is to no one's benefit to become a hired gun. Not only will the researcher lose credibility, but the attorney and the client will lose the case if the researcher is perceived as such. When we take such cases, our philosophy, much as it pains some lawyers, is to take an objective and conservative approach with the goal of finding out what the processes are, and not to help someone win a case.

Surveys

Surveys are a powerful tool that companies can use in protecting their identities, and they deserve to be treated at length here. Consumer surveys should be given close attention and weight by the courts in their examination of whether an act of infringement should be stopped. Surveys are used primarily to assess (a) likelihood of confusion, (b) secondary meaning, (c) genericness, (d) dilution, and (e) tarnishment. They are offered sometimes by plaintiffs (those bringing actions), sometimes by defendants (those defending actions), and often by both. Surveys are expensive, costing anywhere from $25,000 up to $100,000 or more. As such, the law does not require any side to commission a survey. The specific requirements for surveys may differ depending on the court, so the law in any jurisdiction should be consulted. These are the generally accepted standards:

Survey Requirements. Surveys are required to be performed in accordance with accepted scientific techniques. A party offering consumer surveys as evidence ought to satisfactorily demonstrate that:

1. the proper universe or population (in a statistical sense) was identified and examined;

2. a representative sample was drawn from the defined universe;
3. the questioning was unbiased;
4. the interviewers were well trained and had no knowledge of the controversy, the sponsor, or the purpose for which the data would be used; and
5. the data were accurately analyzed and reported.

Three additional—vague but quite important—aspects of the survey to be demonstrated are that: (a) the questionnaire was prepared in accordance with generally accepted standards of procedures in the field; (b) the interviews were conducted in accordance with generally accepted standards of procedure in the field; and (c) the persons designing and conducting the investigation were qualified to perform their tasks.

Hiring Researchers to Perform Surveys. We have conducted a number of such surveys, and offer the following guidance to managers. Typically, your attorney would be the one hiring the survey researchers. Attorneys often choose researchers whom they have used before. As with mutual funds, the choice is often made based on past successes. This is a poor way to choose a researcher, though, since past successes do not ensure future successes. The success may have been due to the case, luck, the sample, etc. Rather, the choice of a researcher should be based upon the following two basic qualifications.

First, a researcher should possess dual knowledge: knowledge of legal standards as well as consumer behavior. That is, the researcher must be able to design studies with knowledge of the consumer behavior underlying the phenomenon at hand as well as the legal issues involved. For what a researcher is setting out to investigate is composed of a legal standard and an application of the legal standard to the consumer-behavior issues being researched. Thus, if the law specifies "likelihood of confusion," a researcher needs to determine what *confusion* means legally and what it means from a consumer-behavior perspective. Designing studies without this dual understanding can lead to miscommunication between attorney and researcher. The true challenge is in applying a legal standard to appropriate measurements of consumer behavior.

And second, a researcher should design studies with anticipation of attacks on their methodology. This means that conservative approaches are important. A researcher who "tries to find an outcome" takes the side of the hiring client. This tactic is all too familiar; but it is dangerous and it violates the ethics of doing research. Yet it is impossible for the researcher to avoid all knowledge of the dispute and how the research is being used. There are two solutions to this: (a) managers and attorneys should not tell the researcher whose side the research is for; and (b) the researcher should take the conservative position, i.e., err on the side that would be favorable to the employer's opponent.

Particularly in defining the population, one must always choose whether one wants to examine the issue wider (using broad population definition) or narrower. For example, a court, determining whether secondary meaning existed for a "red, white, and blue" basketball, saw a population defined as "individuals who played basketball" as overly broad. The survey should have limited its focus to those who had purchased basketballs. On the other hand, in showing likelihood of confusion for the color of Advil tablets, the survey population was deemed too narrow because it looked only at Advil users instead of at users of ibuprofen under any label (i.e., potential Advil users as well). There are thousands of such decisions.

A strong pattern emerges: err on the side of being conservative. In the basketball case, the reason for the selection of a broad population may have been that the survey was commissioned by the side trying to show that no secondary meaning existed. It is easier to show this with a broad population because there secondary meaning is less likely to emerge. In the Advil case, the survey was commissioned on behalf of Advil, which was attempting to demonstrate that a new product was likely to confuse the consuming public. It was easier to show this with a narrow population since they would be more familiar with Advil's color scheme and would be more likely, therefore, to rely on it and to be confused by a newcomer using the same color scheme. In other words, define the population and then err on the side of being conservative. Testing both full and reduced sets of populations is also an option, albeit costly.

Surveys Applicable to Brands, Image, or Identity

Likelihood-of-Confusion Surveys. Testing for confusion is a common endeavor in likelihood-of-confusion cases. The researcher must decide what type of confusion is to be measured: confusion as to source, sponsorship, approval, affiliation, or connection; confusion due to sensory-perception mistakes—"SP confusion"; or, finally, "subliminal confusion." The type of survey must be based on the goal. For the first type of confusion, open-ended questions are appropriate, such as "Who puts out this product/service?" or "Do you think the two products are put out by the same company or different companies?" In either case, side-by-side comparisons should be avoided. For the second type, exposing consumers to the stimuli for a short time and asking what they saw, and then re-exposing them and asking again can provide insight into short- and longer-term effects. For the third type, an open-ended-association question such as "What comes to mind when you see this?" can appropriately test for associational or subliminal confusion. The creativity of the researcher will play a strong part in the experimental design. Controls are often necessary to determine true effects. The above questions are general examples, but cannot do justice to the intricacies of a good experimental design. The principle is that good experimental-design practices should prevail. The threshold for "likelihood" of confusion varies, where the percentage "confused" or "mistaken" (depending on the measure and the meaning of confusion or mistake) varies dramatically. There is no absolute threshold.

Secondary-Meaning Surveys. Secondary-meaning surveys attempt to determine whether a particular aesthetic element or combination of elements embodied in an identity component is identified with a single source (even if the respondents cannot identify which source it is). The idea is to see whether the exclusive use of a certain aesthetic element or combination thereof has caused the element(s) to become distinctive. One can ask whether the element is identifiable by a single source. One can also ask who makes the product. The test usually amounts to whether a "significant" or "substantial part" of the market uses the element to identify a single source. Since we cannot interpret frequencies in isolation, control groups are essential to provide benchmarks for comparing the results. Thus, the survey exposes the respondents to the elements in question and asks them whether the elements come from a single source or multiple sources. Determining the population may be quite difficult, since we want to obtain the "ordinary buyer."

Evaluation Dilution: Parody and Tarnishment Surveys and False Advertising Surveys. A survey to show tarnishment must determine that a company's reputation has been injured. A manager wants to determine whether the offending name or advertisement (or other communication) causes those exposed to it to infer something incorrect about the product or service, or causes a poor association to be made with the product or service. However, if evidence supports a claim made by a competitor in its communication, then the tarnishment claim will not stand.[22]

In terms of consumer behavior, the researcher should focus on (a) associations and beliefs and (b) evaluations or attitudes. Associations and beliefs are determined by asking open-ended questions and analyzing the responses for content. What this means is that all responses are subjectively categorized into what appear to be mutually exclusive categories. These responses are given code numbers, and then the code numbers are tallied to provide frequency distributions of the responses. Evaluations are easily determined by asking a direct question aimed at attitudes and having respondents answer on closed-ended (usually 5-point or 7-point) rating scales. Beliefs can also be measured, using agreement/disagreement (usually 5-point or 7-point) "Likert" or "semantic-differential" scales. The results for each type of measurement can be compared to the performance of a control group not exposed to the offending communication.

Surveys Relating to Brands Specifically

Genericism Surveys (Brand Names Only). Genericism surveys focus on the general consuming public, often comprising actual or prospective users, and come in two general varieties, the "Teflon survey" and the "Thermos survey." Each survey attempts to determine whether or not a name is "primarily" used as a brand name. "Primarily" means that at least a majority must view the name in that way. The Teflon survey focuses on word recognition, but the Thermos survey focuses on word recall. Teflon surveys (named after the *Teflon* case, where this type of survey was introduced), entail explaining to people the difference between generic and brand names. They then are presented with some names to distinguish, the name at issue being one of them. Frequencies are then tallied. The Thermos approach, on the other hand, asks respondents to name the category of product or service that is described to them. This gives a measure of the frequency of various terms used for the category. The follow-up question is to ask what manufacturers or brands of such category they can recall. The test of whether or not a name has become generic is made by comparing the frequency of responses given that a name is generic compared to the frequency of responses given that the same name is a brand. There is no ideal or uniform way to make this comparison.

Recent articles and surveys have addressed the issue that names often have a dual nature. They act differently, sometimes acting as a brand and sometimes as a generic category. (Think, for example, of Kleenex or Xerox as both brands and categories.) Recent trends have addressed this ability by adding a "Both" category in the Teflon test. The Thermos approach already incorporates the possibility that a name is used in a dual way. And, as with the Thermos approach, there is no accepted way to analyze the "both" responses in a Teflon-type survey. Finally, in comparison with the Thermos approach, research has indicated that the Teflon surveys generally produce higher brand scores and the Thermos ones higher generic scores. This methodological difference may indicate that measurement of the truth is difficult, or that we are in effect measuring different things, and the surveys are not quite equivalent in focus.

Typicality-Dilution Surveys. In typicality-dilution surveys, the manager wants to determine how the "distinctiveness" of the brand (or of the other identity elements) is diluted. This requires that we measure for differences between groups: those exposed and those not, or pre-exposure vs. post-exposure. We want to examine whether, upon cueing individuals with the original brand, people think of or recall the new product category. In other words, if I am SUNSHINE and I sell cookie products, and I am concerned that SUNSHINE, selling children's toys, is diluting my mark, I would want to investigate whether there is in fact a dilution in the identifiability of the brand SUNSHINE by giving people the name SUNSHINE and asking them what products come to mind. This associational kind of damage (dilution) is indeed sometimes the same as SP confusion, discussed earlier. Brand recall can be measured in terms of (a) percentage of first mentions, (b) frequencies of the order of mentions, and (c) time to recall (measured up to thousandth of seconds). Brand recall can be used in a similar manner to test brand strength relating to confusion cases. One cues the respondents with a product category and sees how powerful the name is. Example: "What brands of TV set can you recall?"

Registering Trademarks

Generally, trademarks and trade dress become protected once they are placed into commerce. It is not necessary to register the brand or the design since Section 43(a) of the Lanham Act applies equally to registered or unregistered marks. Similarly, dilution statutes and the common law of appropriation do not require registration. Federal registration at the U.S. Patent and Trademark Office on what is called the "primary register," however, affords certain additional benefits: constructive notice of claim to ownership rights, priority rights from the time of filing, prima facie evidence of ownership rights, exclusive right to use the aesthetic element or combination thereof on the goods/services listed in the registration, and prevention of importation of infringing goods (after registering with U.S. Customs Service). In other words, registration can help when you need to bring an action against someone.

To have any parts of an identity registered (under Section 2 of the Lanham Act), one needs to meet the same requirements to make a claim under Section 43(a), i.e., distinctiveness of the elements or secondary meaning and nonfunctionality. Beyond the almost infinite number and variety of names that have been registered, an almost infinite number of designs also have been, like the Century 21 signage, the Juicy Fruit wrapper, and the Coca-Cola shaped bottle, among others.

Once registered, an owner should display the ® or "Registered, U.S. Patent and Trademark Office," or an abbreviation thereof. Even if unregistered, to alert users that you are using an element as an identifying element, one should place a ™ next to the elements for products, an ˢᴹ next to elements for a service (like Delta Sky Miles and the accompanying design of the Sky Miles card), or a ᶜᴹ next to elements for a certification.

Registering Copyrights

A copyright is held in the underlying tangible work once the work is fixed in a tangible medium of expression. As with trademarks, copyrights need not be registered. But registration with the U.S. Copyright Office affords the ability to bring powerful actions against infringers. The protection lasts for the life of the author plus 50 years; or for works made for a company, 75 years from publication or 100 years from creation, whichever is earlier. Copyright protection can be renewed.

While no longer needed technically, to avoid issues of notice, the copyright notice should state "Copyright" or ©. This should be followed by the date and then the author's name. On musical recordings, a ℗ replaces the ©. If the musical composition is also original, it requires a separate copyright notice, beyond that related to the specific sound recording.

Design Patent Application

Patents need to be applied for at the U.S. Patent and Trademark Office. The application is created by using what are termed *claims*, which describe the invention (here, the design). Patent protection holds for 14 years and is nonrenewable. Work can be the subject of both a copyright and a design patent. Details about the interplay of the various laws need to be examined with legal counsel.

SUMMARY

We have reviewed the major laws affecting the protectability of brands, identity, and image, focusing mainly on trademark law but touching the related topics of copyright law and patent law. We began with protection of the brand name and moved toward protection of other aesthetic elements, styles, themes, and overall impressions. The use of surveys as a key tool to protect identity was outlined, and means of obtaining protection was addressed.

As we have seen, aesthetics, identity, and image can be protected. A trade-off between marketing considerations and legal considerations may militate against certain designs that could be more protected and for designs that achieve a better overall impression. Nevertheless, by focusing on the different types of factors that afford greater protection, marketers can secure a great deal of protection for their identities.

PART IV

COMPREHENSIVE
IDENTITY MANAGEMENT

9

Global Identity Management

LEGO: THE UNIVERSAL CONCEPT OF PLAY FROM DENMARK[1]

LEGO products are sold in approximately 60,000 retail outlets in 133 countries. Around the world, more than 300 million children and adults play or have played with LEGO blocks. The LEGO block is so well known that when European countries' postal services celebrated the theme "children's toys and games" in 1989, LEGO blocks were featured on their stamps. In 1987, the organization Action Familiale et Populaire du Luxembourg honored the product with the title "Toy of the Century."

The familiar LEGO products consist of components that can be put together and pulled apart in numerous combinations depending on a child's age, ability, and imagination. The basic LEGO block is a flattened cube of plastic, with studs and tubes, available in a range of mostly bright, primary colors. Just two eight-stud blocks of the same color can be put together in 24 different ways. Six blocks—still of the same color—give 102,981,500 combinations! The international product line includes 378 different Lego sets with 1,720 different elements. The same products, in the same colors and shapes, are sold in all markets where LEGO appears. Sales continue to increase.

Product development, production and marketing are highly centralized. For the production process, LEGO has only five factories. The production process is always the same: molding, decorating, assembling, and packing. There are 1,720 different molds, all of which are made in only three of the five factories—two in Switzerland and one in Germany. The molded items are then sent for coloring and decoration to automatic printing machines. From the warehouses, the products are shipped to sales organizations and distributors across the world. The only localized elements are the sales brochures, printed in 25 different languages, which are added by local organizations and distributors. LEGO is truly a universal toy—a universal product with a global image, or as the organization calls it, the "universal concept of play."

TAMAGOTCHI: THE JAPANESE VIRTUAL PET[2]

The Tamagotchi is a virtual pet that was introduced to the Japanese market in the fall of 1996. The name means "cute egg" (from "tamago," meaning egg; and "chi," a suffix for "small" and "cute"), and shares sound associations with "watchi," the Japanese everyday word for watch. Tamagotchis come in the shape of pocket-sized little green eggs on a keyring with tiny LCD screens on them. They cost about 2,000 yen (approximately $16). The story goes that Tamagotchis hatch from tiny eggs after traveling millions of light years through cyberspace. The owner of the digital pet can feed it, stroke it, scoop its poop, and give it medicine when it is sick by pushing small buttons located underneath the screen. If it is cared for well, within several days it develops into an adult with a variety of shapes and personalities. When it is happy, it coos. If neglected, it will die—and may be buried at a virtual graveyard site on the Internet.

In Japan, Tamagotchis are sold by Bandai Co., Japan's largest toy company, which agreed to merge with Japanese video-game maker Sega Enterprises Ltd. for $1 billion in October 1997. Sega Bandai Ltd. will be involved in computer games and graphics, movies, music, and virtual reality (including the virtual pet industry) and plans to become a global entertainment leader second only to the Walt Disney company.

Market research for the product started in the summer of 1996 when 200 high-school students received a questionnaire on the planned product. The results determined the colors, variety, and design. In October 1996, test-marketing began in Tokyo's Shibuya district, frequented by young Japanese for shopping and entertainment. It was launched in November 1996. Two months after its launch, Bandai had sold more than half a million of the games. After they had sold out in retail stores, street hawkers charged more than 20 times their original retail price. In January 1997, Japanese TV showed pictures of 2,000 people waiting in the early morning hours when a store in the Ginza shopping district in Tokyo announced that they would receive a new shipment—hundreds had camped out overnight in the winter cold. "We've sold far more than expected. We can hardly keep up with demand," said Tomomi Motosu, a Bandai spokeswoman.

In the spring of 1997, demand in Japan among high-school students was estimated to be over six million. Bandai was getting more than one million visits per week on its Internet Web site. Encouraged by the success, the toymaker decided to release "Shinshu-hakken Tamagochi," a newly discovered variety, in early February.

Psychologists have analyzed the hidden desires fulfilled by the pocket-sized creature. They say it fulfills an emotional void experienced by the modern city-dweller. Tamagotchis were originally targeted toward the teenage market. But they are also popular among the middle-aged market of what the Japanese call "salarymen," and "office ladies." Some Japanese companies are raising the chickens as a group project.

In February 1997, Bandai announced that it planned to introduce the virtual pet in the rest of Asia, in Europe, and in the United States at an expected retail price of $35. Will the Tamagotchi craze catch on in the rest of Asia, Europe, and the U.S.? Or is it a uniquely Japanese phenomenon? Will its fate be that of the Sony Walkman or of *karaoke?* At the beginning of 1997, an official of the company was quoted as saying that the toymaker was still mulling over whether it should modify the existing model for overseas market.

To address the potential success of the toy in other countries, we can isolate three parts of the product: (1) concept, (2) name, and (3) visuals and sounds.

Concept: Americans spend more than one billion dollars annually on pet food. But can you imagine American urban youth getting pleasure from feeding a Tamagotchi? Can you imagine a Wall Street trader walking around with a pager and a Tamagotchi and feeding it when it coos? "Cuteness" may easily turn into "silliness" when product concepts cross cultures. Also, part of the fun of owning a Tamagotchi is conversing about it with others. Will this aspect of the toy also work as a success factor in an individualistic society like the United States or will it only work in a collectivist society like Japan?

Name: Bandai calls the pet "Tamagotchi" in its latest U.S. press releases. It is a brilliant name in Japanese, but will this Japanese name catch on in the United States, as well as in other countries? The naming issue goes further. As we said earlier, part of the fun of owning a Tamagotchi is to converse about it with your friends. In the Japanese language, it is easy to create a range of neologisms to describe the various shapes and characters that the chicken might grow into. For example, the creature may turn into a babitchi (a little baby), a kuchitamachi (a fat grown baby with a funny mouth) or in its later stage into a oyaji (a crummy middle-aged man). And while some of these terms may sound sarcastic, there is also an irony to it by adding the suffix "chi" (cute) each time. These ideas cannot be expressed as eloquently in most other languages.

Visuals and sounds: Finally, there is the color, shape, size, and sound of the toy. In Japan, the toy comes in a pastel green color scheme which is very attractive to Japanese people and widely used to express "cuteness." Will these colors also work in other markets or do they need to be adjusted? More serious seems to be the size and shape of the toy. Since Japanese live in tiny spaces, most consumer products and their packaging are much smaller than in the United States. The notion of playing with a tiny toy, and interacting with it by pushing miniature buttons, may be alien to U.S. consumers.

KEY MANAGEMENT ISSUES
IN CREATING GLOBAL IDENTITIES

Most organizations aspire for a global corporate and brand positioning. They express this aspiration in a global positioning statement that identifies a global segment of customers and the benefits provided to this segment. A global positioning statement for Tamagotchis may focus on the benefits of being a virtual pet owner (rather than a real one) and identify teenagers in various countries as the target market. However, global positioning statements are often general and abstract and thus provide only broad guidelines for action. Most "global products" do not fail because of the wrong strategic positioning statement but because of the wrong name, an inappropriate color scheme, a lack of attention to its advertising theme, a culture-insensitive retail environment—in short, they fail because the wrong images are projected through the styles and themes inherent in identity elements. The key issue in global identity management is therefore not only the broad strategic issue of selecting the right target segment and market positioning but whether to standardize corporate and brand identity elements across nations and cultures or whether to localize identity elements to individual markets.

Standardization of Identity

With a strategy of standardization, an organization offers a consistent identity and image worldwide. In a uniform manner, an organization uses aesthetic elements, styles, and themes, and creates consistent overall aesthetic impressions. From a manufacturing, production, and operations viewpoint, standardization is often preferable. LEGO illustrates the enormous advantages in terms of economies of scale of a standardized global image. Using LEGO blocks as an inspiration, Swatch, which changed the traditional Swiss watch from a timepiece to a fashion accessory, reduced the number of components by up to 50%, which cut production costs and enhanced reliability. As a result, Swatch was able to offer an affordable lifestyle accessory to a global consumer market. The two Swatch design labs in Milan and New York create roughly 140 different "collections" each year, which fall into five basic product lines: active, fashion, art, casual, and formal. Certain collections are targeted for specific markets such as the 1993 Europe in concert series of watches playing commissioned melodies. Others are offered simultaneously in all major markets, depending on customer preferences and values.

Localization of Identity

Many organizations must localize across nations and even across target markets within nations because of differences in perceptions and preferences for certain aesthetic elements, styles, themes, and impressions. Effective localization strategies demand meticulous attention to the culture your organization is marketing to—not only broad strategic attention, but attention to aesthetic details.

Amoy Industries of East Asia, a wholly owned subsidiary of French food giant BSN, manufactures a wide range of "local foods" and has created local identities for these foods: soy sauces, ready-to-use savory sauces, natural cooking ingredients, and frozen Chinese dim-sum products. In 1993, Landor Associates in Hong Kong was hired to develop a regional brand identity for Amoy products. The concept selected for the Amoy identity built upon the equities of the Amoy shield, the Chinese characters, and the English bamboo typeface. These elements were integrated into a logo combining the shield with a bold rectangle device, for balance and structure. The background color was bright red, a favorite color in East Asia, and, in particular, in China. The packaging employed newly designed Chinese and English typefaces, a vertical panel format reminiscent of traditional Chinese writing, rich yellow as the dominant color, and a color-coded secondary panel to differentiate between light and dark sauces. This identity provided a contemporary local identity.

DECIDING WHETHER TO STANDARDIZE OR LOCALIZE AN IDENTITY

Differences in corporate and brand naming with respect to primary elements, aesthetic styles, themes, and overall impressions clearly suggest that a localization rather than a standardization approach to global image management works best. In the face of the minefield of these cultural differences, managers might be tempted to throw up their hands and succumb to the lure of a more expensive localization strategy. However, standardization can also be a viable option depending on three major factors that influence the decision whether to standardize or localize an identity. As shown in Figure 9.1, these factors include:

- organizational and competitive factors;
- cultural factors;
- industry and product category factors; and
- attitudes toward foreign images.

ORGANIZATION/COMPETITIVE FACTORS

One important variable that should affect the degree to which an organization uses a standardization or localization approach is the ease with which the identity can be adjusted to local conditions. For example, it is not easy for a national airline to adjust its corporate or brand identity to local conditions. Many of that industry's identity elements (planes, check-in counters, airline tickets) are difficult to adjust. Moreover, given its major customer base of world business travelers, it would be unwise

FIGURE 9.1

A Framework for Standardization vs. Localization in Global Image Management

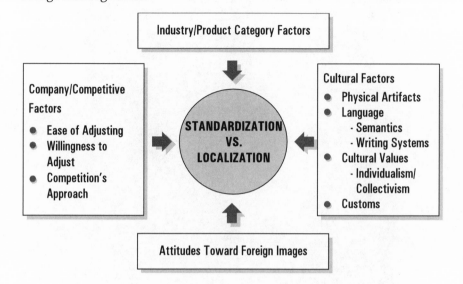

to adjust its reservation offices or even its advertising. Consequently, most airlines pursue standardization as far as possible in terms of image management and make local adjustments only in tactical decisions such as pricing and scheduling.

Another issue for organizations is the degree to which they are *willing* to make the above adjustments. This is determined largely by organizational factors. For example, if the organization strives toward a global image system, is it organizationally set up for such a system? In 1993, the Mary Kay Cosmetics Organization, alarmed by the fact that its competitor Avon derives over 55% of its $3.6 billion in sales from international markets, compared to only 11% out of $1 billion for Mary Kay, initiated a global marketing initiative and set up the goals of establishing and communicating a global image. The organization decided that local subsidiaries would be given more autonomy only after the desired global image had been established. Given such objectives, standardization rather than localization became the primary goal in the years that followed.

The Mary Kay (China) cosmetics company achieves a fine balance of standardized and localized aspects. Mary Kay uses the same logo and organization color—pink—in China and elsewhere. The product line is fairly standard, but is supplemented with a product for whitening the

EXHIBIT 9.1

Mary Kay China Advertisement

MARY KAY is a registered trademark of Mary Kay Inc.

skin, which appeals to Chinese women. The saleswomen in the ads (Asian or Caucasian) are also different—more fashionable and younger than in the United States and Europe (see Exhibit 9.1).

Finally, the degree of global or local image-building also depends on competitive activity—specifically on whether the competition is pursuing a standardized or localized approach. With an increased focus on worldwide retailing, petroleum organizations tend to build global identities. Recently, both British Petroleum and Texaco have built global identities, assisted by Addison Design Company and Anspach Grossman Portugal Inc., respectively. The project for BP provided a new identity for hundreds of organization vehicles and over 32,000 gas stations around the world.

CULTURAL FACTORS[4]

Cultural factors influence aesthetic perceptions and preferences. Four key aspects of a market's culture affect aesthetics. Each of these cultural domains offers challenges to standardization:

- physical artifacts
- language
- values
- customs

Physical Artifacts. Due to technological, political, and historical developments in different parts of the world, different cultures have created unique artifacts that serve to represent them. For example, if we think about silk, jade, and porcelain, the Chinese culture will likely come to mind. Diamonds evoke South Africa; coffee brings to mind certain countries in South America. A region's artifacts, buildings, interiors, clothing, and printing all profoundly affect the sensibilities of the inhabitants. Knowledge of the artifacts of an area will tell a marketer what is familiar to customers there. An examination of the culture's artifacts, their colors, materials, and shapes is crucial to experience the world *aesthetically* the way the native does. No amount of scrutiny, however, can match the insight and intuition of the natives themselves concerning the aesthetic perceptions and preferences of their culture.

Language. Two aspects of language are of major concern to international identity management: semantics and writing systems. Semantics, or the meaning of words, is one aspect of language that design professionals need to be thoroughly involved with. Semantics can cause an otherwise fine standardization strategy to bomb, causing the organization to revert back to a localization strategy.

As we show later in this chapter, marketers in East Asia should be particularly careful concerning semantics. Chinese, for example, has numerous dialects, including Mandarin, which is spoken in most provinces of the People's Republic of China, in Singapore, and on Taiwan; and Cantonese, which is spoken in some of the southern provinces of the People's Republic and in Hong Kong. The pronunciation of these dialects, not just the visual representation, can pose challenges. In Mandarin, for example, a spoken Chinese syllable will have a different meaning depending on whether it is pronounced with a flat tone, a falling tone, a rising tone, or a falling/rising tone.

Another complex issue concerns the writing systems that represent languages. A writing system is a key tool for expressing a corporate and brand identity in the form of corporate and brand names in conjunction with logos. The challenge often is to produce the same impressions via different writing systems. In the history of civilization, three types of systems have been invented for relating a visual symbol to language content: an alphabet (as in English), a phonetic system (as in Japanese *kana*), and a logographic system (as in Chinese).

The contrasts between these primary writing systems have major implications for managing global corporate aesthetics. Chinese writing consists of signs or ideographs, composed of strokes. Unlike our writing system, which uses letters to denote the sounds of words, Chinese provides a different ideograph for every word. There are an estimated 50,000 ideographs in Chinese, far more than any individual can master. There are no nonsense words or acronyms. When "fried" became a negative attribute for Kentucky Fried Chicken, it would have been impossible in Chinese to shorten the name to the equivalent of KFC. In these cases, the whole character—and the spoken name—has to be changed.

Differences in writing and pronunciations may be used to give a product a foreign image, e.g., by spelling or pronouncing it in a foreign language.[5] Häagen-Dazs is the best example. It's American ice cream, but its writing suggests otherwise. The Hong Kong fashion brand *Goldlion* successfully upscaled its image by pronouncing the name in French in its ad campaigns.

Values. Differences between nations and cultures may also be described in terms of social norms, or values. Johnson & Johnson represents a good example. When it entered the Hong Kong market, the name *zhuang-cheng* was used, meaning "an official or lord during feudal times." But this traditional, upper-class association was seen as inappropriate for Communist China. So in China the name *qiang-sheng* ("active life") was adopted, a name with a more upbeat, modern tone that fits well with China's drive for modernization. Thus, Johnson & Johnson ended up with two names in the same culture.

The sociologist Geert Hofstede of the University of Maastricht (Holland) was a pioneer in this type of cultural analysis, distinguishing several value dimensions that result in behavioral differences among peoples as far apart as those of India, Sweden, Norway, Japan, and the United States.

The degree of individualism that a society fosters is a key value to consider in designing an aesthetics strategy. An individualist society like the United States stresses the creativity of its individuals; but the main concern in a collectivist society like China or Japan is social harmony. Thus, on a broad scale, unusual creative expressions that break norms—iconoclastic design—should be valued more in an individualistic society than in a collectivist one. Likewise, in general, harmony and peace would be preferred expressions in a collectivist society, and any symbolism that relates to disharmony or conflict should be avoided there.

Moreover, in a collectivist society, endorsements and testimonials by respected and trusted persons are prominent themes in communications. AT&T, a pioneer in multicultural marketing communications in the United States, used this approach in a campaign that targeted Japanese businessmen residing in the United States. The ad was commissioned from Kang & Lee Advertising in New York, the largest full-service advertising and direct mail agency dedicated to creating in-language multicultural communications programs to target Asian-Americans. The ad includes an endorsement from Professor Yoshihiro Tsurumi, a professor of international business at Baruch College and a prominent figure in the Japanese-American community.

We can also distinguish the traditional time orientation from the modern time orientation. Past-oriented societies would tend to value tradition in aesthetics and design; future-oriented societies would be more likely to value futuristic and avant-garde design. The Ritz-Carlton feels comfortable in Asia. "This is a part of the world that respects tradition and wisdom, even as it embraces the future. Is it any wonder we feel so much at home here," proclaims an ad for The Ritz-Carlton Asia-Pacific.

Customs. Like values, customs vary across the world; they affect purchasing behavior and are of interest to the identity management team. The story goes that when Gerber Foods marketed baby food in parts of Africa, the campaign failed miserably. Why? Gerber put its cute little "Gerber Baby" face on the labels of its jars. Unfortunately, in these regions the custom was to put on the label a picture of the *contents* of the jar! Muslims in Bangladesh were incensed when they thought the Thom

EXHIBIT 9.2

AT&T Advertisement, Professor Tsurumi Testimonial

McAn logo meant "Allah" in Arabic.[6] Custom had been overlooked in the marketing approach. Similarly, the De Beers diamond conglomerate faced a marketing disaster when it went global with its images of a panther wearing a diamond collar; the panther, they learned, is the symbol of death in some cultures.[7]

INDUSTRY AND PRODUCT CATEGORY FACTORS

The degree of difference between cultures varies by industry and product category. Managers must assess the degree to which these differences exist for the particular industry and products in the selected target market or country.

Skin-care products (cleansers and moisturizers) and glamour cosmetics (lipstick, mascara, eye shadow) show the need to consider product category factors. Most cosmetics organizations use the same basic skin-care system around the world, but they may occasionally supplement the basic system with an additional product (e.g., a skin whitener in France or in China). The marketing and image management of glamour cosmetics, however, requires intense localization. South American women wear more make-up and lipstick and brighter colors; they use sun-protection lotion but no make-up that would tend to make their skin look white. Yet looking white and even pale is currently a beauty ideal in France; and looking natural has always been one in Japan. American women, more than women in other cultures, like dramatic eyes. Thus, globalization is far more strategically viable for basic skin care than for the closely related glamour cosmetics categories.

ATTITUDES TOWARD FOREIGN IMAGES

As business across cultures is increasing due to increased trade across borders, more and more consumers worldwide will be exposed to foreign identities and images. The degree and speed with which they will adopt these new identities and images depends on their attitudes toward foreign images.

Like all attitudes, attitudes toward foreign companies and their brands have a cognitive (knowledge) and an affective (feeling) component. The knowledge component relates to the information that consumers in the target market have about the foreign country, organization, and brand being marketed to them. If this knowledge is extensive, consumers in the target culture are more likely to understand the meanings and implications of the image. The feeling component is related to acceptance. Consumers in the target market show high acceptance if they feel positive about the foreign country, organization, and brand, or even admire the country, organization, or brand.

Below we present four strategic alternatives based on acceptability level and knowledge level (see Figure 9.2).

FIGURE 9.2

Knowledge and Acceptance of Foreign Culture

ACCEPTANCE

	High	Low
High	Standardization	Image Improvement
Low	Education	Education or Image Improvement

KNOWLEDGE (left axis label)

Quadrant 1: High Knowledge and High Acceptability

High knowledge and high acceptance allows for standardization despite some differences between cultures.

Example: Italian upscale kitchenware manufacturer Alessi has successfully exploited the knowledge and acceptance that consumers worldwide have of Italy as the center of avant-garde fashion and design. Alessi's self-declared goal is to address the needs of "a keen and culturally curious public. . . . Our object is to offer to this public, with the valuable collaboration of retailers sharing our programme, the results of research carried out by some of the most interesting personalities of the contemporary international industrial design scene." These include designers Aldo Rossi and Philippe Starck, architects Frank Gehry and Robert Venturi, and others. The series of products bears such Italian names as "Antologia Alessi," "Tea & Coffee Piazza," and "La Casa della Felicità," to reinforce the Italian image. The brochures are printed in both Italian and English and provide Italian recipes on the side.

Quadrant 2: High Knowledge and Low Acceptance

High knowledge alone does not provide managers with adequate assurances of success. High knowledge and low acceptance requires image improvement.

Example: When Disney opened its European theme park, "EuroDisney," near Paris in May 1992, it faced a difficult situation, one that can be characterized as "high knowledge but low acceptance." Europeans were familiar with U.S. culture, Disney, and Disney characters and themes. Many Disney characters are in fact based on European imagery. However, certain aspects of American culture and of Americana in Europe had low acceptance, especially among the French. One French critic called EuroDisney "a horror made of cardboard, plastic, and appalling colors; a construction of hardened chewing gum and idiotic folklore taken straight out of comic books written for obese Americans." Paris theater director Ariane Mnouchkine called it "a cultural Chernobyl."

Still, Disney's top management was optimistic: CEO Michael Eisner said, "This is the most wonderful project we have ever done," and Robert Fitzpatrick, chairman of EuroDisney, predicted, "I think we'll help change Europe's chemistry." Disney forecast profits of hundreds of millions of francs, and many investors believed it: EuroDisney's shares soared to an all-time high of about 150 francs just before its opening. Unfortunately, Disney had barreled ahead blindly and done little to address the potential image problem. In February 1994, before it changed its approach drastically, EuroDisney was close to bankruptcy and the stock was worth just barely 30 francs.

Quadrant 3: Low Knowledge and High Acceptance

Low knowledge and high acceptance requires education about the foreign country, corporation, or brand.

Example: In contrast to EuroDisney, Tokyo Disneyland has been wildly successful ever since its opening; with 16 million visitors, it has surpassed the Disney theme parks in the United States. As a result, Disney reportedly plans to open a second theme park in Japan and is scouring Asia for additional theme-park sites. It can be argued that Disney faced a situation of low knowledge but high acceptance in Japan. The Japanese were somewhat familiar with and knowledgeable about American culture and Disney characters, but much less so than Europeans. At the same time, Japanese are crazy about and open to anything foreign and American. (An advisor to Jacques Chirac, then mayor of Paris, has called the Japanese "sponges of foreign culture.") Moreover, the Japanese were willing to expose themselves to Disney and learn about its American values, which offered opportunities for experiential education when visiting the theme parks. For example, Japanese visitors were impressed by the cleanliness, orderliness, good service, and high technology of the Tokyo theme park—features that they did not expect to find based on their stereotypes of American culture.

Quadrant 4: Low Knowledge and Low Acceptance

In the case of low knowledge and low acceptance, the organization should either reconsider the selected target or go through the difficult process of education and image improvement.

Example: Bang & Olufsen, the Danish stereo and TV manufacturer, is known among stereo experts for its striking minimalist design. But Bang & Olufsen faces in many markets a "low knowledge and low acceptance" situation. (Absolut Vodka faced a similar situation when it entered the U.S. market, as discussed in Chapter 1.) To enable the potential customer to learn more about and accept the brand, the organization, and Danish design, Bang & Olufsen uses an unusual niche-marketing strategy. It can be described as a combination of both education and image enhancement.

Recent brochures for Bang & Olufsen's stereo equipment describe its "BioLink technology" and explain "the way it looks" and "the way it works." Brochures illustrate how the Bang & Olufsen system is an integrated sound system for the whole house, with pictures and graphics of "BioLink" in the kitchen, living room, bedroom, bathroom, and study. Testimonials throughout the brochures talk about how the product meets representative customers' "visual and musical needs perfectly," "appeals to all the senses," and creates the feeling of "being there." Showrooms and selling boutiques in major cities around the world reinforce the image and provide further opportunities to educate the public about Bang & Olufsen's products and Danish design.

STYLES AND THEMES
IN GLOBAL IDENTITY MANAGEMENT

To illustrate the complexities of decisions regarding global identity, we now discuss issues related to the two key aesthetics concerns: styles and themes. We begin with the most important theme, corporate and brand names; we then discuss colors, shapes, styles as a whole, and overall impressions.

We provide examples from around the world, with a specific focus on East-Asian examples. Focusing on these more distant cultures (compared to the U.S.) allows us to discuss the intricacies of global identity management more succinctly. As a Chinese proverb says, "When drawing dragons, pay attention to the eyes" *(hua long dian jin)*. As we will show, it is critical to pay meticulous attention to aesthetic issues in a global identity management.

Corporate and Brand Names

Naming decisions in an international context can be mind-boggling. Names usually sound different across various languages. Translated, they can often carry negative associations. For example, German's Hoechst, a healthcare, agriculture and chemicals manufacturer, spent lavishly on an ad campaign to get U.S. consumers to say the name (about) right: "Just say Herkst," the ad advised. At least the company has a name for itself in this industry. To select a new name in the pharmaceutical industry that does not infringe on one of the about 500,000 pharmaceutical trademarks registered worldwide can be a formidable task.

Most U.S. organizations rarely consider the linguistic complexities involved in corporate and brand naming. As a result, there have been a number of image disasters, due to inappropriate names.

- The king of consumer packaged goods, Procter & Gamble, reeled when they learned that Puffs brand tissues had a quite unexpected and undesirable connotation in Germany, where *Puff* is a colloquial term for "brothel."
- Chevrolet had a "challenge" on their hands when they used a standardized name to market the Nova brand automobile to Spanish-speaking countries. *No va* in Spanish means "It does not go," hardly a desirable association.
- Coors Beer also had a Spanish-language challenge when its slogan "Turn it loose" was seen to imply "suffer from diarrhea."
- When Braniff tried to tout its upholstery with the slogan "Fly in Leather," it came out in Spanish as "Fly Naked."
- Perdue also had a Spanish problem with its slogan "It takes a tough man to make a tender chicken." This translates into Spanish as, "It takes a sexually stimulated man to make a chicken affectionate."

EXHIBIT 9.3

"Coca-Cola" in Different Languages

European companies are more sensitive to the intricacies of languages due to the sheer number of different languages spoken on their one continent (Romance and Germanic languages and even non-Indo-European languages such as Hungarian). They know how easily a successful name may be misunderstood in another language. Also there are numerous agencies that specialize in name development in France, Germany, and Great Britain. "Entering a market is getting more expensive, and the more expensive the launch, the more important it is to get the name right," states Marcel Botton, a partner at Nomen, a naming agency in Paris.[8]

Corporate and Brand Names in China.[9] The makeup of the Chinese language (as discussed earlier in this chapter) imposes stringent requirements for attractive corporate and brand names: the Chinese names must sound good, look good in writing, and have positive associations. Few Western brand names fulfill all three of these criteria. Coca-Cola does. The Chinese name for Coca-Cola (shown in Exhibit 9.4 underneath "Always Coca-Cola") is not a sequence of meaningless words (nor could it be, given the structure of the Chinese language). It does not merely suggest the ingredients of the drink, either. Coca-Cola (*Ke-kou-ke-le* in Mandarin and *Ho-hau-ho-lohk* in Cantonese) means "tastes

EXHIBIT 9.4

Coca-Cola in Chinese on Outdoor Advertisement

good" and "makes you happy," thus conveying the essential positioning of the brand. Through the repetition of syllables, the name has rhythmic characteristics, as it does in English. In addition, its tonal characteristics are beautifully enhanced by the tonal nature of the Chinese language. And the characters look good, even to Western eyes. Other brand names with excellent meanings and look in Chinese include Mercedes-Benz ("striving forward fast"), Boeing ("wave of sound"), and Sharp ("treasure of sound").

Most organizations, however, end up with suboptimal Chinese-name solutions, perhaps out of necessity, or worse, out of a lack of thorough research. For example, some Western organizations have kept their Western name and Western spelling. This approach may be appropriate in Japan, where consumers are familiar with the Roman alphabet, but it is less appropriate in a fast-growing market such as China, where only a minority of consumers know the Roman alphabet. Keeping the original alphabetic name seems to work, however, for organizations or brand names that are short and catchy, such as 3M, IBM, AT&T, and M&M. In these cases, the names themselves become visual symbols or logos and are remembered for their graphic qualities rather than as linguistic units.

Most organizations that have transliterated their names have done so by sound (e.g., Ford or Winston), without considering the Asian name's meaning. Other organizations have translated their names by meaning (e.g., United Airlines, Northwest Airlines, SAS, as well as General Electric, Digital Equipment, and Westinghouse Electric), regardless of how the name sounds in different languages.

Misuse of calligraphy can have negative consequences. Delta Air Lines used a map of its Asian destinations that suggested a novel mock-Chinese character. Although the ad was visually striking, Asian consumers were confused when they searched for, and failed to find, a meaning in the mock-Chinese character. As we discussed in Chapter 1, Hong Kong's Cathay Pacific also used a calligraphic approach in its identity campaign—but the effect was to celebrate calligraphy and Chinese culture rather than to seem to ridicule them.

Brand Names in Japan. Modern Japanese uses four writing systems simultaneously: *kanji* (based on Chinese characters), two phonetic systems called *hiragana* and *katakana,* and the Roman alphabet *(romaji).* In any one sentence, different words can be spelled in different writing systems; occasionally even one word may use two systems. And some words have both Chinese and Japanese pronunciations.

Corporate names are typically spelled in *romaji* (and sometimes, in the case of foreign organizations, in *katakana*). While brand names may be spelled in any of the four systems, the systems themselves carry certain associations, and are therefore more or less appropriate for certain product categories. Brands that use the oldest writing system, *kanji,* are perceived to be traditional; as a result, *kanji* may be appropriate for tea products but not for technological products. For high-tech products, the most modern language system, *katakana,* is the best. The *katakana* system was introduced into the Japanese language in the nineteenth century and is designed specifically for foreign words. It is most appropriate for foreign products and products associated with foreign lifestyles. *Hiragana*, used exclusively for the first time in the famous novel *Genji Monogatari (The Tale of Genji,* written in the eleventh century by a courtesan), has a somewhat feminine connotation. It is frequently used for the names of beauty products, hair salons, and kimono stores, and it was used for Tamagotchi (the introductory example at the beginning of the chapter). Clearly, organizations entering the Japanese market should be familiar with the impact of the different writing systems and writing styles on their corporate and brand images.

APPLICATION: BOSCH IN EAST ASIA

Branding decisions in Asian-Pacific markets are often made on an *ad hoc* basis as the organization enters market after market, rather than on a pan-Asian basis. As a result, the organization may have chosen a name that works in one market but does not transfer well to another market. For example, name awareness and positive associations may be established with a Cantonese name in South China, but as the organization expands into North China it discovers that the name has negative associations in Mandarin. This happened to Robert Bosch, a German multinational organization that manufactures high-quality vehicle parts and electrical appliances. The organization had been using a certain name since 1986 in Hong Kong and South China, where Cantonese is spoken. In 1988, this name was registered as a trademark. At the same time, another name had also been widely accepted in China, especially among clients such as Volkswagen in the diesel-fuel-injection equip-

EXHIBIT 9.5

"Bosch" in Chinese

ment field, one of Bosch's key business sectors. When Bosch considered opening an office in Beijing during the same year, name uniformity seemed necessary. The options were considered carefully. The goal was to select a name (i.e., a combination of characters) that sounded like Bosch when pronounced in both Mandarin and Cantonese, that had positive meanings that related to Bosch's core business or image as an organization, that had no negative sound associations, and that was distinct from other corporate names so as not to raise trademark infringement issues.

One name considered by the company had established name recognition in South China but had negative connotations in the second character (the first element, or radical, means "death"). Another name did not sound as good in Cantonese as in Mandarin. In Mandarin another name had the association of "academic education"—a positive association but not appropriate for an industrial organization. Still other names had been registered by several other organizations, including one organization selling generators and oscilloscopes, thus potentially contributing to customer confusion.

The new name (shown in Exhibit 9.5) that was ultimately selected sounded less good in Cantonese than the original name used in Hong Kong and in South China. However, those names that would have sounded better in Cantonese would, in Mandarin, not have sounded like Bosch or would have had associations with a welfare organization. The new names' connotations are favorable (the name may be interpreted as "winning all over the world").

Similar problems occur as the organization entered the Japanese, Korean, and Vietnamese markets. Even Asian organizations operating in the Asia-Pacific Region are not immune to this phenomenon. When Matsushita first entered the Chinese market through the South, *le-sheng*, meaning "merry sound," was used for its National brand. Later, in the North, *song-xia* was used.

Color

Managers should also arrange for studies of the cultural meanings and impact of particular colors that are considered for use in a campaign. Certain colors have uniform meanings throughout the world (red means "stop," green means "go") and colors can cause similar physiological responses across cultures. Also, certain colors are universally associated with certain cultures or countries, such as green for the Irish. Flag colors carry a national identity into international markets, which may or may not be desirable. When United decided to create a more global image for its airline, it worked with CKS Partners to replace its American-identified red, white, and blue color scheme with a blue and gray one.

But colors also bear cultural associations leading to different perceptions and evaluations; they have different meanings and aesthetic appeal in different parts of the world. Pastel tones expressing softness and harmony rather than loud colors are particularly appealing to Japanese. They were used for the Tamagotchi virtual pets in Japan. In Chinese culture, red has been appreciated for centuries as the most appealing and luckiest color. Red appears frequently on packaging, on the awnings of

---

COLOR COMBINATIONS IN KOREA

The colors red, yellow, blue, and green have become a color signature of Korea. The four colors, originally found on Korean dresses and other festive clothing, are nowadays frequently used in advertising and shine brightly on neon displays at night in the streets of Seoul and other South Korean cities. A common design alternative is to use red and yellow as a pair, bundled with either blue or green. Major Korean companies have used these color combinations as part of their logos or in the packaging of their products including several Korean banks (e.g., Seoul Bank, Peace Bank, and Koram Bank), Hyundai Electronics, Ssang Yong Oil, Oheh fruit juice and Mini-Stop, a local alternative to the popular 7-Eleven stores. Asiana, one of the two South Korean airlines uses a red-yellow-blue color combination in their logos and on flight attendants' uniforms. DC&A, a strategic design consulting firm based in Seoul, has created several successful identities using these color combinations for Korean companies (e.g., music channel m-net and supermarket chain Da-Mart). For IBM, DC&A used the colors in pavilions for trade shows and as part of IBM's retail identity (e.g., posters, packaging, and signage).

Source: Research by Bernd Schmitt.

fine Chinese restaurants, and on buses and taxis. Blue, on the other hand, America's most frequently used corporate color, is considered to be a cold color in Chinese culture, connoting evil and the sinister. Yellow is seen as pleasant and associated with authority.

In Singapore (as elsewhere in East Asia), prominent enterprises such as Singapore Telecom, Singapore Technologies, Wuthelam Holdings, and the Urban Redevelopment Authority use red in their logos. Blue is almost universally found in logos of organizations whose business is related to the sea. The logo of the Sembawang Group, a diversified conglomerate with core business in the marine and process engineering industries, is blue. So is the logo of the Singapore Navy. Other organizations use blue only in the writing of their corporate name but not in the actual logo. For example, the name of Singapore Airlines is written in blue but its crane logo is brownish-yellow.

Shape

The associations with shape that we discussed in Chapter 4 are particularly pronounced in East Asia. Angular shapes, associated with conflict, are often a bad choice in a culture that values harmony.

In Hong Kong, the buildings of two banks feature prominently on its skyline: the Bank of China, designed by the Chinese-American architect I. M. Pei, one of the tallest buildings in Hong Kong, and the Hong Kong and Shanghai Bank by Norman Foster. In its architectural design, the Bank of China building is the essence of angularity, with triangular pattern throughout and two sharp poles on its top. The style represents a dynamic display of power, but also of conflict. Accordingly, the Bank of China has been associated with strife and bad luck; given Hong Kong's unique political situation, the poles on its top had been compared to a dagger hanging over the British Governor's Mansion, which was located nearby. In contrast, the Hong Kong and Shanghai Bank building uses a variety of shapes including numerous round ones; it is not remarkable that it has become a center of civic pride and a place for socializing throughout the day. We reemphasize: aesthetics are powerful. Shapes should be thoroughly tested prior to use. Designers need creative freedom; however, decisions on shapes, like all other aesthetic decisions, should be bolstered by cultural analysis, customer input, and managerial deliberation.

FENG SHUI

The ancient Chinese art of *feng shui* is an important part of designing corporate and retail spaces in Asia, and is increasingly coming into use in the United States. The term *feng shui*, which translates literally as "wind and water," refers to what Westerners call geomancy—the placement and location of buildings, man-made structures, and interior objects so as to harmonize with and benefit from the surrounding natural environment. The Chinese believe that the proper orientation of a house or building and of the objects within it will bring the inhabitants or customers good fortune. Good *feng shui* allows the cosmic energy—*chi* or *qi*—to flow freely through the structure.

The addition or incorporation of water is one of the most powerful ways to bring the environment into harmony. In the predominantly Asian Flushing area of New York City's borough of Queens, the recently completed China Trust bank building was subjected to a pre-construction *feng shui* review, and a fountain was added to the lobby of the building to counteract the potentially negative effect of the bank's corner entrance. In addition, the core of the building was moved to a more auspicious location, desks were moved out of the sight line of the entrance, the specific orientation of some desks within offices was established, and the location of certain lights and mirrors was specified. At the New York corporate offices of Tahari Ltd., an upscale clothing manufacturer, a *feng shui* review resulted in the alteration of almost every employee's work environment by shifting desks, adding plants, changing the way doors open, and in some cases relocating entire offices.

In Minnesota Brian Broughten, owner of Saltwater Specialist, a retailer of high-quality exotic sea-life and aquariums and proprietor of a business called Advanced Aquarium, which designs and maintains customized aquariums for homes and businesses, uses *feng shui* principles to design and place aquariums in commercial settings such as the Holistic Health Care Center in St. Paul. "It's really catching on," says Joe Pryweller, senior editor for the American Society of Interior Designers (ASID). In line with the trend, *Fortune* recently published a *feng shui* analysis of the Oval Office.[10]

(continued)

(continued)

Some general *feng shui* tips:

1. When choosing a retail or office space, try to find a building facing east–west, rather than north–south.
2. Try to eliminate angles and walls and create an open feeling in the entrance. The main entrance to a building is like the mouth of a person, according to Chinese beliefs.
3. In an office, position desks so that they afford a maximum view of the entire room and those who enter.

Source: Evelyn Lip, *Feng Shui for Business* (Singapore: Times Books International, 1989); Joan A. Podell, "Bank Design as a Marketing Tool," *Bank Marketing*, May 1994; "Tropical Fish Retailer Makes a Big Splash," *PR Newswire*, July 10, 1995.

Styles

Differences in aesthetic styles may be illustrated best by examining two of the key dimensions of aesthetic styles that we discussed in Chapter 4: the complexity dimension and the representational dimension.

Whereas the U.S. seems to be truly multicultural in terms of preferences along the complexity and representational dimensions, there are other parts of the world where there seem to be a more pronounced preference for certain types of overall representations. In general, South American style preference tends to fall into the "ornamentalist/realist" quadrant. Quite appropriately, advertising and packaging of Brahma, the Brazilian beer and soft-drink giant, is full of colorful, complex, and realist imagery. European style tends to be more minimalist and abstract. This is especially true for Germanic and Scandinavian cultures. Mediterranean cultures are far more realist and less minimalist. The Middle East is often characterized by an ornamentalist abstract style and Africa by minimalist realism.

With the exception of Japan, East Asian cultural preferences are clearly in the ornamentalist/realist quadrant of the aesthetic perceptual space. East Asians value complexity of expression and decoration; they love the display of multiple forms, shapes, and colors. This feature can be found in the aesthetics of the Chinese, Thai, Malaysians, and Indonesians. East Asians also value naturalism. In the Chinese culture, symbols and displays of natural objects—of mountains, dragons, and phoenixes—prevail, and are frequently found in packaging and advertising. In Southeast Asia, the natural world of wild animals dominates the imagery.

The Shangri-La Hotel Group, a luxury hotel group with properties all over Southeast Asia and China, makes prominent use of this ornamentalist/realist symbolism in its corporate and brand identity. From the corporate name (Shangri-La echoes the name of a magical mountain in Tibet described in James Hilton's famous novel *Lost Horizon*), to the abundant use of realist imagery in the lobby and hotel rooms, to the location of most of the hotel properties near mountainsides or scenic environments, Shangri-La has made use of East Asia's preferred visual style to create the image of a "paradise on earth."

Themes and Overall Customer Impressions

Successful themes in East Asian regions focus more on harmony and affiliation, than do those in the West, where they focus more on independence and other individualistic values. Knowledge of and respect for these common themes is crucial for an organization's success.

APPLICATION: MOTOROLA IN CHINA

Motorola, in its extensive ten-year report on "Milestones in China (1987–1997)," used appropriate Chinese symbols and proverbial slogans to illustrate various developments. The phoenix, a symbol of happiness and prosperity with the accompanying slogan "The Phoenix soars toward the sun," is used to illustrate China's economic growth and modernization; the tiger, a symbol of a powerful mission with the accompanying slogan "Giving wings to the tiger," is used to illustrate Motorola's investment of $1.2 billion up to 1995; the plum, orchid, bamboo, and chrysanthemum, symbols of courage, integrity and flexibility, with the accompanying slogan "Putting down deep roots in China," are used to illustrate its strategies; and the sailboat, a general symbol of good business, is used with the accompanying slogan "Sailing toward a shared destiny."

As we discussed in Chapter 6, themes come together with styles to create overall aesthetic expressions that can be traditional, contemporary, or futuristic. For most consumer products in Asia, the preferred aesthetic is modern/contemporary with a traditional twist. We encountered this type of overall aesthetic already in the identity for the Amoy brand featured earlier in this chapter. The Asian preference for a modern/con-temporary aesthetic may be explained on the basis of the economic development of the region. Contemporary expressions reflect change without the daring uncertainty of an avant-garde look. The traditional twist relates to East Asians' traditional time orientation, which we discussed at the beginning of this chapter.

Domain-specific themes and overall impressions can be found in many countries. In Germany, environmentalism, which is heavily promoted by the Green Party, is the rage. A green or environmental aesthetic is used for a large variety of supermarket brands ranging from yogurt and shampoo to deodorants and detergents. In Japan, cuteness is "in." Female models in Japanese TV ads are predominantly in their teens or early twenties, always smile and behave in a funny way, and are often dressed like children. Product displays of ice creams and many other categories are styled to look playful and "cute." To many South American male consumers, a machismo image plays well. Clearly, these specific themes and their aesthetic representations are reflective of broader cultural values, such as the roles of men and women, and indicative of the relationship of human beings to their surrounding environments.

SUMMARY

Global identity management, as we have shown, is fraught with dangers. Aesthetic perceptions and preferences can vary significantly between cultures. The key decision for managers, whether to standardize or localize, should be influenced by four key factors: possible limitations imposed by the organization itself or its competition; the nature of the target market's culture; differences among cultures within the industry or product category; and cultural attitudes toward the foreign culture or brand. While it is a difficult arena, global identity management can be successful with careful preplanning. We have not presented hard and fast rules, however—nor could we. Success for any international organization will rest in part on research, in part on planning and analysis, in part on intuition, and in part, as the Chinese would say, on good luck.

10

Retail Spaces and Environments

GODIVA: A MEMORABLE IN-STORE CHOCOLATE EXPERIENCE[1]

Godiva Chocolatier, acquired by the Campbell Soup Company in 1967, needed help in the early 1990s when its new president had a mandate to boost sales. The products were excellent, but the stores' image was not. Their former design, using elements such as black and chrome to create an ornamentalist, static, potent, abstract style with an overall customer impression of chic and modern, was geared to the upscale 1980s. The less lofty 1990s required a different approach. Cato Gobe & Associates Inc. (now Desgrippes Gobe and Associates), the identity and design firm specializing in retail image and store design, described the tone of the old approach as rigid, sterile, aloof, hard, and intimidating.

The new approach employed a revolutionary change intended to create an overall customer impression of fluidity, warmth, entertainment, sensuousness, and invitation. With this design positioning of corporate expressions, the Art Nouveau art style was used with a European theme to match the product—the fluidity and sensuality of chocolate —with the candymaker's geographic origin, Belgium. The style dimensions are dramatically different, still ornamentalist and static, but soft and realistic rather than potent and abstract. The aesthetics of the identity elements were carefully chosen to create the styles, theme, and overall customer impressions. "Curved cherry cabinetry, display cases and mirror frames, wrought-iron pedestals and tables decorated with gilded leaves. Vintage Art Nouveau knickknacks in vitrines help to set the tone."[2]

"Creating a store image is tougher than designing a store. Image creation starts earlier, goes on longer, and involves considerations far beyond the store" states Marc Gobe, president and CEO of Desgrippes Gobe. About creating the Godiva Chocolatier retailing image, Gobe states:

> Godiva Chocolatier has an image that communicates with a customer's extravagant side. The product relates to values that urge us to live for the moment and enjoy life now. When we were asked to look at Godiva Chocolatier's

EXHIBIT 10.1

Godiva Chocolatier Store Interior

Architecture Photography: Andrew Bordwin

image, we found the stores did not project this kind of image. They did not communicate with the senses. They did not make you want to browse. They weren't places to go in and feel and experience something. Yet the product itself is very sensual. When we redesigned the stores, we aimed at communicating sensuality. We use an Art Deco look, which is an example of the extravagance characteristic of the end of the last century.[3]

This approach created repeat purchase, not just occasion-based purchase. It boosted sales 10% to 30% in the stores where it was first introduced, prompting a national design shift.

NIKE: FROM SPORTS SHOES TO AESTHETIC TOTALITARIANISM?[4]

What kind of retail space might we expect from a sneaker company? If we were living in the 1980s or before, the answer would be that manufacturers would not create retail spaces at all. If a manufacturer had created a retail space, it would probably have been to sell defective merchandise or poor sellers from last season's merchandise by way of a factory outlet. The early to mid-1990s have brought a spate of manufacturer-based retailing. Names like Speedo, Levi's, Reebok, and Nike were joining the fray.

The Nike factory outlet stores are large, with the Nike name and swoosh symbol in red and white on the outside of the building. Entering the Nike store immediately fills the consumer with the overall customer impression that he or she is obtaining warehouse no-frills shopping and pricing. Sneakers are displayed by size numbers on racks located around the large room. Stock is below the display, within the wall. Within the retail space, basic display cases have sneakers sitting above with stock below in the case. Find the sneaker you like (either on the wall or in the case), and look for your size below. Sneakers are also on racks without stock nearby—get-what-you-see type selling. The store is bright but its aesthetics are short on detail. It matches its purpose. You will not find finely polished woods, metals, or glass; you will not find sophisticated or subtle lighting schemes; and you will not find ornamental sports displays; you will not find any overt themes except a straightforward sports orientation.

Contrast the factory outlet approach of Nike with Nike Town, introduced in 1991. "For us, Nike is an inclusion brand. Everyone can find something to be a part of it. That is much different from our neighbors," explains Gordon Thompson, vice president of research, design and development. And Nike means it. The New York Nike Town, the flagship, contains 66,000 square feet of selling space on four floors, with an entire floor devoted exclusively to women's shoes and clothing. Nike Town is the result of a sophisticated aesthetics strategy, where styles and themes create a grand overall customer impression of a sports theme park.

You enter more than a retail establishment; you get more than a shopping space. You walk into what seems to be an interactive museum and information center on sports. The theme of confidence contributes strongly to this overall customer impression. You experience large glass-encased photos and other sports-related objects. You are kept up to date by instant results of worldwide sporting events, or video and audio information at your request on sports figures like Carl Lewis or Michael Jordan. Enhancing the confidence theme, swoosh logo-marked information booths act as museum guides to take you where you need to go and personnel cruise the floors clad in Nike apparel and footwear to help you with your experience. Messages appearing throughout the store carry the theme forward, such as "To all the athletes and the dreams they chase, we dedicate Nike Town New York." Your purchases are made part of sports history, connecting you and your life to the very best sports performers in the world. The aesthetics creating the styles, themes, and overall customer impressions begins on the outside, where you enter what appears to be a vintage Manhattan public-school gymnasium, with P.S. 6453 etched above the entrance, reflecting the number equivalents of NIKE and the last four digits of the store's phone number. Grand all-capital sans-serif metal letters spell NIKE TOWN above the entrance on a convex, crescent-shaped lintel that reflects movement and confidence.

As you enter the store, you experience aesthetics reflecting sports and power and movement. You enter through turnstyles as though entering a sports event and are faced with seven videos, some showing live sporting events. Nearby, the Nike brand is reinforced within the identity through a 36- x 22-foot square movie screen that runs various promotional videos every few minutes. The Nike identity is tied to this space through other aesthetic devices like the continued appearance of the Swoosh logo, which is built into displays, door handles, and even staircase banisters.

The gym theme is reinforced by a style reminiscent of gyms: an open

EXHIBIT 10.2

Nike Town in New York City

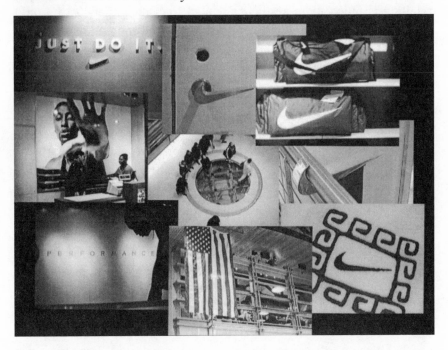

atrium, giving a sense of a gymnasium (or as if we were entering a very fancy sports club), mats on the floor, a basketball-court look, outer brick walls, wooden bleachers, clocks, and protective caging. The identity elements creating the style contain brushed and polished aluminum (reflecting high technology), light satin-finished woods (reflecting a bright, clean gym-floor color), angular ornamentation (reflecting a chiseled athlete appearance), all designed to create an overall impression of high technology along with superior sports performance.

With Nike Town, however, we question whether Nike is in danger of moving beyond a reasonable aesthetic toward what we term "aesthetic totalitarianism."

AESTHETICS IN RETAIL AND ENVIRONMENTAL SPACES

Headlines tell the story: "Reinventing the Store: How Smart Retailers are Changing the Way We Shop,"[5] "Attention, Shoppers: Brand-Name

Stores,"[6] and similar pieces tell us that retailing is "hot" again. Traditionally, retailers have been concerned with utility and efficiency. But retailing is much more aesthetics-related than its earlier focus would have one think. Landor Associates defines selling environment or retail identity in terms of product displays, "the physical environment in which the company's products or services are presented and offered for sale to customers." The definition should be further expanded to state that the company itself, through its retail environments, is making a statement about itself, not merely about its products and services.

Nowadays, traditional retailers have begun to realize the importance of store image and want to link this image to the images of their other stores. Moreover, manufacturers have learned that expansion into retailing is a viable option to enhance their identities. Here, the interior of the store should reflect the image of the brand or the entire organization.

Spatial design and the image of a space is not only of concern to retailers or manufacturers. It is also the concern of city planners and architects. Like retailers, architects and city planners were in the past concerned with the spatial object itself—in their case, to make a building or city work structurally and operationally. The United States Holocaust Museum, designed by Pei Cobb Freed and Partners, is a quintessential example of using aesthetics even for the most important messages. Clients (private or public) are concerned about their image. Corporations fund and design the subway stop next to their headquarters to facilitate employee access and pleasure. Entire cities and countries select positioning for themselves with clear aesthetic implications: Singapore is the "intelligent island," Atlanta is the "pearl of the South," and Korea is the country of "morning calm." And European cities in general with their hallmark pedestrian malls create a unique "European" feel.

In this chapter we first discuss strategic issues and choices that retailers have in expanding beyond the type of retailing that they are known for or even beyond retailing altogether. Next we discuss the issues involved in the trend of manufacturers toward using retailing to enhance their identities. We then review the essential characteristics of modern retail identities as well as environmental spaces in general. We conclude the chapter with management issues regarding retailing and environmental aesthetics.

STRATEGIC ISSUES FOR RETAILERS
AND MANUFACTURERS

Retailers Expanding from Their Core Identity

1. *Store-Bound vs. "Cyber"-Bound.* The first choice of a retailer trying to achieve a broader image is whether it should remain store-bound or whether it should become independent of a physical location. Expansion entails a new strategy for finding and targeting consumers. It may ensure long-term benefits by reducing physical expansion needs and maintaining demand even when shopping patterns and demographics in particular locations shift. Along with this, the retailer must expect a large communications budget to pull off the transition. For example, Barnes & Noble, a book chain retailer, faces the issue of whether it should pursue the image of a leisure-time provider in retail outlets or whether it should massively market itself on the Web and become independent of its retail origins.

2. *From Books to Coffee to* **?** The ability for a company to extend its image is directly tied to how powerful that image is in terms of recognizability, likeability, and persuasiveness. Barnes & Noble teams with Starbucks to provide coffee shops in the bookstores simply because their name is not powerful enough to extend credibly to coffee. An Armani boutique, on the other hand, tied to upscale images, powerful in likeability and persuasive as a leader in taste, would have an easier time opening a no-name coffee shop on the premises. It would be designed to fit the identity of the store and would, over a short time, be accepted as part of the natural decor and functioning of an Armani boutique.

3. *From Boutiques to Strip Malls.* The new identity that a retailer emerges with in the minds of the consumer will be highly dependent on the execution of the aesthetics in the identity elements, i.e., the vision of the designers. But it will also be highly dependent on the strategic visions articulated by management, i.e., what kinds of retail we are expanding into. What channels should we avoid and which should we pursue from an aesthetics standpoint? Expanding into different channels is perfectly fine when one chooses a new identity for the new retailing. Consider Old Navy with its factory-like centers vs. The Gap with its boutique aesthetic.

People are not told of their connection so the identities stand on their own. But if a connection is made, the aesthetics should be of similar caliber and type. Consider the analogous situation of a manufacturer and designer like Donna Karan, that has a branded Donna Karan couture line and also DKNY casual lines. The problem with such a strategy is that image dilution of the higher name is likely. This is often far worse than the benefits of using the powerful Donna Karan name or DK designation on the casual wear: it can lead to a vicious circle where the casual line dilutes the couture line and then the couture line, having been diluted, no longer helps or even hurts the image of the casual line.

Manufacturers Entering Retailing

Edward Friedman, president of retail services at Newmark & Company Real Estate, a commercial brokerage in Manhattan, stated in 1994 that "we're seeing an evolution in retailing . . . brands are staking out their own identity in the marketplace." The trend continues today. Examples of manufacturers entering retailing (or more broadly, spatial design) include Godiva and Nike, Harley Davidson and Disney, Coca-Cola, and M&M's.

HARLEY-DAVIDSON:

DO MOTORCYCLES AND RESTAURANTS FIT TOGETHER?

Numerous companies have recently expanded into retailing. One of them has been Harley-Davidson. If you were to ask branding experts if motorcycles and restaurants go well together, they would list a number of criteria to evaluate the fit: complementarity, substitutability, attribute relatedness, technology relatedness, and image fit. None of these criteria would explain why a motorcycle manufacturer and a restaurant are in fact perfectly matched. But theme cafes, like the Harley-Davidson Cafe, have changed the dining experience of millions throughout the world. They do it not by any of these "fit" criteria but by the experiences they create. The experience of a Harley-Davidson Cafe enhances the Harley-Davidson motorcycle experience. The aesthetics of the store enhances the emotional tie with the brand.

Manufacturers selling directly to the public through traditional retailing need to consider three major strategic decisions.

1. *Flagship vs. Neighborhood Approaches.* Should the manufacturer develop a few flagship retail stores (e.g., in core cities) or should it strive for a saturated image through a large number of stores? The choice depends on the objectives of the extension into retailing: is it to reinforce and promote the core brand image or is the purpose to add to the core business a profitable line of business extension that extends the core image into new terrain? Nike Town, at this point, is exclusively limiting itself to prime city spaces to promote the image of Nike: performance, commitment, and innovation. Starbucks, on the other hand, was set from the start for expansion and by now has hundreds of coffee shops and expands into bookstores and music stores. Starbucks, however, like Häagen-Dazs, starts in an exclusive fashion when it enters new, foreign markets by first opening a flagship store in a core location in a new city.

2. *Stand-alone or Submerge.* Manufacturers often fear getting lost in the information clutter of a department store. Some manufacturers, therefore, opt for a stand-alone retail presence that does not get confounded with those of other retailers. In this case, the manufacturer creates an exclusive boutique or otherwise self-contained space; in the latter it strives to be one among many by selecting a location where similar merchandise may be found, by selecting mall locations or locations in a department store. The choice depends on the degree of leverage gained or lost by association. Without the cost of stand-alone stores, however, manufacturers have the potential for powerful identity creation within department stores. For example, Unilever decided to sell its CK ONE® fragrance for men and women through an innovative retailing approach that mimicked the entry of a manufacturer into a stand-alone retail outlet by selling the fragrance on stand-alone displays in music stores such as Tower Records. This reinforced the image of the brand as a casual, everyday fragrance for the contemporary woman and man. It also allowed for a wider range of shoppers to be exposed to the product.

3. *Reinforcing the Core Identity.* The last issue is not a matter of choice between dichotomies but the procedural question of how to achieve the objective of reinforcing the image. What kind of aesthetics should we use? Traditional factory outlet type? Theme-store type? A hybrid? (Like Ann Taylor's Loft, for example, discussed later.) Which store elements, i.e., which colors, shapes, materials, relate to the image? How can the conservative country look of a fashion brand or the clean performance look of a sports brand be expressed in a store design?

The success of the transition is directly geared to whether the identity of the core franchise is consistent with the new retail environment in some way that is meaningful to consumers. Thus, as in the case of Harley David-son, while we would think that motorcycles have little in common with cafes, they in fact share a distinct image bolstered in the cafe via various visuals and sounds. Ralph Lauren has translated both positionings very successfully in the store designs for its "Polo/Ralph Lauren" and "Polo Sport" brands. The Polo/Ralph Lauren stores have the look, feel, and smell of an American country house; they are ornamentalist/realist, dark and rusty, and full of natural materials. Polo Sport stores, in contrast, are mini-malist and no-frills; bright and clean, and full of man-made materials.

MODERN RETAIL IDENTITIES

Aesthetics creates the image or the tone of a space. A storefront with small windows with one or two displays of exclusive items indicates a high image or a classy image; a store with panel signs (non-three-dimensional) typically suggests cheapness. Inside, aesthetics clue us into the image; in-consistent displays may indicate sloppiness or poor quality, while pol-ished floors might suggest cleanliness and higher-quality products or services. Colder and more delicately fashioned materials such as glass and metal ornamentation surrounding a window or on a typeface might sug-gest strength and class, while plastic letters for signage might suggest lower-end performance in product or service. The particular combination of aesthetics creates this overall image or tone. The space can be described by polar adjectives, such as happy vs. sad, playful vs. serious, alive vs. dull, classy vs. garish, noisy vs. quiet, cheap vs. upscale, etc. These and numerous other adjective pairs are often used in research to create indices of image or personality through various multivariate techniques (such as factor analysis).

The aesthetics, and thus the identities, of retail environments vary tremendously depending on the type of retail location. Major aesthetic differences can be found across (1) department stores, (2) regional malls,

FIGURE 10.1

Modern Retail Identities

(3) strip malls, (4) supermarkets, (5) boutiques, (6) superstores, (7) factory outlets, (8) theme stores, and (9) restaurants.

Department Stores. Among the best practices of aesthetics by department stores has been Bloomingdale's, particularly the flagship New York City location. You enter a multisensory environment that uses numerous identity elements to create an overall customer impression of chic, class, and strength. Orange-hued woods add to the sense of strength, while black-and-white motifs in floor patterns and uniforms add to the chic character of the store. The use of identity elements, however, also creates the representation of affordability. "Sales" signs are conspicuous, and clothing and shirts are accessible and in abundance. Tables and racks are filled with merchandise, as in other wide-market department stores such as Macy's, Dillard's, Hecht's, etc. Contrast this presentation with Bergdorf Goodman, Saks Fifth Avenue, or Nordstroms, all upscale department stores, which create a very different representation. Here, personnel are dressed more formally; clothing is laid out in small quantities, suggesting higher price; the variation between low-end products and high-end products is less, with more uniformly higher-end products; displays use better woods and metals; fixtures are fancier; the furniture tends to be more ornamental and classic, and there is more open space on the selling floor. The result is a more subdued, quieter, more elegant approach where personal service seems readily available and the shopping experience is more refined.

In other words, as one moves to lower-end department stores, fixtures become cheaper (plastics, not metals), displays more disorganized, more merchandise displayed, less open space, all creating a feeling of mass merchandising rather than boutique shopping. Using these guidelines, Takashimaya, the Japanese retailer, has created an identity of high refinement and class. Galeries Lafayette in France, Harrods in England, El Corte Ingles in Spain, Horten in Germany, and other European department stores mirror well the aesthetics of a Macy's or a Bloomingdale's. The same is true for department stores like Seibu, Mitsukoshi, and Takashimaya in Japan. In Singapore and Hong Kong, however, all Japanese department stores have positioned themselves above local department stores as well as above their Japanese competitor Yaohan, and thus often use a more sophisticated aesthetics.

Department stores have tremendous leeway in creating new aesthetics, because the various departments need not be consistent (either in style or theme) with one another in the way that the elements of a hotel, for example, need to be. People enter different departments for different reasons; often they belong to different segments who self-select themselves to the right merchandise. The variety of aesthetics can lend a pleasant edge along with a desired level of arousal and attention grabbing. The overall customer impression can be one of eclecticism and choice as opposed to sloppiness or inconsistency.

Regional Malls and Megamalls. The aesthetic landscape of the United States has changed dramatically in the past thirty years with the invention of the regional (covered) mall. Sociologists equate the regional mall with the equivalent of the pedestrian mall in the centers of European towns, usually near the central church. These gathering places fulfill such community needs as commerce, social interaction, entertainment, child and teen activities, and relaxing. In the suburban setting, which has been dominating the United States since the mid-1950s to 1960s, these needs are more typically met through the regional mall. This implies that the aesthetics of the regional mall need to be designed with these multiple purposes in mind. Varieties of services are one way to assure this (like movies, selection of stores, child care, food courts, etc.), but its aesthetics are what truly distinguishes the modern mall from a mere collection of stores under one roof.

Megamalls such as the famous "Mall of America" in Minneapolis, take the regional mall to grand aesthetic proportions, giving consumers entire villages to play in. The Mall of America, for example, heralded a shift from mundane cookie-cutter malls to a new entertainment experience. The entire aesthetic theme is intended to match the feel of an amusement park. The shops within malls are also becoming aesthetically aware, with varying styles and themes, accentuated by numerous identity elements. The collage of colors from products to displays in the Body Shops, H_2O, or Bath & Body Works, for example, highlight the keen attention that mall stores are paying to form and style. The scents, designs of packaging, and displays of the Crabtree & Evelyn stores are typical of the wide use of aesthetics strategy in most regional mall stores.

Strip Malls. The most underdeveloped retail space aesthetically has been the strip mall. Still far behind the times, most strip malls give the impression of being cheap, low-level, sometimes dirty or sloppy, and always without flair. One ad might have a large blue-and-yellow "Blockbuster" sign, while the other a bright red "Walgreen's" sign. Colors, typefaces, shapes, and materials are usually not coordinated and are poorly managed. The ease with which the aesthetics of various identity elements can be managed in a strip mall (signage, walkways, etc.) makes it all the more illogical that sales aren't tapped through identity management.

Supermarkets and Mega-Supermarkets. Supermarkets have moved into the world of identity management. A notable example is the Publix supermarkets in the southern states where design has played an integral part in the shopping experience. Loeb, Inc. (IGA supermarkets in Canada) worked with designers from Lippincott & Margulies to alter signage, layout, vehicles, advertising and private-label branding to create a bold new identity in food shopping. In general, the modern supermarket's aesthetic tends to have wider aisle spaces, better and more refined lighting (vs. the traditional long, exposed fluorescent-light fixtures), highly designed fancy gourmet sections, upscale floor tiling, and sleeker displays and check-out counters. Its styles tend to be minimalist, with identity elements often employing angularity, the color white, brightness, and lack of ornamentation. Private-label designs have learned to compete on design with the major brands, pioneered, in part, by the D'Agostino supermarkets in New York, who introduced their designed "President's Choice" line in the late 1980s. Others have followed suit.

There tend not to be themes in supermarkets except for ethnic-brands displays such as Goya, but thematic supermarkets may be an aesthetic device whose time has come. Supermarkets could play on thematic-based aesthetics by dividing the shopping experience into cuisines, across brands: the Southwestern section, the Italian section, for example, and, by concept, the sportsperson's section, the Older America section, the teen section, etc. This is a novel concept, but one that could flow directly from an infusion of themes into the aesthetic.

Beyond infusion of themes, supermarkets, like other retailers, often use international expansions as an opportunity to change or refocus their image. Ahold, a Dutch supermarket giant, with TOPS and BILO branded supermarkets in the U.S., positioned its TOPS supermarket as a "fresh" supermarket to differentiate itself from the "canned foods" image of other Western and Asian supermarket chains operating in the People's Republic of China. One of us (Schmitt) was involved in the name testing and name selection for TOPS. Several names were tested in focus groups and mall intercepts, and the final name selected used the Chinese characters for "fresh food" to express the supermarket's distinct identity.

Boutiques. Boutiques occupy a strong segment of retailing. A stroll down any major upscale boutique section in any city worldwide reveals specialty stores using aesthetics designed to create overall customer impressions of exclusivity, high-end merchandise, expansiveness, high quality, and high-level, personally involved customer service. Their very names have come to stand not only for quality, but for aesthetics and taste: Fendi, Steuben, Tiffany, Bulgari, Christian Dior, Gucci, Cartier, and Louis Vuitton are but a handful of these high-end aesthetic centers. Here aesthetics strategy meets aesthetics products per se. In other words, here, more than in any type of product or service, an aesthetics strategy is virtually synonymous with a marketing strategy, primarily because the products and services themselves are inherently aesthetic—fashion, jewelry, crystal, etc. The aesthetics of a boutique are usually unique, expensive to create, and often classically elegant. The timeless nature of elegance should militate against rapid aesthetics shifts.

Boutiques marked by comprehensive identity management are popping up everywhere, including clothing boutiques like Talbots, Ann Taylor, J. Crew, Eddie Bauer, and miscellaneous general-merchandise boutiques like Sunglass Hut, Things Remembered, Pier 1 Imports, and Crate & Barrel, among numerous others. Many are chains. For chains, the consistency of the aesthetics of their stores allows the parent company to maintain strong recognizability of its name and its aesthetic.

How comprehensively boutiques manage their identity and image can be illustrated by the store image of Pottery Barn. Pottery Barn with stores in major cities in the U.S. is a retailer of home furnishings owned by Williams Sonoma, the kitchenware retailer. The stores have an attractively bright color scheme to convey an image of casual elegance. Sales staff wear white shirts with khaki pants. Jazz music plays in the background. Boxes and shopping bags are made of natural brown paper, representing the natural wood of most of the products.

APPLICATION: ANN TAYLOR

Ann Taylor represents another good example of comprehensive identity management through the subtle evolutionary design approach (discussed in Chapter 4). Research by design firm Desgrippes Gobe & Associates revealed that attributes and values that women wanted in a clothing store were authenticity, naturalness, and simplicity balanced by sensuality and a sense of adventure and humor. Numerous design elements were changed to accomplish this (see Exhibit 10.3) including details down to the packaging of the new fragrance line "Destination." Nature-based shapes, gunmetal and glass for the bottle design, and wood and textured paper for the box were designed to encourage the shopper to be attracted to and touch the product (thereby increasing likelihood of sales). The change helped evolve Ann Taylor from a store to a brand identity. The identity has become so powerful that many refer to Ann Taylor as a "trusted friend," despite the character's fictional nature.

EXHIBIT 10.3

Various Identity Elements of the New Ann Taylor

Architecture photography: Andrew Bordwin

Superstores or Megastores. Wal-Mart, Sam's, Price-Costco, and Home Depot all have one thing in common. These superstores cater to bargain hunters, to large families, and to a wide range of incomes for an ultra-wide range of products and services. The aesthetics should evoke for the customer the unfinished, rough, aggressive, economical. Achieving this requires the use of strong materials, large spaces, organized aisles, visible stock, bright lights, large carts, minimalist styles, and cost-savings family-oriented themes.[7]

Not all superstores, however, need to imply this kind of aesthetic. Barnes & Noble is a successful example of a company that has created "megastores" with aesthetics that create an overall customer impression of being in a friendly, relaxing, pleasant, good-looking, modern, library-like, and artistic environment. They create this impression with carpeting; wooden display shelves; polished metal ornamentation; green and brown organic colors; classic wooden chairs, matching the wooden displays, beside large, sturdy modern tables; plush, relaxing living-room-like armchairs; and the inclusion of Starbucks cafes. The theme is that you've entered a relaxing library, and the styles resonate with this to create an impression that makes people stay. And the longer people stay, the greater their likelihood of purchase.

By the time Barnes & Noble was coming out with megastores, Boston's Waterstone's booksellers had already created a strong identity with its aesthetics in a megastore environment. Crimson carpeting, chandeliers, custom built wood fixtures, and wrought iron and oak trim created what a trade journal called "Athenaeum-like" interiors.[8]

Factory Outlets. The factory outlet typically uses an aesthetic hybrid of strip mall and regional (covered) mall. The malls are usually outdoors, but employ uncovered walking spaces that are flanked by stores on all sides. The aesthetic is often village-like. Wooden signs, wooden benches, and food pavilions typically mark the shared commons experience. The stores included in the factory outlet can fit into the required overall casual, low-key customer impression despite being "high end," like Barney's New York for example. Similar signage and logos connect the consumer to the higher-end counterpart, and matching the aesthetics of the particular retail environment can create the required consistency of image. A departure from the typical factory outlet impression is that of Ann Taylor's "Loft." Maple-trimmed display racks, skylights, and white brick walls create a unique balance of an upscale boutique image with the size and feel of a factory outlet.

Theme Stores. The themed retail environment has ushered in a new era of retailing, culminating in stores like Nike Town. In theme stores the aesthetics focus primarily on creating and supporting a story or a motif. Theme stores include most notably Disney, Coca-Cola, Harley Davidson Cafe, and the Warner Brothers Studio Store. Themed retail spaces require multisensory stimulation in order to overcome the natural lack of variety that often accompanies these "one-pony" shows. Attracting the first-time customer is an important part of an aesthetics strategy. Most of these stores employ a variety of identity elements to highlight the theme, with style flowing from thematic considerations.

Restaurants. Restaurant design incorporates numerous identity elements, each of which is heavily noticed, like walls, floors, tablecloths, napkins, silverware, plates, uniforms, bottles, etc. Theme cafes are a unique mix of restaurant and general theme store; examples are Planet Hollywood, Harley Davidson, Hard Rock Cafe.

ENVIRONMENTAL SPACES

We are faced every day with aesthetics in our surroundings that are often managed by public officials of various sorts. Whether we are in a city, suburb, or rural area, numerous such spaces affect us. These environments include transportation systems (airports, bus and train stations, buses and trains themselves, subways in cities), recreational spaces (parks, playgrounds, pools and golf courses, beaches and docks), cultural spaces (outdoor concert arenas, opera houses, museums, and schools), and political complexes (state houses, governmental offices, and courts).

Management of such spaces usually falls into the hands of urban planners or industrial designers or architects. Urban designers engage in strategic planning similar to the work of those in corporate and brand identity. The city's identity is crucial for tourist dollars, convention bookings, immigration, etc. If we consider a city space, for example, the identity elements would consist of the buildings, street signs, lampposts, trash cans, sanitation trucks, police cars, public phone booths, newsstands, etc. Most cities in the United States do not control their aesthetics as much as cities in Europe. The identity of New York City, for example, is marked by inconsistencies, overlapping time periods, varieties of styles, disorganization, lack of cleanliness, and age. But Washington, D.C., with its angular and mundane buildings and flat skyline, is controlled stringently to maintain its representation. If we turn to cities like Rome, Athens, or Jerusalem, with structures dating back some 2,000 years we see marked overall aesthetic differences, with classic stone structures, but with a strong attention by governmental authorities to aesthetics and to the zoning needed to maintain these overall classic impressions for visitors. The older the area, the more difficult it is to build and plan due to the numerous aesthetic constraints, which indeed often lead to legal constraints.

Large environments like cities have more identity elements (both manageable and unmanageable) than any other identities in the world. Here the concept of centrality, discussed in Chapter 6, becomes extremely important for urban planners. One element can dramatically transform the impression. Consider the European city street, for example, and the typical American city street. If we were to view a photo of a city street from anywhere in Europe (removing any names indicating language), it is virtually certain that we could identify it as European; the same thing for an American street. Why is this? One major difference is the pedestrian mall. City streets in Europe are often flanked by small and large pedestrian malls, while those in the United States typically are not. These minor differences create a large impression. Similarly, Europe's tree-lined streets differ dramatically in aesthetics and overall customer impression from the treeless ones in the U.S.

MANAGING RETAIL AND ENVIRONMENTAL AESTHETICS

Environmental aesthetics drive business. Nowhere else in the retail environment are there so many simultaneous aesthetic expressions that can affect the bottom line quickly and directly. Retailers are learning "tricks" that enhance the retailing experience. Promotions in stores, for example, lengthen the time that consumers stay in the store, and the longer they stay in the store, empirical evidence has shown, the more they tend to purchase. But promotions are a tiny part of how retailers can affect sales. Rather than focusing on gimmickry, savvy retailers are focusing on aesthetics to lure the customer in and keep him or her there much longer. The FAO Schwarz toy store is a quintessential example of an early leader in this movement toward aesthetics in retailing. You enter a music-filled environment, with colors, clown-costumed employees, stuffed animals, huge rotating dolls, and a new toy everywhere you look. The multisensory approach is compelling.

Optimal Level of Arousal

How much sensory expression is too much? Consumer-behavior studies on arousal suggest that people have individual optimal levels of stimulation or arousal.[9] Below the point of optimal stimulation boredom sets in, sometimes accompanied by sadness and apathy. Above the point of optimal stimulation, nervousness and irritability can set in (see Figure 10.2).

The mall provides a wide range of stimulation levels via the different retail stores located in it. The common spaces of the mall itself should provide a moderately high level of stimulation, rather than extremes. The "moderate level" of stimulation is geared to the target markets frequenting the mall. Likewise, department stores can modify their levels of stimulation based on the demographic and psychographic characteristics of the target market for each department. Thus, there is often varied music playing in the different departments, as well as varied lighting, displays, colors, and personnel types.

Research on Effects of Environments

Research on the effects of environments has been flourishing for the past twenty years. *Atmospherics*, as academics term the environmental identity elements, have been experimentally tested as well as observed

FIGURE 10.2

Levels of Arousal

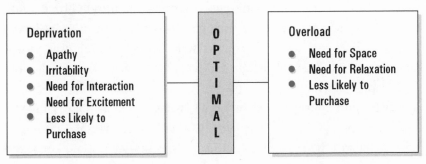

directly in the field. Bitner[10] has synthesized much of the material in this area, but only to conclude that "through careful and creative management of the servicescape, organizations may be able to contribute to the achievement of both external marketing goals and internal organizational goals." General implications were broad, like "the physical environment can serve as a differentiator in signaling the intended market segment, positioning the organization, and conveying distinctiveness from competitors."

In the 1930s the famous architect Morris Lapidus, in addition to making his mark on Miami and on Art Deco design in general, was also revolutionizing retail-marketing research. As a preeminent retail-space designer, when he set out to discover what lures people to various retail environments—what attracts them—he performed what has become a state-of-the-art research technique. He observed people going in and out of boutiques and other stores and made qualitative observations of what appeared to lure them. "A lady wants to buy a pair of 69-cent nylons. What I had to do was think of ways to get her inside the store," Lapidus is quoted as saying in the *Washington Post*.[11] (Curves and colored lights did the trick in this instance.)

Lapidus observed consumer behaviors in a quasi-experimental setting. This observational technique has been honed by a number of companies, such as leader Envirosell Inc. of New York City. The work of these firms focuses on analyzing what to do in retail spaces and what not to do. The methodology is based on observations of spaces and consumers via video and human observers. The interactions and subsequent reactions are monitored, quantified, tabulated, and analyzed (see Figure 10.3). Cognitive and emotional responses are obtained from supplemental interviewing.

When one of us (Simonson) interviewed Paco Underhill, founder of Envirosell, he told us that the bottom line seemed to be that what appears to be complex is often simple. The trick is to take the time to observe. A department store, for example, learned to place a seat in the luggage department when a customer was seen on an Envirosell videotape throwing luggage to the ground in order to take a seat on the luggage display table.

What might appear to be functional issues—such as display layouts and placement of merchandise, among others—really revolve around issues of sensory perception. What do people see when they enter and

FIGURE 10.3

Observation of Retail Spaces

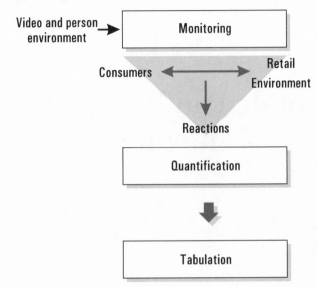

how do they react to that? What do they hear and how do they react? What causes them to stay longer? The Gap, discussed in Chapter 1, uses tactile strategy to maximize customer time and purchase. Woolens are laid out on tables for people to look at and, as Underhill found, to touch and experience. This "petting" (Underhill's term) builds the relationship between consumer and product. Grocers have learned the value of the sensory effect of retail: many are placing fruits and vegetables near the entrance to provide smells, bright colors, feelings of freshness and organicness, and an ability to touch the products.

CYBERSPACES

The newest spaces are cyberspaces. Visit some Web sites like Nike, Reebok, or Adidas and you are transported into a retail environment. Tower Records has virtual stores, and virtual malls are popping up throughout the Web mimicking the "village square" of the regional mall.

The Internet and its World Wide Web subpart are transforming retail environments. A consumer may visit the store or the Web site. The management of aesthetics within a Web site and across identity elements including Web sites is discussed in Chapter 11.

11

Corporate and Brand Identity on the Internet

In 1994 Volkswagen, Europe's largest car manufacturer, announced that it would revive one of the commercial and design legends of this century: the "Beetle." In that year the organization presented a prototype of the New Beetle at the two major motor shows in Geneva and Detroit and pledged to manufacture the New Beetle before the end of the century.

As this book goes to press, the New Beetle exists only as a concept and a prototype, not as a finished car. Volkswagen has invited Beetle fans worldwide to actively contribute to the final shape of the idea. It has chosen to use the latest medium available for identity and image creation—the World Wide Web—to revive the legend.

A Brief History of the Beetle

On January 17, 1934, Ferdinand Porsche submitted a design proposal for a "people's car" to the German government. At that time in Germany, cars were luxury items for the rich; less than 2% of all Germans owned one. But Porsche was committed to change this situation by building a user-friendly, well-designed small car. The first prototype was an outstanding example of modern small-car construction: full steel bodywork, space for five people, and superb performance set it apart from other designs. The shape of the car was distinctive and easily recognizable.

In 1938, when the car was first produced, it was instantly nicknamed the "Beetle" by the *New York Times* because of its odd shape. The outbreak of World War II, however, brought production to a standstill.

After the war Volkswagen became the largest car producer in Europe with this same high-quality small car. In 1948, the organization produced 19,244 cars, 64.4% of all cars built in Germany. The Beetle was soon exported to Denmark, Luxembourg, Sweden, Belgium, and Switzerland. In 1949, the Beetle was shipped to the United States, where it was displayed at the German Industrial Exhibition in New York.

In the United States, initial distrust and resistance to the Beetle soon turned into enthusiasm. The car became accepted as an unconventional, classless vehicle, and became the car of choice for individualists as well as design maniacs. In the summer of 1960, the 500,000th Volkswagen was exported to the United States. In the same year, construction began on the U.S. headquarters of Volkswagen of America in Englewood Cliffs, New Jersey. Volkswagen's advertising was taken over by DDB Needham, which produced many award-winning advertisements in the years that followed.

In 1972, the 15,007,034th Beetle came off the production line, overtaking the legendary Ford Model T, produced between 1908 and 1927, as the most-produced car ever. Production of the Beetle in Europe came to an end in 1976, although it continued in a Mexican plant.

The New Beetle

In 1994, Volkswagen presented a prototype vehicle ("Concept1") as "the return of the Beetle." As J. C. Mays, who headed the design team, explains, the point was "to combine the past and the future. Customers can directly relate to Concept1—and they have confidence in it. At the same time, it features state-of-the-art technology." As Mays further explains, the car design and the image campaign surrounding it are based on four principles:

> Simplicity, honesty, reliability, and originality—these are the Volkswagen traditions that are being focused upon. We started out from the point of view of the engineer, just as Ferdinand Porsche did when he designed the legendary

Beetle. What is absolutely necessary? What elements of design and form-giving lines are superfluous? We selected individual geometric elements and integrated them to produce modern and harmonious proportions. Concept1 is the embodiment of Volkswagen.

The shape of the prototype vehicle recalls the famous shape of the original. It has no aggressive lines, and none of its lines gives the impression of speed. Likewise, only straight lines and spherical elements are featured in the interior, giving it a simple style. The interior has a Porsche-style glass sliding roof and is decorated in a light gray and yellow fabric/leather combination to give an impression of lightness and fun. The exterior color is also highly original: a pearlescent "cyber" green. An extremely economical 1.9-liter turbodiesel engine with direct fuel injection and 81 kW (110 hp) power expresses simplicity and reliability. The instruments focus on essential functions. All these features reflect the design philosophy of simplicity, honesty, reliability, and originality.

The public and the press responded exuberantly. Volkswagen instantly received several blank checks from car enthusiasts. Matthias Wissmann, the German Minister of Transport, called the concept car "A classic for the future!" Christiane Weilmann, the editor of *Bild,* Germany's largest newspaper, wrote that "the neo-Beetle is a great car— round, aesthetic, and cuddly."

The New Beetle in Cyberspace

To support the introduction of the New Beetle, in March 1996 Volkswagen launched a Web site devoted solely to the car (http://www.beetle.de). Like the car itself, the Web site is stylish, original, fun, and experiential. Extending the Volkswagen Beetle aesthetic into cyberspace, the site uses the Internet medium to its fullest potential for image management.

The Web site consists of several interlinked Web pages of text, graphics, and downloadable components as well as links to relevant e-mail addresses and other Volkswagen Web sites. All the site's pages include the same basic design elements. A copy of some pages of the site are shown in Exhibit 11.1.

Several features of the Web-page design are noteworthy. On the right side of each page, almost half the space is occupied by a dark blue color block—a clever design approach that serves as a constant reminder of

EXHIBIT 11.1

New Beetle Web Site

Concept1 is the new Beetle.

Detroit 1994

Streaming Video

ISDN (527kb)

Geneva 1994

Tokyo 1995

german | hot | tech | the idea | facts & figures | sign in | gallery |
feedback | in the public | help

Reprinted from the New Beetle Web page, copyright 1996 by Volkswagen AG.

Volkswagen's corporate color. The only other element in this huge space is a well-designed, original, flowchart-type navigation bar which looks like a road with cars. It allows the user to navigate the Web site easily and conveniently. The top left of the home page has eye-catching graphics with a "retro-techno" feel, stylistically and thematically inspired by the Beetle legend. For example, the News page is graphically represented by a vintage megaphone, and Public Relations by a funky news column. The remainder of each Web page consists of informational text (appropriately kept to a minimum number of words), pictures, or graphics. Each page loads quickly, due to the monocolor blue on the right and the small, color-reduced graphics. At the bottom of each page is an icon that can be clicked on for more information, a convenient feature that saves users scrolling time.

Another feature of the Web site that creates an image of simplicity and convenience is a separate Web page that provides "pointers for smooth navigation" of the site as a whole. On this page, we find an explanation for each component of the stylish navigation bar at the right of each page ("To go back one level, click on the word BEETLE") as well for the text links at the bottom of each page. This page also gives information on different browsers and on the software that is needed to run the VRML (Virtual Reality Modeling Language) models of the car that are available at the site.

The Beetle Web site is highly interactive, fostering the identity of Volkswagen as a user-friendly organization that focuses on people. A visitor to the site can view a detailed rendering of the interior and exterior of the New Beetle by downloading the VRML software from the Web site. This feature allows users to stroll, in effect, around the car's interior and exterior. Users are also invited to submit their feedback, ideas, and preferences via e-mail to Volkswagen. The organization evaluates the ideas and feeds them into the New Beetle development process. A visitor to the site can also sign up as an "Official New Beetle Fan" and receive ongoing e-mail updates from Volkswagen about the development of the new car.

Most important, users are encouraged to develop their own designs for the new vehicle. To do this, they can download a template of the car, redesign it, and submit their design via e-mail. The most interesting designs are displayed by Volkswagen in a cyberspace art gallery on the site. Some of them are reproduced in Exhibit 11.2. As our selected examples

EXHIBIT 11.2

New Beetle Cyberart Gallery

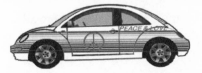

Picture created by Mark and Shelly Perkins

Picture created by Claudio Prado, Rio de Janeiro

Picture created by Arru Weis, Israel
"It is a vehicle for times of peace."

Picture created by Kristen Schroeter, Bonnie
Marshall, Thai Pham, Scott Dawson, Mike Guy
and Mary O'Neil in Michigan in the United
States

Picture created by Mayo, ConceptCinelle One

Picture created by Yvon Paquette, Canada

show, the Beetle, unlike almost any other car, is indeed a cultural icon, packed with meaning and able to inspire intense emotion. In their designs users relate the Beetle to other cultural icons like the Mona Lisa and Hollywood.

The Beetle Web site is linked to other Web sites of the organization: the German corporate Web site (http://www.volkswagen.de), the U.S. corporate Web site (http://www.volkswagen.com) as well as the Web site for other brands, such as the new Volkswagen Passat (http://www.passat.de). Strategically, the separate Web pages for new VW brands are intended to be discontinued a few months after the launch of each new car and to become part of the corporate Web sites.

Every Volkswagen Web site has a simple graphic design. Yet they are all suffused with the Volkswagen aesthetic—they are attractive and personable as well as original, exciting, and high-tech. The German-language Web site uses a strikingly minimalist design with white background and colorful and friendly graphics. The high-tech-looking Web site for the new VW Passat allows the user to download a video clip of the car. The U.S. Web site, set up in 1996, starts like a movie: the words "On the road of life, there are passengers and there are drivers" gradually fade in and fade away, while the slogan "Drivers wanted" appears with the blue VW logo. Visitors are informed: "You are about to enter the Volkswagen Web site."

The same philosophy and design principles are present in each of the organization's Web sites: simplicity, personal attention, and originality. Each thus becomes an integral component of Volkswagen's corporate aesthetic, moving it into the new medium and reinforcing the organization's identity and image.

NETSCAPE AND YAHOO!

The Web identities of two related organizations, a Web browser and a search engine—both virtually unknown just a few years ago but now in everyone's lexicon—offer a stark contrast of differing Web identity approaches.

Netscape, the first big player in the browser market, has a distinctly corporate look. In March 1995 the organization decided on a new logo to go with the release of its new Netscape Navigator 1.1 software. The logo was designed not only for use on traditional corporate materials, such as letterhead, business cards, labels, and packaging, but also for use on line. Landor Associates produced the dark global scape dominated by a bold uppercase N (set in a serif typeface to soften the letter's towering stature). To add a whimsical note to the screen interface of its new N logo, Netscape held an on-line contest for animation ideas. Naturally, the contest was also a brilliant publicity move and gave users a high level of interactivity with the organization. The "shooting-stars" animation, a variation of popular screen-savers familiar to many computer users, was the winner of this contest. To reach its final form, Netscape's own designers refined the animation to work on a variety of software platforms, adjusting the range of colors so that the logo would work in a Windows PC environment with as few as sixteen colors.

Netscape's 32 x 32 pixel billboard, set at the upper right of millions of computer displays, is now the cornerstone for a distinctive identity. When a user logs onto the Internet, the browser runs and the logo comes alive; shooting stars in a night sky surround the monumental-looking "N." But when seen standing still, on line or in print, the logo has a more formal, classic, and corporate flavor. It is appropriate to an organization doing business with large, established corporations such as AT&T, MCI, and other Fortune 500 organizations.[2]

In contrast, the search engine Yahoo!'s new funky graphic identity is quite the opposite of Netscape's soft corporate look. Started by two Stanford graduate students who put together lists and directories of Web sites for their own amusement, Yahoo! drew its name from a college catchphrase, "Yet Another . . ." What began as a goofy hobby has become one of the Web's best-known locations. Early in 1995, when Yahoo! found financing and incorporated, the time had come to formally establish its own brand identity, starting with the logo.

The first priority set by Yahoo! and their designers at CKS Partners was performance. They set ambitious targets of 2.5 to 3 seconds for loading—as fast or faster than the old site without graphics. To achieve this goal, they kept their graphics small—under 4K—and limited colors to black, yellow, red, and transparent.

As important as the speed of the graphics was their style: Yahoo!'s founders wanted to keep the look of a site put together by a couple of guys who were not all that different from their primary audience. For two months before the new look made its debut, users were greeted with an on-line questionnaire that asked their opinions about Yahoo!'s future and its use of graphics. The 65,000 responses helped to shape the beta site; its URL, in turn, was sent to 24,000 users, leading to 15,000 further comments. Confident that they had their audience with them, the new Yahoo! went live.

Yahoo! changed its corporate identification—but succeeded in keeping its identity. By building from the ground up, the site maintained its character as part of a community whose members had a voice in its development.[3]

Both of these organizations were savvy about using the properties of the Web to establish their identities—not surprising, since they are Web-based organizations. But each managed to create a distinctive sort of aesthetic while still achieving high interactivity. Netscape's call to users to help design the corporate logo invited the public in, but the final result was still polished by the organization itself. The final look of the logo, in keeping with the corporate identity of the organization, is lively but austere. Yahoo! solicited input from users at every step of its conversion, creating the feeling of a community, one in which communication flows freely. The final look of the site is zany and casual, with unusual color mixes and adventurous graphics.

THE WORLD WIDE WEB AS A MARKETING TOOL

As the examples of Volkswagen, Netscape, and Yahoo! make clear, digital media such as the World Wide Web have become key instruments for corporate and brand identity and image creation. And the Web style—the prominent use of visuals, and the nonlinear writing style—has already influenced other media. Gigantic visual images are in vogue again in outdoor city advertising, and printed copies are becoming more and more modular and less and less linear.

In most industries, a Web presence is absolutely essential to competitiveness. But as Alan Siegel, chairman of Siegel & Gale, a New York-based identity firm, observes, establishing a presence on the Internet must be done strategically: "Many corporations are rushing headfirst into electronic communications without a realistic set of priorities that will help them focus on the user and intelligently extend their corporate identity into the new media."[4]

The Web is a system on the Internet that allows a business to be present and open on a 24-hour basis through its Web site, which is made up of special files (text, graphics, and sound or video) that are placed on a computer connected to the Internet. Users logged onto the Internet can get to any Web site via so-called browser programs. (Netscape and Microsoft Explorer are currently vying for dominance in the browser market.)

Organizations must focus on the unique features of the Internet and use the medium to its fullest identity-creating potential. The Internet is far more than just a new platform on which to post traditional promotional materials. To express their corporate identity on the Web, organi-

CREATING A WEB BRAND: CONDENET

Creating a Web brand is a strategy that has been extremely successful for some companies. The magazine company Conde Nast, publisher of glossy, upscale magazines such as *Glamour, GQ, Conde Nast Traveler,* and *Bon Appetit,* has two Web brands: Epicurious and Swoon, both ranked among the "Top 100 Money-Making Sites" by *P.C. Computing* magazine in September 1996. These sites are free to users and are completely supported by advertising revenue. In 1996, the two sites' advertisers included Saturn, Le Meridien Hotels, Bank of America, and Stolichnaya. Each of the two brands has created a distinctive look that is carried through in the site's graphics and layout. While the sites do post appropriate articles from the Conde Nast magazines, the CondeNet sites take advantage of the Web's capacity to involve customers. Swoon, the site devoted to "Dating, Mating, and Relating," is aimed at the 18-to-34-year-old market. The site offers a free Personals service on which users who are looking for love can post advertisements and can respond by e-mail to others' ads. Forums such as "Roommates From Hell" invite users to sound off about the relationships in their lives. Quizzes such as "Who's Doin' Who" test users' knowledge of the latest celebrity pairings. Eighty percent of the material is created directly for the site, with the other 20% consisting of reprints of relationship-related articles from Conde Nast magazines.

The Epicurious brand is divided into two sites, Epicurious Travel and Epicurious Food, which sport the same distinctive retro style Epicurious logo and busy but orderly graphic layout, with each feature enclosed in its own box. The target market here is older users, who can find articles from *Gourmet, Bon Appetit, Conde Nast Traveler,* and much more that only the Internet could make possible. The Epicurious Food site features an international restaurant guide searchable by city; a wine guide; an Epicurean foods-and-drink dictionary; a recipe file with more than 4,000 dishes that can be searched by ingredient; a "Recipe Swap" forum; and "What's Ripe," weekly reports from farmer's markets across the United States. The Epicurious Travel site offers a database of travel destinations searchable by topic or destination: "Flight Stimulators," an updated list of the cheapest fares on major air routes; a "Deal of the Week"; Travel Forums, on which users ask each other questions and post travel stories; and five-day weather forecasts for 1,200 cities.

Source: Materials provided by CondeNet.

zations must consider the full array of electronic options available—text, striking visuals and graphics, audio and video, interactive sections, e-mail links, links to other Web sites, and so on. The choices seem to be endless, and new options are constantly added. There can be a temptation to do too much, a temptation that companies should resist. A poorly designed Web site reflects poorly on a firm's identity.

In what seems like a brief span of time, corporations and organizations have used their vast resources to create sophisticated, alluring, and profitable Web sites of every imaginable variety for a variety of purposes such as

- public relations management
- providing corporate, product, and service information at one's finger-tips
- defining and dominating a new channel of distribution
- demonstrating corporate or product capabilities
- customer service
- direct sales
- providing services (news, stocks, erotica, etc.).

Some companies have launched original new products on the Web that reinforce their core identity. For example, the "Warren Idea Exchange" Web site, offered by the S. D. Warren company, a paper manufacturer, serves as a content-rich resource for thousands of designers working in companies by providing more than 10,000 samples in over 120 categories of design and production as well as address books that list suppliers and vendors. Ernst & Young's Web site features Ernie, a cyberspace character who represents a consulting service by Ernst & Young with a direct line to Ernst & Young's business consultants. Both Web sites were created by Siegel & Gale, a firm that believes in simple, clear, and value-added communications with customers.

THE WORLD WIDE WEB AS AN IDENTITY ELEMENT

The Internet is a powerful tool for expressing a corporate or brand identity. As Jill and Matthew Ellsworth, authors of *Marketing on the Internet: Multimedia Strategies for the World Wide Web*, note, "The Web has the ability to level the playing field for businesses dramatically. For people who encounter your business through your Web page, that page provides them with the image of your company."[5]

What Web users see is not just words: when the medium is exploited to its fullest, users are treated to a full mix of graphic images, sounds, and moving images, and they are invited to interact with parts of the site. Visitors to the most sophisticated Web sites can use their eyes, ears, and imagination to enjoy a rich and varied experience.

At a corporate Web site, the choices are almost limitless: viewing text or logos, "visiting" the factory, listening to sound or music clips, watching a commercial, product demonstrations, or informational clips. Users may also fill out surveys, enter sweepstakes or participate in other promotional events, order products, and send feedback or complaint letters.

In November 1995, there were 100,000 Web sites; that number has doubled every two and a half months.[6] Worldwide, users were estimated to be around 60 million. Several identity firms derive the majority of their business from creating Web identities and have created catchy acronyms for their work. For example, David Boorstin Associates service-marked the identity creation process on the Web as IDNetity (Leading Internet Identities).

Managers faced with numerous other ways in which to express an organization's identity and image will naturally ask, "Why the Web?" Why turn to a Web site for identity management instead of relying on the same traditional media that we have been successful with?

THE UNIQUE PROPERTIES OF THE WEB

Proactivity

Given that a computer is currently the only way for people to enter the Web, marketers have to make their communications stand out. Above all, in concert with other communications media, such as television, the Web site needs to draw people. Think of it this way: the communicator must be proactive enough in order for the consumer to proactively find the communication. Advertisements on other Web sites are an effective way to lure visitors to your site. They are small and relegated to a small part of the screen; not only do they deliver your message, but if you can lure a viewer of your ad to click on it, he or she can be taken right to your site.

The current method of finding sites is through "search engines" like

Yahoo!, Alta Vista, Magellan, or InfoSeek that list all Web sites relevant to the key word or words the user types in. The average Web user visits the Yahoo! site at least once every time he or she connects to the Web. To some degree, the popularity of search engines determines the lay of the land for marketers. Consumers make aesthetic and other comparisons not only or not necessarily between direct competitors, but between all the organizations that appear under a certain heading. What other organizations do on their Web sites—their look, style, and theme—is now relevant to an organization's Web strategy. Communicators need to conduct a competitive assessment, as we discussed earlier in Chapter 7 on research, for their Web presence. It is important to do Web searches in all the categories under which an organization appears, in order to see who it is competing with.

Increasing proactivity can enhance identity by providing order and understanding to customers. For example, maintain key words so that search engines can find you in appropriate searches. Some organizations are excellent at thinking of every word that someone might use to find your site. Consider using competitor names as well. If your organization or brand has more than one Web site, be sure to have an easily understood and easily found home page as the center of the "village" of all your sites.

Interactivity

Interactivity usually refers to interaction between a communicator and the person to whom a communication is addressed, for example a Web site that entices a user with questions that he or she must click on to answer and bring on more options. The communicator needs to take advantage of the benefits of interactivity. When a user enters an organization's Web site and finds nothing but scanned brochures, the communicator misses an excellent opportunity to form an interactive relationship with the consumer. Moreover, this kind of move has the potential to do serious harm to the identity of the communicator, because unfavorable comparisons are easily made to other organizations' presence on the Web.

Early television was merely radio with still photographs for background. TV was able to move toward greater interactivity, aiding identity formation. Interactivity in the Web also needs to go even further. The individual entering the Web is entering a world with connections to various villages. Some sites are only imitation villages; others hint at a sense of a specific place and community through such features as chat rooms. But what true interactivity requires is for the communicator, not merely the communication, to interact with the intended recipient. When entering a Web site, people need to experience being there as they would experience any new environment.

A communicator has to cater to people's basic needs when they come across a new space: the need to explore—to exercise curiosity and have some freedom of movement; the need for sociability—to interact with others; and the need to have privacy and anonymity. Communicators on the Web must cater to these needs by creating interactive sites that stimulate and excite people, that make them feel that the communicator is there for them—not merely that computerized responses to their queries have been programmed. Relationships on the Web should mimic our interactions in the real world with potential communicators. Allowing for demonstrations or movement, for example, is useful to create a sensory experience that is desired and remembered. Contrast this with Microsoft's Web site, which is an example of an encyclopedic but dull site. If users ask for product information, there are no demonstrations or easy-to-see replicas. Instead, there is prose, as though a brochure just came in the mail.

This realism is what separates the Web from a fad like Magnavox Odyssey, which tantalized because of its novelty but quickly died out. The game provided a quick exploration cycle that was easily exhausted, and it lacked the potential for easy sociability. Unless many people were around to play with, consumers lost the desire to play, not because they had conquered the highest level of the game, but because playing it became lonely and isolating.

Imagine the following site, which is not far off technologically, but which communicators need to develop. A user enters the site on a TV set or other easily accessible device. An image of a communicator appears, who talks to the user. The user can respond by touch (or voice) and truly interact. Videos of the user and other people in the site at the time can be seen, and those visiting the site can interact with each other. At the most advanced sites, something approaching this level of interactivity is currently possible. But even more interactivity is on the horizon. Clearly, as we progress, we are simply inventing a real-world style through electronic means. While there are still some limits on what kind of electronic world can be achieved, organizations should use the current technology to create for consumers as lifelike a situation as possible.

CREATING IDENTITY ON THE WEB

Our position, reiterated throughout this book, is that creating a corporate or brand identity requires more than providing information, awareness, or association. In keeping with this approach, we contrast below three of the basic types of Web pages that roughly mirror the three phases discussed in Chapter 1: the benefits phase, the branding phase, and the sensory experiences/aesthetics phase.

Some Web pages focus on (1) information and products—the benefits phase; others focus on (2) recognition and associations—the branding phase; and still others focus on (3) the users and their experiences—the aesthetics phase. The last are the richest for creating strong identities.

1. *The Information and Product-Driven Web Site.* The information or product-driven Web site portrays the corporation or brand using a serious tone, either with much text and impoverished graphics, or with pictures of products or their packaging. In the auto industry, in 1996 the Web site of Peugeot, Europe's third-largest car manufacturer and the maker of Peugeot and Citroën cars, was a good example. Its home page, with yellow as the dominant color, showed a billboard-like display with its motto "Traffic fluid," and listed the following headlines: Corporate Profile, Vision and Strategy, Finance and the Economy, Research and Technology, and Press Information Center. The following buttons could be clicked to access additional Web pages: Identity form, Officers and executives, Research data, Organization, Automobiles Peugeot, Automobiles Citroën, An international group, Automobile-related subsidiaries, and Innovation.

Volvo's Web page had a similar (though a bit less extreme) corporate approach. A world map showed its three Web sites in Europe, two in America, and one in Australia. Icons that can be clicked on included: The Volvo Group: Facts and Figures; Research: Environment; Insurance; Museum; Sports; Opportunities; News Releases; Support and Service.

2. *The Recognition or Association Web Site.* Recognition or association Web sites treat the Web like any other promotional medium to create brand awareness and associations. They frequently repeat the slogans and taglines created in advertising or elsewhere.

Ford's Web page (all in blue) is an example of this type of Web page. Ford positions itself as a global brand, as the viewer notices immediately

GENERAL PRINCIPLES FOR CREATING IDENTITIES
ON THE WEB

1. *Use icons clearly and consistently.* Small pictures and graphics are used as icons that serve as click-on anchors for links to other sections or Web pages. Too many icons may be confusing. Icons embedded in pictures and graphics may take time to access and may be difficult to find. The size, color scheme, and layouts should match and be consistent. Icons are key elements to express styles and themes on the Web.

2. *Use the Web writing style.* Writing Web documents is quite different from top-down book, brochure, or even journalistic writing. Documents on the Web are often accessed in a nonlinear fashion. Home pages are supposed to draw attention and to serve as advanced organizers and summaries of information that is treated in more detail on subsequent pages. Home pages provide a first impression of the organization. However, when the viewer uses a search engine (Alta Vista, Excite, or the like), then the first impression of the organization may occur on one of the subsequent pages. Therefore, every page must repeat some of the information and impressions and must provide clear links to the home page. Otherwise, the identity is scattered all around the Web site.

3. *Link the Web site to other communications.* The Web is only part of the total communications mix that makes up an identity. It should reflect a corporation's identity and image and at the same time contribute to it. Therefore, Web sites must be referred to in other communications, and Web sites should allude to, or explicitly feature, other forms of communications, such as TV ads.

4. *Test the Web page* using different browsers. All Web browsers interpret the HTML format in which the site is created slightly differently. This means that fonts and colors as well as the correspondence between icons and text are processed and appear differently depending on the browser used. In unfortunate cases, the wrong text may appear under an icon, diluting the value of the page and giving a sloppy impression of the identity. Also, test for the response times of various pages, using, for example, different modem baud rates, especially if the page is full of pictures, sound, or videos. Larger documents take a

(continued)

(continued)

long time to load. However, long documents with many links reward the patient viewer with fast links within the document. Check the download time for downloadable components. If documents take too long to load or download, customers may become impatient and may miss your Web identity entirely. Consider offering a "fast" text-heavy version coupled with a slower graphics-heavy version.

5. *Update and upgrade the Web site.* Launching a Web site is only the first step. The challenge is to maintain a website by updating and upgrading it. Users will only "bookmark" a website if it provides value on an ongoing basis. And a website is only useful for identity management over time if users access the identity.

6. *Create (ultimately) a global Web site.* One of the unique features of the Internet is its worldwide access. This may require, for example, using different languages, aesthetic styles that appeal to different cultures and universal symbols. The pay-off is that you are one step closer to offering a global corporate or brand identity.

---

as he or she accesses the Web site. A rotating globe, the slogan "Ford World Wide Connection" and a toolbar with numerous countries—from Africa (yes, they seem to consider Africa a country!) and Andorra to Sweden—position Ford as a global brand. Icons include: Around the World, Ford News Briefing, Career Center, Environment, and Stockholder Relations.

General Motors' Web page, entitled "People in Motion," positions the organization and its products as family and people oriented. The Web page shows happy dogs and families, and navigation topics use the imperative verb form: Meet the family, Choose a finance plan, Discover new frontiers, etc. BMW of America's Web site pushes the theme of its corporate brand: "The Ultimate Driving Machine" derived from its nineties advertising slogan. Finally, several car manufacturers (Fiat, Toyota, and Porsche) have designed their Web pages pictorially yet statically around a "passion" theme.

3. *The Viewer-Focused/Experiential Web Site.* What matters for image creation is not only the information-recognition and associational value of a Web page but its experiential value for the user. Users must have fun;

FIGURE 11.1

Types of Web Sites

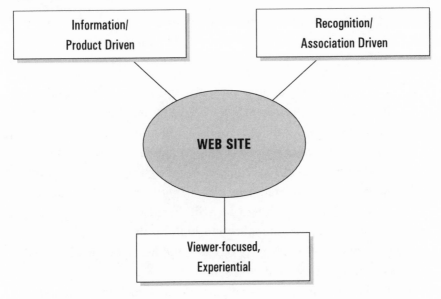

they must find something intriguing or newsworthy in a Web page in order to want to revisit it. Experiential Web sites like the New Beetle Web site discussed earlier seem to fulfill these user needs best. This type of Web site provides information and positions the brand, but also adds involvement via sensory experiences and aesthetics. Experiential Web pages do not push a product or a logo; they create experiences. They are genuinely user-focused. The experiential Web page, however, is currently still the exception rather than the rule on the Web.

THE FUTURE IS NOW:
TRANSIENT IMAGES AND VIRTUAL IDENTITIES

What does all this mean for identity and image creation? The explosive growth of new media, along with more sophisticated features that create increasingly complex searches and experiences, greatly expand the possibilities for identity and image management.

As a result, consumers will be confronted increasingly with dynamic virtual identities. As a consequence, the concept of corporate identity as such will expand. Organizations will no longer express their identities just by logos and signage, packaging and brochures, buildings and offices.

WHERE TO FROM HERE?

The Internet is constantly and rapidly changing. Predicting the future of the Internet is difficult. However, the following developments seem certain.

1. The Internet has grown explosively, and will continue to do so. The business sector particularly is ripe for more growth, with estimates that there will be more than 100 million users on the Internet by the end of this decade. The commercial on-line services such as America Online, CompuServe, Prodigy, and the Microsoft Network are also bringing new, more diverse users to the Internet.
2. New compression technologies will drastically speed page transfers, allowing more complex and high resolution graphics to be used. Increased availability of ISDN and fast speed modems will also allow for faster data transfer.
3. New kinds of tags and operations and new capabilities such as tables and animation will be developed constantly. Authoring and Web creation has already become as simple as using a word processor and will allow easy updating by anybody anytime.
4. The search engines and services on the Web will grow in number and sophistication. Search tools will become increasingly personalized, intelligent "searchbots" (search robots) that will be able to sniff out the specific information you want.
5. VRML and multimedia will become more commonplace, and all kinds of virtual malls, showrooms, and product demos will become part of the Internet. Customers will be able to use an object, walk through a mall, or even "drive" a car. Images on the Internet will move from 2D to 3D and include three-dimensional moving images as well.

They will create transient images that result in ever-changing consumer experiences. The anchor point—the consumer's resting point from which he or she will form an overall impression of the organization—will be an organization's aesthetics, the expression of its style and themes via various media.

NOTES

Chapter 1. Aesthetics: The New Marketing Paradigm

1. Appealing to consumer needs is one of the key ideas of marketing. Throughout this century, psychologists and marketers have classified needs into different categories (See Anthony H. Murray, *Explorations in Personality*, New York: Oxford University Press, 1938; David McClelland, *Personality*, New York: William Sloane, 1951; George Katona, *The Powerful Consumer* (New York: McGraw-Hill, 1962). According to Abraham Maslow in *Motivation and Personality*, 2nd ed. (New York: Harper & Row, 1970), needs are organized in a hierarchy ranging from basic needs (survival and safety) to higher-order needs. Following Maslow, experiential and aesthetic needs are higher-order needs, which individuals seek only when basic needs have been satisfied.
2. This case has been written, in part, based on material provided by Absolut's ad agency TBWA/Chiat Day and the following articles: Andrea Adelson, "Unusual Ads Help a Foreign Vodka to the Top," *New York Times*, November 28, 1988; Ken Frydman, "Dick Costello of TBWA: The Man Behind the Spirits Industry's Most Dazzling Advertising," *Market Watch*, March 1990.
3. GAP, Inc. 1994 Annual Report, 1995, 10-(k), Hoover's Company Profile Database 1996; Lisa Schultz, "How Gap's Own Design Shop Keeps Its Imitators Hustling," *Wall Street Journal*, March 13, 1997, B1, B5; and interview with managers, Fall 1996, by A. Simonson.
4. The Cathay Pacific case is based on materials provided by the company, McCann-Erickson and on Miriam Jordan, "Cathay Hopes New Logo Helps Airline Sport a More Asian Look," *Asian Wall Street Journal*, Sept 1, 1994, p. 5.
5. See, for example, Morris B. Holbrook and Elizabeth C. Hirschman, "The Experiential Aspects of Consumption: Consumer Fantasies, Feelings, and Fun," *Journal of Consumer Research* 9 (September 1982), pp. 132–140.
6. Philipp Kotler, *Marketing Management*, 9th ed. (Upper Saddle River, NJ: Prentice-Hall, 1997).

7. Glen Urban and Steven Star, *Advanced Marketing Strategy* (Engelwood Cliffs, NJ: Prentice-Hall, 1991), p. 141.

8. Larry Keeley, "Getting Your Unfair Share of Attention: Decentralizing the Concept of a Brand," *Design Management Journal*, Spring 1992, pp. 64 ff.

9. David A. Aaker, *Managing Brand Equity* (New York: The Free Press, 1991).

10. Important books include: David Aaker, *Building Strong Brands* (New York: The Free Press, 1996); David Aaker, *Managing Brand Equity* (New York: The Free Press, 1991); Jean-Noel Kapferer, *Strategic Brand Management* (New York: The Free Press, 1993); Charles Pettis, *TechnoBrands: How to Create and Use "Brand Identity" to Market, Advertise and Sell Technology Products* (New York: American Management Association, 1995).

   Influential articles include: Edward M. Tauber, "Brand Leverage: Strategy For Growth in a Cost-Control World," *Journal of Advertising Research*, August/September 1988, p. 26; Birger Wernerfelt, "Umbrella branding as a signal of new product quality: an example of signaling by posting a bond," *RAND Journal of Economics*, Vol. 19, No. 3 (Autumn 1988), pp. 458–466; David A. Aaker and Kevin Lane Keller, "Consumer Evaluations of Brand Extensions," *Journal of Marketing*, Vol. 54 (January 1990), pp. 27–41; C. Whan Park, Sandra Milberg, and Robert Lawson, "Evaluation of Brand Extensions: The Role of Product Feature Similarity and Brand Concept Consistency," *Journal of Consumer Research*, Vol. 18, No. 2 (September 1991), pp. 185–193; Peter H. Farquhar, "Managing Brand Equity," *Marketing Research*, September 1989, pp. 24–33; Kevin Lane Keller and David A. Aaker, "The Effects of Sequential Introduction of Brand Extensions," *Journal of Marketing Research*, Vol. XXIX (February 1992), pp. 35–50; David M. Boush and Barbara Locken, "A Process-Tracing Study of Brand Extension Evaluation," *Journal of Marketing Research* 27 (February 1991), pp. 16–28.

   We have also contributed to this literature in the following articles: Bernd H. Schmitt and Clifford Shultz, "Situational Effects on Brand Preferences for Image Products," *Psychology and Marketing*, Vol. 12, No. 5 (August 1995), pp. 433–446; France Leclerc, Bernd H. Schmitt, Laurette Dube, "Foreign branding and its effect on product perceptions and attitudes," *Journal of Marketing Research*, Vol. 31 (May 1994), pp. 263–270; Daniel Sheinin and Bernd H. Schmitt, "Extending brands with new product concepts: the role of category attribute congruity, brand affect and brand breadth," *Journal of Business Research* 31, 1994, pp. 1–10.

11. Aaker, *Building Strong Brands*, p. 84.

12. John W. Bender and H. Gene Blocker, *Contemporary Philosophy of Art: Readings in Analytical Aesthetics* (Engelwood Cliffs, NJ: Prentice-Hall, 1993).

13. James J. Gibson, *The Perception of the Visual World* (New York: Houghton Mifflin, 1950); Kurt Koffka, *Principles of Gestalt Psychology* (New York: Harcourt Brace, 1935); Rudolf Arnheim, *Visual Thinking* (Berkeley: University of California Press, 1935); John A. Bargh, "Automatic and conscious processing of social information," in Robert S. Wyer and Thomas K. Srull, *Handbook of Social Cognition*, Vol. 3 (Hillsdale, NJ: Erlbaum), pp. 1–44, 1984.

14. John Anderson, *Cognitive Psychology and its Implications* (San Francisco: W. H. Freeman and Co.), 1980.

Chapter 2. Creating Identity and Image Through Aesthetics

1. Based on materials provided by Landor Associates and McCann-Erickson, interviews with Landor and McCann-Erickson managers, and the following article: David Barbuza, "Now That It Is a Separate Company, Lucent Is Spending $50 Million to Create an Image," *New York Times,* June 3, 1996, p. D9.
2. Tony Spaeth, "Corporate Identity: A Watershed Year? New Corporate Logos," *Across the Board,* Vol. 29, No. 1–2 (January 1992), p. 57.
3. "What Are the Best Brands?" *Business Week,* April 7, 1997, p. 6.
4. Charles J. Fombrun, *Reputation: Realizing Value from the Corporate Image* (Boston, MA: Harvard Business School Press, 1996); James R. Gregory, *Marketing Corporate Image: The Company as Your Number One Product* (Lincolnwood, IL: National Textbook Co. [NTC], 1993); Marion G. Sobol, Gail E. Farrelly, and Jessica S. Taper, *Shaping the Corporate Image: An Executive Guide for Executive Decision Makers* (New York: Quorum Books, 1992).
5. This information is based on brochures supplied by Lippincott & Margulies as well as exhibits included in the show "Mixing Messages. Graphic Design in Contemporary Culture in America," at the Cooper-Hewitt National Design Museum, Smithsonian Institution, Fall 1996–Spring 1997.
6. Information on the history of industrial design in America is based on "Packaging the New: Design and the American Consumer: 1925–1975," Cooper-Hewitt National Design Museum, Smithsonian Institution, February 8–August 14, 1994.
7. The section on identity firms is based on material supplied by Landor Associates, Lippincott & Margulies, AGP, the Design Management Institute, and the Corporate Design Foundation.
8. Alan Siegel, "Beyond Design: Developing a Distinctive Voice," *Design Management Journal,* Fall 1989. The quotation is from a Siegel & Gale promotional brochure entitled "Voice," 1996.
9. Alice Rawsthorn, "A Rough Ride Ahead—The U.S. Market, Financial Times," *International Design* 2 (October 1, 1990), p. 20.
10. Dieter Kretschmann, "Consulting in Germany: Where we Stand," *Design Management Journal,* Spring 1996, pp. 32–37; John M. T. Balmer, "Corporate Identity: The Power and the Paradox," *Design Management Journal,* Winter 1995, pp. 39–44. The quote is from promotional material by Zintzmeyer & Lux.
11. Motoo Nakanishi, *New Decomas: Design Conscious Management Strategy* (Tokyo: Sanseido, 1994 [Japanese]); Motoo Nakanishi, *PAOS Design: Corporate Aesthetics, Creative Identities and Management Culture* (Tokyo: Kodansha, 1989 [Japanese]).
12. Roz Goldfarb, "On the Art of Consulting," *Design Management Journal,* Spring 1996, pp. 16–20; quotation from p. 19.
13. Bernd Schmitt, Alex Simonson, and Joshua Marcus, "Managing Corporate Image and Identity," *Long Range Planning* Vol. 28, (1995) pp. 82–92.
14. Alex Simonson, Bernd Schmitt, and Joshua Marcus, "Processes for Managing Identity and Design Within a Corporation," *Design Management Journal,* Winter 1995, pp. 60–63.

15. See Bernd H. Schmitt, "Gustav Ichheiser's Early Work: The Forgotten Roots of Person Perception and Attribution Theory," *Contemporary Psychology,* Vol. 12, No. 3, August 1987; and Gustav Ichheiser, *Appearances and Realities: Misunderstandings in Human Relations* (San Francisco: Jossey-Bass, Inc., 1970).

16. Egon Brunswik, *Perception and the Representative Design of Psychological Experiments* (Berkeley: University of California Press, 1956); Fritz Heider, *The Psychology of Interpersonal Relations* (New York: Wiley, 1958).

Chapter 3. Corporate and Brand Expressions

1. Alexandra Ourosoff, "Brands. What's Hot. What's Not," *Financial World,* Vol. 163, No. 16 (August 2, 1994), pp. 40–56; Laurie Mays, "Abstractionist Practically Reinvents the Keyboard," *Wall Street Journal,* March 6, 1995, p. B1; Charles Pankanier, talk, "Design in IBM," Design Leadership Symposium, June 27–30, 1993 at IBM's Advanced Business Institute in Palisades, NY; Stephen Wildstrom, "IBM's Butterfly is a Beauty," *Business Week,* March 20, 1995.

2. Wally Olins and Elinor Selame, *The Corporate Identity Audit,* Uster-Zurich: Strategic Directions Publishers Ltd.

3. GE Identity Program Case (Boston: Corporate Design Foundation, 1992).

4. Jin Han and Bernd Schmitt, "The relative importance of product-category dynamics and corporate identity in brand extensions: A comparison of Hong Kong and U.S. consumers." *Journal of International Marketing,* Vol. 5 (7), 1997, pp. 77–92.

5. Wolff Olins, *The New Guide to Corporate Identity* (Cambridge: Cambridge University Press. 1995).

6. What is called *brand personality* these days is projections, analogies, or metaphors. They are comparisons of the brand with something else— whether it is an animal, a person, personal relationship or a ship; see also David Aaker, *Building Strong Brands* (New York: The Free Press, 1996). It may be most convenient for consumers to use animals, traits or other means to express their perceptions and feelings toward brands—but what people give us are their impressions. Therefore, we prefer to use the term *character* rather than *brand personality* in the realm of corporate expressions.

7. Based upon material supplied by Sametz Blackstone Associates, and Roger Sametz's article, "Creating a Principles-Based Identity System to Build Brand Equity," *Design Management Journal,* Summer 1995, pp. 23–35.

8. Jean Bouchenoire, "Consultants in Concert: The Making of Bell's New Corporate Identity," *Design Management Journal,* Spring 1996, pp. 21–26.

9. Birgit Helene Jevnaker, "Designing an Olympic Games in the Face of Chaos: The Case of Lillehammer," *Design Management Journal,* Summer 1995, pp. 41–49.

10. Bonnie Briggs, "How We Developed 'Communicating Caterpillar: One Voice,'" *Design Management Journal,* Winter 1995, pp. 53–59.

Chapter 4. Styles

1. Bill McDowell, "Starbucks is Ground Zero in Today's Coffee Culture: Brand Goes Beyond Cup By Embodying Attitude," *Advertising Age,* December 9,

1996, p. 1; "Starbucks Earning More Than Double," *United Press International*, November 14, 1996; Robin Pogrebin, "New Yorkers & Co.; Starbucks Pours it On," *New York Times*, June 25, 1995, pp. 13–14. Sylvia Wieland Nogaki, "Advertising—Starbucks' New Splash," *Seattle Times*, May 18, 1992, p. B1.

2. Linda Dono Reeves, "Coffee Firm's Plans to Go National are Percolating," *USA Today*, September 8, 1992, p. B5.

3. Meyer Shapiro, "Style," in Alfred Louis Kroeber, ed., *Anthropology Today* (Chicago: University of Chicago Press, 1953).

4. Matthew Erdelyi and John Kleinbard, "Has Ebbinghaus Decayed with Time? The Growth of Recall (Hypermnesia) Over Days," *Journal of Experimental Psychology: Human Learning and Memory*, Vol. 4 1978, pp. 261–275.

5. "Who Owns That Color?," *At Issue: The Journal of Business and Design*, Vol. 2, No. 1 (1996).

6. David Burrows, *Sound, Speech and Music* (Amherst, MA: The University of Massachusetts Press, 1990).

7. Mason Adams is a good example of a well-known voice in advertising. In the U.S., the "Smucker's" voice is his.

8. Diane Ackerman, *A Natural History of the Senses* (New York: Vintage Books, 1990).

9. Lawrence Ingrassia, "Marketing: Gillette Ties New Toiletries to Hot Razor," *Wall Street Journal*, September 18, 1992, Section B, p. 7; "The Best a Plan Can Get," *The Economist*, August 15, 1992, pp. 59–60.

10. Material supplied by Desgrippes Gobe and Associates.

11. Robin Lee Allen, "Dunkin Donuts to Fight 'Stale' Image with Upgrade Plan," *Nation's Restaurant News*, November 18, 1996, p. 3.

12. Colin McJinn, "Metaphysical Fitness: A Philosophical Celebration of Manhattan's Latest Super Phenomenon—Reebok's Way-Pumped-Up Gesamtsporthalle," *New York*, May 8, 1995, pp. 50–53.

Chapter 5. Themes

1. "Top Cookie Brands," and "Top Cookie Brands by Sales," *Market Share Reporter*, 5th ed., 1995; Ray Lahvic and Dan Malovany, "Total Freshness and Rapid Response," *Bakery Production and Managing*, Vol. 27, No. 10, p. 170.

2. Rebecca Quick, "Betty Crocker Plans to Mix Ethnic Looks for Her New Face," *Wall Street Journal*, September 1, 1995, pp. A1 and A9.

3. Paul Schoemaker, "How to Link Strategic Vision to Core Capabilities," *Sloan Management Review*, Vol. 34 (1), September 22, 1992, p. 67.

4. Material on Knoll provided by the company.

5. The research on brand personality conducted by Jennifer Aaker is summarized in David Aaker, *Building Strong Brands* (New York: The Free Press, 1996).

6. AT&T publication, "Corporate Identity Program: Overview and Guidelines."

7. Milton Rokeach, *The Nature of Human Values* (New York: Free Press, 1973).

8. David Glen Mick, "Consumer Research and Semiotics: Exploring the Morphology of Signs, Symbols, and Significance," *Journal of Consumer Research*, Vol. 13, September 1986, pp. 196–213; Grant McCracken, *Culture and Consumption*, Bloomington and Indianapolis: Indiana University Press.

9. Alvin H. Schechter, "Measuring the Value of Corporate and Brand Logos," *Design Management Journal,* Winter 1993, pp. 33–39.

10. Philip Shenon, "The Last Stewardess," *New York Times,* October 25, 1993, p. C3.

11. "Kobe Gathering Ponders 'Toilet Culture,'" *Japan Times,* June 8, 1993, p. 1.

12. J.A. Edell and R. Staelin, "The Information Processing of Pictures in Print Advertisements," *Journal of Consumer Research* 10, 1983, pp. 45–60.

13. Bernd H. Schmitt, Nader T. Tavassoli and Robert Millard, "Memory for Print Ads: Understanding Relations Among Brand Name, Copy and Picture," *Journal of Consumer Psychology,* Vol. 2, No. 1 (1993), pp. 55–81.

14. K.A. Lutz and R.J. Lutz. "Effects of Interactive Imagery on Learning: Applications to Advertising," *Journal of Applied Psychology* 62, pp. 493–498.

15. Joan Meyers-Levy and Alice Tybout, "Schema Congruity as a Basis for Product Evaluation," *Journal of Consumer Research,* Vol. 16 (June 1989) No. 1, pp. 39–53.

Chapter 6. Overall Customer Impressions

1. Information about the Four Seasons is drawn from: Barbara Sturm, "Weekend at Manhattan's Four Seasons is a Luxurious High," *Asbury Park Press,* September 22, 1996, Section F, p. 3; Ruth Reichl, "Restaurants," *New York Times,* June 21, 1996, Sec. C, p. 22; Sonia Reyes, "Four Seasons Sold. Hong Kong Investors Pay $190M for Hotel," *Daily News,* August 6, 1996, p. 31; Amy Felman, "Japanese Bank Seeks to Unload Four Seasons: High Occupancy, Rising Room Rates Push Up Price Tags On City's Hotels," *Crain's New York Business,* June 10, 1996; Witold Rybczynski, "How Suite It Is; A Visit to a Four Seasons Hotel in Palm Beach, Florida," *Saturday Night Publishing,* Canada, May 1996; Bruce Serlen, "Debut of Four Seasons Stirring Luxury Market; Newcomer Posing a Challenge to Posh Neighboring Hotels," *Crain's New York Business,* Executive Travel, p. 33.

2. Barbara Sturm, "Weekend at Manhattan's Four Seasons is a Luxurious High," *Asbury Park Press,* September 22, 1996, p. F3.

3. Ruth Reichl, "Restaurants," *New York Times,* June 21, 1996, Section C, p. 22.

4. John R. Anderson, *Language, Memory, and Thought* (Hillsdale, NJ; Erlbaum, 1974).

5. This classic study was performed by Solomon Asch, "Forming Impressions of Personalities," *Journal of Social Psychology* 41 (1946), pp. 258–290.

6. Richard Bagozzi and Robert Burnkrant, "Attitude Organization and the attitude-behavior relationship," *Journal of Personality and Social Psychology,* Vol. 37 (1979), pp. 913–929.

7. Tom Peters, "Design Is . . ." *Design Management Journal,* Winter 1995, pp. 29–33.

8. Geoffrey Smith, "Sneakers that Jump Into the Past," *Business Week,* March 13, 1995, p. 71.

9. Silvia Sansoni, "Full Steam Ahead for Diesel," *Business Week,* April 29, 1996, p. 58. The examples have been selected from company material.

10. Information on Sonae was provided by the company.

11. Materials were supplied by the St. Regis Hotel in New York and are based on

an article entitled "Gray Kunz and His Fabulous Ideas," *Art Culinaire*, Vol. 24, 1992.

12. Alex Simonson and Morris B. Holbrook, "Consumer Evaluations of Brand Imitations," unpublished working paper.

13. Mitchell Pacelle, "U.S. Architects in Asia: Only Way to Go Is Up," *Wall Street Journal*, March 21, 1994, B1; "Towers of Powers," *South China Morning Post*, March 26, 1994, pp. 1–2; "For the Debut of a Virgin Megastore, Everything is on a Grand Scale," *New York Times*, April 17, 1996.

Chapter 7. Assessment and Research Tools for Identity Management

1. Pamela W. Henderson and Joseph A. Cote, "Designing Positively Evaluated Logos," Working Paper, Marketing Science Institute, Report No. 96–123, 1996.

2. Alvin H. Schechter, "Measuring the Value of Corporate and Brand Logos," *Design Management Journal*, Vol. 4, No. 1 (Winter 1993), pp. 3–39.

3. Interview by Alex Simonson, Bernd Schmitt, and Joshua Marcus, Spring 1994.

4. Discussion by Dr. Deming with Prof. Simonson's class on Product Quality, Columbia University, Fall 1990.

5. See Alfred E. Goldman and Susan Schwartz McDonald, *The Group Depth Interview: Principles and Practice* (American Marketing Association), 1987.

6. William G. Zikmond, *Exploring Marketing Research*, 6th ed., (Orlando: Dryden Press, 1997); Melvin Crask, Richard J. Fox, Roy G. Stout, *Marketing Research Principles and Applications*, Naresh K. Malhotra, *Marketing Research: An Applied Orientation*, 2d ed, Prentice Hall, 1996; William R. Dillon, Thomas J. Madden, and Neil H. Firtle, eds., 3d ed. (New York: Irwin, 1987), *Marketing Research in a Marketing Environment*, for a thorough treatment with many practical identity-related applications.

7. Pamela L. Alreck and Robert B. Settle, *The Survey Research Handbook*, 3d ed. (New York: Irwin 1996); Seymour Sudman and Norman M. Bradburn, *Asking Questions: A Practical Guide to Questionnaire Design* (San Francisco: Jossey-Bass Publishers, 1982).

8. Brand Strategy, *Briefs*, October 25, 1996, p. 3.

Chapter 8. Protecting Aesthetics and Identity

1. Information for this case is drawn from *Two Pesos, Inc.* v. *Taco Cabana, Int'l, Inc.*, 112 S.Ct. 2753, 2764 (1992) and *Taco Cabana, Int'l, Inc.* v. *Two Pesos, Inc.*, 932 F.2d 1113 (5th Cir. 1991).

2. *Two Pesos, Inc.* v. *Taco Cabana, Int'l, Inc.*, 112 S.Ct. 2753, 2764 (1992).

3. 15 U.S.C. 1125 (a) (1946).

4. *American Chicle Co.* v. *Topps Chewing Gum, Inc.*, 208 F.2d 560 (2d Cir. 1953).

5. *Charles of the Ritz Group Ltd.* v. *Quality King Distributors, Inc.*, 832 F.2d 1317 (2d Cir. 1987).

6. *Qualitex Co.* v. *Jacobson Products Co., Inc.*, 115 S.Ct. 1300 (1995).

7. *Ferrari S.p.A.* v. *Roberts*, 944 F.2d 1235 (6th Cir. 1991) (applying standards from *Inwood Laboratories, Inc.* v. *Ives Laboratories, Inc.*, 456 U.S. 844 (1982).

8. Ibid. at 1144.

9. Restatement (Third) of Unfair Competition, @17 cmt c. (from Tent Draft No 2 1990).
10. *NutraSweet Co. v. Stadt Corp.*, 917 F.2d 1024 (7th Cir. 1990).
11. *Qualitex Co. v. Jacobson Products Co.*, 115 S.Ct. 1300 (1995).
12. *Playboy Enterprises v. Chuckleberry Publ., Inc.*, 486 F. Supp. 414 (S.D.N.Y. 1980).
13. *Stern's Miracle-Gro Products, Inc. v. Shark Products, Inc.*, 823 F. Supp. 1077 (S.D.N.Y. 1993).
14. Alexander F. Simonson, "How and When Do Trademarks Dilute? A Behavioral Framework to Judge 'Likelihood' of Dilution," *The Trademark Reporter,* 83 (2), 1993, pp. 149–174.
15. *Polar Corp. v. Coca-Cola Co.*, 871 F. Supp., 1520 (D. Mass 1994).
16. "The Rational Basis of Trademark Protection," Frank I. Schechter, *Harvard Law Review,* Vol. XI (6) 1927, reprinted in *The Trademark Reporter,* January–February 1970, 60 TMR 334.
17. *Jordache Enterprises v. Levi Strauss & Co.*, 841 F. Supp. 506 (S.D.N.Y. 1993).
18. Federal Trademark Dilution Act of 1995, 15 U.S.C. 1125 (c)(1).
19. *Jordache Enterprises v. Hogg Wyld, Ltd.*, 828 F.2d 1482 (10th Cir. 1987).
20. Rhonda M. Abrams, "When Life Gives You Lemons, Make Lemonade," Gannett News Service, September 5, 1996; Nancy Millman, "Creativity Is Name of the Game," *Chicago Tribune,* April 11, 1993, p. 3.
21. Alexander F. Simonson, "How and When Do Trademarks Dilute? A Behavioral Framework to Judge 'Likelihood' of Dilution," *The Trademark Reporter,* 83 (2), 1993, pp. 149–174.
22. See Jacob J. Jacoby, Amy Handin, and Alex Simonson, "Survey Evidence in Deceptive Advertising Cases Under the Lanham Act: An Historical Review of Comments from the Bench," *The Trademark Reporter,* Vol. 84 (5) (1994), pp. 541–585.

Chapter 9. Global Identity Management

1. The LEGO case is based on "LEGO Toys Earn National Awards for Quality and Play Value; Duplo Water Park and Fort LEGOREDO Lead the Way," *Business Wire,* November 22, 1996; Chris Partridge, "Lego Locks into Cyberspace," *The Times,* November 6, 1996; Stephen Ohlemacher, "Lego Systems Celebrates: New Headquarters a Symbol of Growth," *The Hartford Courant,* August 22, 1995, p. 6; "Lego Builds Internet Among Girls, One Pastel-Colored Block at a Time. . . ," *Los Angeles Times,* July 13, 1995, p. D4.
2. This story is based on interviews by Bernd Schmitt with Tamagotchi owners as well as on the following articles: "Japan's Bandai to Sell Hot 'Virtual Pet' Overseas," *Reuter Business Report,* February 4, 1997; Masatoshi Sato, "Electronic Peeps Hatch Nationwide Sensation as Young Shoppers Flock to Purchase 'Cute Eggs,'" *Daily Yomiuri,* January 29, 1997, p. 3; Kevin Sullivan, "A Demanding Toy Chicken Takes Over Japan," *International Herald Tribune,* January 25, 1997, p. 13.
3. Vern Tapestra and Ravi Sarathy, *International Marketing* (Chicago: The Dryden Press, 1990).

4. Phillip Harris and Robert T. Morran, *Managing Cultural Differences* (Houston: Gulf Publishing Company, 1987).
5. France Leclerc, Bernd H. Schmitt, and Laurette Dubé, "Foreign Branding and Its Effects on Product Perceptions and Attitudes," *Journal of Marketing Research*, Vol. 31 (May 1994), pp. 263–270.
6. Harry Berkowitz, "Marketing Gets Lost in Translation: International Ads Subject to Gaffes." *The Houston Chronicle*, June 21, 1994, p. 1.
7. Suzanne Bidlake, "Growing By Design," *Marketing*, April 26, 1990, p. 46.
8. Cäcilie Rohwedder, "Global Products Require Name-Finders," *Wall Street Journal*, April 11, 1996, p. B 8.
9. The section on East Asia draws on the following articles: Bernd H. Schmitt, and Yigang Pan (1994), Managing corporate and brand identities in the Asia-Pacific Region. *California Management Review, 36 (4)*, 32–48; Bernd H. Schmitt, Yigang Pan, and Nader Tavassoli, Language and consumer memory: The impact of linguistic differences between Chinese and English. *Journal of Consumer Research, 21* (1994), 419–31; and Yigang Pan, and Bernd H. Schmitt, Language and brand attitudes: The impact of script and sound matching in Chinese and English. *Journal of Consumer Psychology* (in press, 1997).
10. "Hail to the Chi," *Fortune*, February 24, 1997, p. 10.

Chapter 10. Retail Spaces and Environments

1. Suzanne Slesin, "So Flows the Chocolate," *New York Times*, June 16, 1994, p. C3; Marianne Wilson, "New Store Design: Just Do It Now," *Chain Store Age Executive*, March 1, 1994, p. 66; Campbell Soup Co. 1995 Annual Report and 10(k).
2. Suzanne Slesin, "So Flows the Chocolate," *New York Times*, June 16, 1994, p. C3.
3. Company materials from Desgrippes Gobe & Associates.
4. Suzy Menkes, "The Nike Experience: Don't Forget to Shop," *International Herald Tribune*, November 19, 1996; Megan Kummer and Vanessa Correira, "Kidsday / Let's Take A Trip / Nike Town in New York City / Kids in the Kitchen," *Newsday*, November 19, 1996, p. B44; "Nike-Reebok: Retail Faceoff. Nike Inc. Opens 95,000 Sq. Ft. Store in New York, NY to Compete with Reebok International Ltd.," *WWD*, October 31, 1996; George Mannes, "Nike Jumps in with Megastore," *Daily News*, November 2, 1996, p. 6.
5. Mary Kuntz, "Reinventing the Store: How Smart Retailers are Changing the Way We Shop," *Business Week*, November 27, 1995, pp. 84–96.
6. Susan Schherreik, "Attention, Shoppers: Brand-Name Stores," *New York Times*, August 14, 1994, p. 9-1.
7. See Philip Langdon, "Breaking Out of the Box: Architectural Planning for Big Box Retail Superstores in New York, N.Y.'s Large Urban Areas," *Progressive Architecture* Vol. 76, No. 12 (December 1995), p. 45.
8. Marianne Wilson, "The Next British Invasion? Waterstone's Booksellers Ltd. Increases Market Share in the U.S.," *Chain Store Age Executive with Shopping Center Age*, Vol. 68, No. 12 (December 1992), p. 136.

9. See, e.g., David M. Sanbonmatsu and Frank R. Kardes, "The Effects of Physiological Arousal on Information Processing and Persuasion," *Journal of Consumer Research* 15 (December 1988), pp. 379–385.

10. Maray Jo Bitner, "Servicescapes: The Impact of Physical Surroundings on Customers and Employees," *Journal of Marketing*, 56:2 (1992), p. 57.

11. William Booth, "For Architect Morris Lapidus, A Kitschy, Kitschy Coup: The Public Loved His 'Architecture of Joy,' But Critics Scoffed. Now He's Getting the Last Laugh," *Washington Post*, July 2, 1995.

Chapter 11. Corporate and Brand Identity on the Internet

1. The profile of Volkswagen is drawn from information available on the Volkswagen Web site.

2. Company and Web site material from Netscape and material from Landor Associates.

3. Company and Web site material from Yahoo!

4. "Digital Voice," *Design Management Journal*, Winter 1996, pp. 17–23, quotation on p. 20.

5. Jill and Matthew Ellsworth, *Marketing on the Internet: Multimedia Strategies for the World Wide Web* (New York: John Wiley, 1995), p. 56.

6. Vic Sussman and Kenan Pollack, "Gold Rush in Cyberspace," *U.S. News and World Report*, November 13, 1995, pp. 73–80.

INDEX

ABOUT THE AUTHORS

BERND SCHMITT holds a Ph.D. in psychology from Cornell University. He is Associate Professor in the Marketing Department at Columbia Business School and holds a marketing chair at CEIBS in Shanghai. He has taught courses on corporate identity, advertising, consumer behavior, and strategic marketing. He has also been a visiting professor at M.I.T., in Germany, Poland, and Hong Kong. He has contributed more than 30 articles to academic and management journals. Dr. Schmitt consults and lectures in the United States, Europe, and all over Asia.

ALEX SIMONSON holds a J.D. from New York University School of Law and a Ph.D. in marketing from Columbia Business School. He practiced trademark-related law at Phillips, Nizer, Benjamin, Krim & Ballon primarily for fashion designers for a few years prior to entering academia. Currently he is Assistant Professor in the marketing department at Georgetown University School of Business and vice president of Guideline Research Corp. in New York. He specializes in research relating to brands, identity, and trade dress, particularly brand confusion, dilution, genericism, trade dress confusion and dilution, and advertising claims. Dr. Simonson has consulted for various Fortune 100 and 500 companies and has published in leading academic marketing, strategic, and intellectual property journals. His pastimes include piano playing, singing, woodworking, and photography.